In appreciation of your interest & cooperation

Edward R Schinman

Jacob Epstein

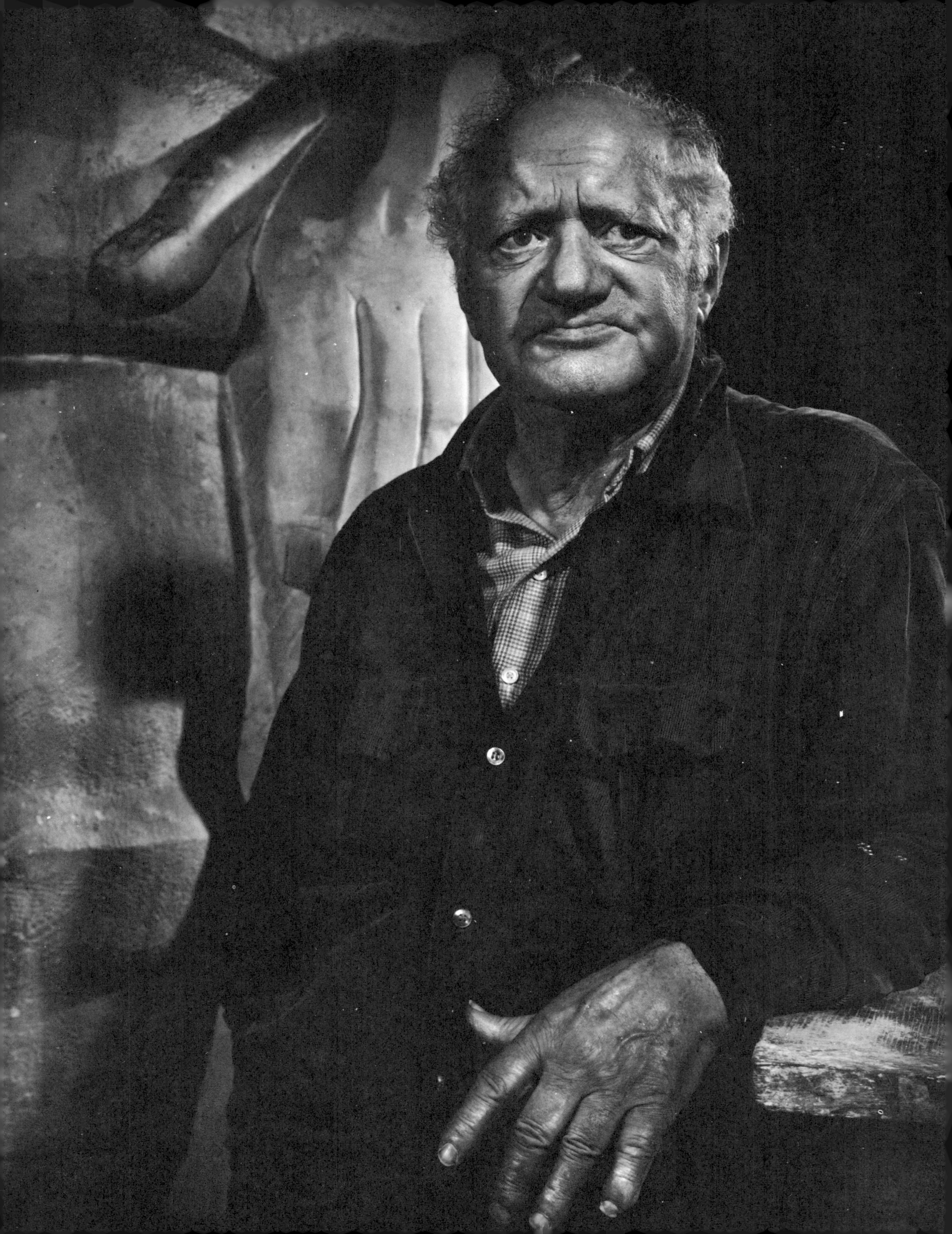

Jacob Epstein

A Catalogue of the Collection of Edward P. Schinman

Edited by
Edward P. Schinman
and
Barbara Ann Schinman

Rutherford · Madison · Teaneck
Fairleigh Dickinson University Press

Library of Congress Catalogue Card Number: 67-29137

Associated University Presses, Inc.
Cranbury, New Jersey 08512

SBN: 8386 6958 1

Printed in the United States of America

Contents

Acknowledgments

For what has become an absorbing and devoted interest the writer wishes to express his deep gratitude to those people who in their various timely actions influenced the writer in his acquisition of a major collection of the works of Sir Jacob Epstein.

First, to my wife, Pauline Schinman, at whose gentle urging I visited the Tate Galleries in London, which had on exhibit a large collection of Sir Jacob Epstein's portraits and sculptures. This visit was to spark the tremendous enthusiasm for the art of this man whom I consider the greatest sculptor of the century, if not of all time.

I am particularly indebted to Mr. John P. Nicholson of the John Nicholson Galleries, New York City, who together with his friend Mr. Robert Jackson enabled me to acquire in less than one year's time a collection which ordinarily would have taken many years to amass (Mr. Robert Jackson was a friend of the Epstein family). The cooperation and knowledge of John Nicholson was particularly helpful because of his expertise in the field of English art. When I approached him with the idea of acquiring works of Sir Jacob Epstein in chronological order, he indicated that such an idea was unique, not having been done by other collectors in connection with any other artist. This kind of collection would not only be advantageous from an artistic standpoint but would also prove of immense educational value to connoisseurs and students who would thus be given an opportunity to view the development of one of the world's greatest sculptors.

Among the numerous friends who helped in so many ways, I would like especially to mention Mr. and Mrs. Murray Reiffin, whose active interest in art and particularly in Sir Jacob Epstein encouraged me in carrying out this project.

I also wish to acknowledge the beneficent and scholarly interest of Dr. and Mrs. Peter Sammartino who, after seeing some of Sir Jacob Epstein's works, felt that it would be desirable to have the entire collection on exhibit at Fairleigh Dickinson University. At their prodding the collection was placed on view in its entirety for the first time from February 19 to April 1, 1967.

Also my sincerest thanks go to Mr. W. Norman Hudson for his extraordinary effort in the preparation of the catalog and the setting up of the exhibit at Fairleigh Dickinson University, and particularly to all of those persons involved in the preparation of this first exhibit.

I am also indebted to Mr. John Reardon for his painstaking care and technical performance in making the photographs of the Epstein works and especially his ability to bring out the beautiful coloring in *Epstein Flowers* and *Epping Forest.*

Comments of many of those who attended the exhibition, including many relatives of Sir Jacob Epstein, have been most gratifying. Mrs. Aline Saarinen of NBC News in showing the collection on the *Today* Show on March 15, 1967, helped to create additional enthusiasm for the exhibit at Fairleigh Dickinson University and make the works of Sir Jacob Epstein known on a national scale.

Reviews of the Fairleigh Dickinson exhibition by Mrs. Katharine Kuh (reprinted with permission of Saturday Review, Inc. and Mrs. Kuh) and Mrs. Emily Genauer follow the bibliography.

And last but not least, I wish to express my appreciation for the extensive research work done by my daughter, Barbara Ann, for the preparation of the bibliography and for her original comments on the Epstein drawings. As Curator, her keen interest and devotion to the collection has been most gratifying.

I hope to be able to keep this collection intact so that my original purpose may be maintained. I shall do my utmost to have the collection as a whole shown at public museums throughout the country so that everyone may have the opportunity to appreciate the works of one of the world's greatest sculptors, Sir Jacob Epstein.

EDWARD P. SCHINMAN

Jacob Epstein

Sir Jacob Epstein
1880–1959

It is a fitting climax to a life devoted to doing one job extremely well that the fame of Sir Jacob Epstein will live in perpetuity as the greatest sculptor of his time.

After the unveiling of Epstein's great work *St. Michael and the Devil* at the Cathedral at Coventry, England by his widow, Lady Kathleen Epstein, the world awoke to the fact that it had indeed lost a great man and one of the greatest sculptors in history.

Sir Jacob was born in 1880, on the Lower East Side of New York City, a predominantly Jewish area at that time. This area was later vividly portrayed (1902) in his famous illustrations for Hutchins Hapgood's *The Spirit of the Ghetto* (recently reissued [1967] by the Harvard University Press with an introduction by Moses Rischin, Associate Professor of History at San Francisco State College).

Sir Jacob Epstein was an unassuming youth who seemed to have but one burning ambition—the perpetuation of life through his sculpture. Today, there is much evidence that he succeeded far beyond anyone's dreams. His portraits in bronze of the famous men of his time—in whom he saw greatness and had the ability to express it—are as remarkable for the selection of their subject as for their rendering. It was typical of Epstein that after six modeling sessions with Sir Winston Churchill he should have felt that his superb clay was still only "an interesting character study." This man was original, temperamental, and absolutely demanding of himself in all of his works—whether done on commission or for his own pleasure.

Epstein's love of humanity was directly translated into a constant sketching of the teeming life around him. In his early youth he set out to become a painter. To achieve that goal he studied drawing and painting at the Art Students' League in New York. At that time the human face and form especially interested him and he would be dominated by it throughout his life. Some of his earliest sketches appeared in the magazine *Critic* for March, 1900.

At the age of twenty, however, Epstein decided to abandon painting for sculpture. He sought instruction from the popular and successful American sculptor, George Gray Barnard. His contact with Barnard served principally to fire Epstein's enthusiasm, with the predictable result that the young artist determined to study further in Europe. The irresistible lures were Rodin—whose reputation was already international—and the great masters of the Italian Renaissance, whose works Epstein longed to see in the great museum collections.

Paris, then the undisputed art capital of the world, was a magnet for artists at the turn of the century and Epstein finally arrived there in 1902; his trip had been financed by the sale of illustrations for Hapgood's book. The city, a stimulating environment for any artist, was for Epstein, at the start of his career, an overpowering inspiration.

Epstein's three years in Paris were spent modeling at the Ecole des Beaux-Arts and the Julian Academy. Several small portraits survive from his formative Paris years. Among those are his *Baby Sleeping* and *Baby Awake.* He familiarized himself with the sculpture collection at the Louvre and traveled to Italy to see the monumental works of Michelangelo, Donatello, and Ghiberti. However, after a relatively short time, Epstein felt the need for new surroundings and left Paris for London.

Epstein's productivity increased from the time of his arrival in London. He was encouraged by his circle of new-found friends, which included the painter Augustus John, T. E. Hulme, Sir Muirhead Bone, Bernard Van Dieren, Richard Sickert, W. G. Constable and Ezra Pound. While London lacked the intense creative life of Paris, Epstein found there a sympathetic climate that better suited his own special requirements. He was especially attracted to the ethnographical collections in the British Museum, which were to have an influence on his drawings and sculptures of such exotic types as *Sunita, Betty Peters, Olive,* and others. Except for an occasional trip abroad, Epstein remained in England the rest of his life.

He was awarded his first important commission to decorate the British Medical Association Building in the Strand in 1907. His eighteen large figurative sculptures quickly established Epstein's reputation as a rising young artist, and unexpectedly made him the center of controversy among groups who objected to the statues' nudity.

In his Strand commission, Epstein made an outstanding contribution to the then neglected area of architectural decoration. The statues "blended into the building." At the age of twenty-six, he had proved himself capable of executing a major project, which he conceived as symbolizing the "passage of man and woman through life." In little more than a year, he had carved from stone and set in place forty feet above the street eighteen larger-than-life-size figures on the British Medical Association building in the Strand.

It was characteristic of Epstein that unlike Rodin, Maillol and other famous sculptors he did everything himself. No pupils nor talented assistants were allowed to do any work on his carvings. In view of this fact his lifetime production of more than five hundred major pieces will always be an amazing tribute to his personal productivity as well as to his greatness.

With the Strand commission successfully completed, Epstein immediately began another work, the *Tomb for Oscar Wilde.* It consisted of a great rectangular stone dominated by the form of a Flying Angel.

During the half dozen years before the outbreak of World War I, Epstein showed signs of an increasing interest in primitive and abstract styles. In this collection are several examples of this influence, notably in the carvings *Sunflower*, *Flenite Figure*, and *Flenite Relief.* To some extent this abstract quality persisted in his handling of various later carvings, such as *Chimera* and *Elemental Man.*

In his commissioned portraits, Epstein retained realism, but his other experimental works indicated he was responding to the influence of aboriginal sculptures on display in ethnological museums. The tendencies in these works were reinforced through contacts with Picasso, Modigliani, and Brancusi during the course of a stay in Paris in 1912. His carving *Sunflower* showed he had been a cubist before Braque and Picasso had even defined the term.

In 1913 Epstein helped found "The Vortex," an association of artists who detested the lingering academic traditions of nineteenth-century art and embraced forms they considered more vital to the times. Epstein's unusual *Rock Drill*, symbolizing the dehumanization of man in the modern world, incorporated the point of view of the Vorticists. Several Venus figures of this time are also powerfully evocative of primitive form and emotion.

The effects of World War I are visible in some of his portraiture of that era—notably *Tin Hat*, a study of a soldier. The artist, now an English citizen, served for a year in the British Armed Forces. In 1917, while still in the Army, Epstein was granted his first exhibition at the Leicester Galleries. It was a complete artistic success.

Epstein's *Risen Christ,* a powerful revival of an ancient theme, was the first of a series of imposing religious subjects that he was to produce during the next four decades.

Splendid portraits poured forth from Epstein's studio during the postwar period. These were characterized by masterly control of the medium and psychological penetration of the subject, as for example in the *Joseph Conrad* and the *Dolores* series. Epstein's major works seemed almost alive because of their humanistic outlook and dramatic vitality. In 1924 Epstein received a commission to execute a memorial to W. H. Hudson, author of *Green Mansions.*

There has been much discussion of Epstein's magnificent talent for surface treatments of portraits. A most amazing aspect is that Epstein was able to visualize his finished interpretation of the subject even at the very start of his work. In order to attain his goal he was concentrating on the surfaces even while the work was gradually growing. He added dab after dab of clay as his feelings dictated without any apparent effort to control the surface until the portrait was completed. In this way the Epstein surface was completely integrated in the finished art, in contrast to other artists' methods of completing the basic work and then deciding on a particular finish. Each form became more alive and dramatic as the light hit the uneven plane surfaces. Thus, his portraits attained a delineation of personality not achieved by any other sculptor. His abstract works were smooth-surfaced, thereby lending importance to cold shape. In others, such as *Tin Hat*, both smooth and rough surfaces were harmoniously combined.

In *Visitation* and *Madonna and Child*, Epstein resumed his religious subject matter. He was fascinated by head shapes and the personalities they revealed. Anything that exuded life was in his eyes beautiful. In 1927, the artist came to America to attend an exhibition of his work at Ferragil Gallery, New York. While there he modeled portraits of the philosopher and educator John Dewey, the anthropologist Franz Boas, and the singer Paul Robeson. He also revisited the scenes of his childhood.

During his New York visit, Epstein also testified at the Brancusi trial in which the U. S. Customs was seeking to levy an import duty on Brancusi's famous *Bird in Flight.* U. S. Customs held that this sculpture was a manufactured article and not a work of art. Epstein exhibited a 5000-year-old piece of Egyptian sculpture that lacked detail and naturalism but supposedly represented a hawk. He thus demonstrated that Brancusi had followed a long tradition of abstract sculpture. Confronted with such evidence, the Customs Bureau was eventually forced to reverse its decision.

Epstein was commissioned in 1928 to create two groups for the Transport Headquarters Building, consisting of *Day,* a man with his son, and *Night,* a woman with a boy lying across her lap. Epstein continued to produce powerful portraiture during the 1930s and added to his growing gallery of the world's eminent people. Among these were *Bernard Shaw, Albert Einstein* and *Chaim Weizmann.* Exhibitions of his sculpture, drawings, and watercolors drew thousands of people.

In 1931, he did a series of drawings based on the Old Testament. In the summer of 1933, he produced more than one hundred water colors of flowers and of Epping Forest. He illustrated an edition of Baudelaire's *Les Fleurs du Mal,* and he also did seven water colors for *The Book of Affinity,* a collection of poetry by the mystic poet Moysheh Oyved. In 1938, he was awarded an L.L.D. degree from Aberdeen University and two years later he published his autobiography under the title *Let There Be Sculpture.* In 1955, he revised and enlarged this book, calling the new edition *Epstein: An Autobiography.* The decade's work is dominated by his forceful and colossal *Ecce Homo* and other large-scaled sculptures such as *Genesis, Primeval Gods* and *Consummatum Est.* In these monumental carvings of the 1930s, Epstein revealed the depth of his comprehension of primitive styles and his ability to adapt them to his important sculptural concepts.

During World War II, Epstein remained in London, maintaining a steady stream of production. Among the many portraits of exceptional quality were his *Winston Churchill, Yehudi Menuhin* and *Myra Hess.* (The latter reflected his love of music.) The powerful and mysterious *Jacob and the Angel* also made its appearance. Another angel, *The Fall of Lucifer*, was completed at this time. It had evolved from sketches and a relief. The sculpture was later gratefully accepted by the people of Birmingham.

Epstein's portraits were widely admired and much in demand. His skill in manipulating his medium never deserted him and he easily laid claim to the position of the greatest portraitist of the century. Like Picasso, Epstein was capable of several styles in any one period. In 1949, he obtained the first of a series of architectural commissions which brought his career to its pinnacle in the 1950s.

The first was for a *Madonna,* commissioned by nuns of the Society of the Holy Child Jesus. This was followed by *Youth Advancing* for the Arts Council for the Festival of Britain. The Fairmount Park Trust of Philadelphia asked him to make a group for the Philadelphia Museum of Art. Epstein traveled to the United States to inspect the site, and eventually produced the monumental group *Social Consciousness.* He was also commissioned to execute a *Christ in Majesty* for Llandaff Cathedral. Interspersed among these gratifying indications of public approval were other accolades: in 1952 the Arts Council honored him with a retrospective exhibition at the Tate Gallery; in 1953 Oxford University gave him the honorary degree of Doctor of Letters; in 1954 Epstein was knighted by Queen Elizabeth.

Then followed three large works: The *Liverpool Giant,* a gigantic figure commissioned for the facade of Lewis's, a Liverpool store; the *T.U.C. Memorial*; and, of course, Epstein's *St. Michael and the Devil* for the rebuilt Cathedral at Coventry.

St. Michael and the Devil climaxed the completion of the new Coventry Cathedral just a little more than twenty years after its total destruction by the Luftwaffe on November 14, 1940. Mounted on the west wall beside the main entrance, the mighty work weighs nearly five tons and the head of the saint is thirty feet above the ground. Surely it is here that Sir Jacob Epstein's fame will live on with his victorious St. Michael.

Although he was ill much of the time during his final years, he continued to work as if propelled by some unseen force. He even insisted upon undertaking the arduous task of carving on the site his T.U.C. War Memorial.

Stricken in 1957 and hospitalized for a time, Epstein maintained a steady pace of demanding work. On August 19, 1959, after working all day on his last commission, *Bowater House Group,* Epstein on leaving his studio said to his wife, "All's well. The group is finished." He went to his room and died in the night.

Jacob Epstein: A True Romantic

MARCH 1967

While in London during 1960, Edward Schinman, a New Jersey businessman, was persuaded by his wife to steal a few hours from work and accompany her to the Tate Gallery, where an exhibition of Jacob Epstein's sculpture was on view. From that moment Mr. Schinman was hooked. He had never collected or even been interested in modern art before. "I was so impressed," he said, "I couldn't think. Epstein's carvings and bronzes seemed to talk to me. At that time we had no idea they could be purchased."

After returning to Wayne, New Jersey, where Mr. Schinman lives, he was unable to shake Epstein's images from his mind, so back to London he went, and with dedicated devotion began acquiring the artist's work. Now, less than eight years later, he owns the largest and most comprehensive Epstein collection in the world, as evidenced by the current exhibition at Fairleigh Dickinson University in Rutherford, New Jersey—an exhibition, by the way, that closes shortly. On view are 140 works, including bronze and stone sculpture, drawings, watercolors, and one oil painting, reputedly and wisely Sir Jacob's only known effort in this medium.

The exhibition proves that Epstein was first, last, and always a sculptor. His best drawings, almost invariably preliminary sketches for bronzes or stone carvings, have a springy viability, an assurance and élan sadly lacking in the watercolors, which are often over-explicit. Sir Jacob was rarely a colorist, though a few flower still lifes recall the explosive radiance of Nolde. It is, however, the heavy-handed watercolors of nudes and landscapes that indicate how alien Epstein found the painter's brush.

Eighty-three bronzes focus on the artist at his best—a best sometimes underrated in America. The exuberant bronze portraits and small, taut, quivering bronze nudes are a testament to the artist's genius for investing clay with expressive content. And, to be sure, it is always Expressionism that underlies Epstein's work, a fact which may explain why he excelled in a spontaneous medium like clay but faltered when he attacked the more formal problems of stone. The speed of his eye, the nervous intuition of his hand were hampered by the laborious process of carving.

A true romantic, Epstein explored and exploited every nuance of human expression, searching for individual meaning in faces, hands, hair, and even in external adornment. Often beards, curls, and coils of hair detach themselves, and, coming to life with snake-like vehemence, characterize the personality of the sitter. Though he was born in America and lived most of his adult years in England, Sir Jacob seems entirely a European artist, influenced more by Rodin, Negro art, and the School of Paris than by Anglo-Saxon memories. One of the few twentieth-century sculptors to pursue the mysteries of portraiture, he remained essentially loyal to earlier traditions, and this despite the furor he occasioned in Britain. Indeed, when he tried to abandon the past he was least successful. One thinks of his vorticist drawings where academic neatness substituted for the excitement of Italian Futurism.

Today we try to understand why England reeled at each successive Epstein onslaught. It was the stone and marble carvings that upset the public, rarely the portraits. Now we look at these carved figures (there are several in the Schinman collection) and realize that the British were offended less by technical innovations than by savage symbolism. Like numerous colleagues in Paris, Epstein borrowed from primitive African sculpture. His hope was to emphasize generic meanings through favorite themes like those that inspired the works, *Maternity, Genesis,* and *Elemental Man.* At times the stone carvings are convincing in their heavy brutality, but more often they tend to be mannered, linear, and overstated.

In contrast, Epstein's small bronze nudes and portraits avoid philosophic pretense and deal with the specific, with his own direct experience. Here one feels the sculptor's hands at work; one feels his electric presence hovering over images that are in part autobiographical. Yet when he tried for monumentality, he often ended up with a rigid tour de force, with large stone carvings that are curiously frozen and pompous.

To compare the tender head, *Baby Awake,* done in Paris before 1905, with the later likeness of Epstein's own child, *Peggy Jean Laughing,* is to understand the sculptor's steady progression toward freer working methods. The early bronze —smooth, simplified, and restrained—becomes a haunting generalization of all babies, but *Peggy Jean Laughing* is an individualized child caught at a specific moment. Hair, open mouth, heavy cheeks, and asymmetrical features vibrate with life and yet there is no attempt to suggest more than an overall impression.

Like Rodin, Epstein broke up the surface of his bronzes so that light both invigorates and transforms them. Deep clefts forge exaggerated shadows that dramatize these pliant, roughly-kneaded heads and charge them with volatile emotions. Yet one senses the underlying structure of jutting chin and sloping shoulder. Take, for example, the bold Slavic features and strong torso of *Girl from Baku.* More contained but no less tense is the likeness of Haile Selassie, his robes, hands, and face all combined in an elegant evocation of authority. Each Epstein portrait is, above all, the study of a personality. From each emanates the quality of the sitter, but also from each emanates the ardent sensibility of the artist himself. He comes across with astonishing intensity.

KATHERINE KUH.

Remember Jacob Epstein?

FEBRUARY 1967

Over the river to Rutherford (N.J.) is where I recommend that New York art-lovers drive one afternoon—or evening, or even Sunday—during the next couple of weeks. There, Fairleigh Dickinson University is presenting in its Nessler Library, on campus, what is probably the largest exhibition of sculpture by the late Sir Jacob Epstein ever held in America.

The unforgettable Sir Jacob, dead only since 1959, has, at least on his native side of the ocean (he was born on New York's Lower East Side), been almost forgotten. Ours is a time, remember, when the mobiles of Alexander Calder and the mountainous near-abstractions of Henry Moore are described—I read it in a newspaper last week—as the conventional "musts" for every major new architectural project.

It's possible Epstein isn't known at all to a generation brought up on such new forms as sculpture fashioned, sometimes very handsomely, of nuts, bolts and assorted debris picked up off a junk-heap, and on the huge, impersonal, machine-smooth geometrical constructions known as "minimal" sculpture. In any case, the bronze portrait heads and the large marble and alabaster symbolic figures which Epstein was famous for are out of fashion.

Actually the old man knew what was happening when he made his last visit to this country from his home in England, late in the '50s. And he was very bitter about it. He had himself been the veteran of countless controversies with the esthetic, social, even religious Establishment. In 1913 he was one of a group of dissident artists who formed "The Vortex." Protesting against the Academy elders who imitated the art of Greece and Renaissance, they turned for inspiration to primitive art, principally the monumental heads of the Easter Islands.

And yet when the still burly old rebel was here he ran into some abstract sculpture by David Smith, who's also dead now, and counted a major figure and inspiration for a new generation of sculptors. And he sounded off thunderously in precisely the old no-foundation-anywhere-down-the-line clichés which old revolutionaries so often throw at the new avant-garde.

No matter. Epstein's pieces, in or out of style, will stand up as what they are, the most vital sculptured portraits of our century. Maybe that's a reckless statement, since we've more than 30 years still to go. But then portraiture itself may never come back—possibly because the human race begins, these days, to look as stamped-out as everything else.

Still, it should be pointed out that Epstein's subjects included some singularly arresting characters, like Shaw, Churchill, Haile Selassie, Paul Robeson. They're all to be seen out in Rutherford now, a battery of men so intensely alert, so charged with nervous energy, a group of such acutely listening, waiting presences, as to be eerie. They're so alive that as I looked at them the other day, I remembered the things Epstein told me, on that last visit to America, about sittings, about Shaw arguing with him because he had a "plan." ("You shouldn't have a plan. Each day I begin with brand-new ideas." And Epstein's reply, "Try altering a big block of stone each day!"); about Haile Selassie's posing while the whole Abyssinian court stood around and conducted its business with him; about Paul Robeson's keeping the sculptor's little daughter quiet by singing lullabies as he posed.

The monuments in the exhibition don't catch the transient but profoundly revealing gestures that the portrait heads do. Their gestures, broader and heavier, but no less tense, have the quality of eternity in them. But it is through rhetoric, rather than direct speech. And this should be no surprise, in view of Epstein's admiration for the sculpture of primitive peoples. Those weren't direct speech, either, but commanding symbols communicating aspects of deep and universal human experience, of death, sex, sacrifice, bondage. Sometimes, in the monuments, the artist declaims about them as if he felt they were indistinguishable.

And that, I think, is why the drawings and paintings in the show afford such unexpected pleasure. The paintings are mostly landscapes in watercolor. By anyone else they would be admirable but not really exceptional views of sun-lit forests and flowers. For Epstein, so dedicated to capturing the character of his subjects, so sternly, grimly, even melodramatically given to projecting big ideas in his monuments, these must have meant complete release. Here one feels a free man, reveling in the movement of motes in the sun, in the green and mysterious depths of the woods, in brilliantly colored flowers that seem as alive on their stalks as human heads on their bodies.

More satisfying even than these are Epstein's drawings. In these the bridling energy is suddenly set free. Now the line, instead of tracing nervous tension, is all relaxed sensuousness. The naked female bodies stretch out as languidly as those of Modigliani, or Pascin. The aggressiveness of the monuments, the vigilance of the portrait heads, are in these replaced by voluptuousness. Quick linear rhythms of thigh, breast, belly, slip into each other in sequences which suggest that only in these did Epstein directly identify with the essence of nature rather than with ideas and forms, or even the image of nature as we see it in the landscapes.

They bring to mind something Epstein once wrote, recalling his beginnings on New York's Hester Street, before he went abroad to study with Rodin in Paris, and eventually to become not only a famous British citizen, but knighted by the Queen. The Lower East Side, when he was born there in 1880, had he remembered the character of an Oriental city. One remembers that, seeing the drawings of luxuriating, sensuous odalisques in the new exhibition. The factual, evangelistic, messianic sides of the ghetto-born New York Jew who became a titled but never-quite-proper Englishman, took over only in his public works.

The Epstein collection on view at Fairleigh Dickinson now (83 bronzes, 28 drawings, 20 watercolors, eight stone carvings, one oil), belongs to Edward P. Schinman, who is a member of the university president's council.

It is the latest in a series of events held in the college library and open not only to students but to residents of this community which hasn't a museum in the area. Another exhibition, a group show of sculpture assembled recently especially for the blind, came with labels and wall-notes in Braille.

I learn, moreover, that the university, not yet 25 years old, has a unique art program that reaches beyond temporary exhibitions. It hasn't to do with anything as formal as art classes (the school doesn't even offer an art major yet), but rather with developing an awareness of art in the students' daily lives on the several university campuses.

Dr. Peter Sammartino, chancellor, spoke about it as we sat in his office hung with exceptionally good works by Reginald Marsh and Marsden Hartley. Then we went in and out of classrooms on the campuses in both Rutherford and Teaneck, seeing pictures and sculpture everywhere.

Some works were very good. Others ranged from mediocre to poor, which was a great pity, especially since what was shown was not student work, where poor quality might be justified, but works by artists in the community.

On the Teaneck campus I found the students were involuntarily involved not only with the visual arts but also with music, theater and dance. Notices were posted on bulletin boards about freshman and sophomore class tickets for *Measure for Measure,* the American Symphony Orchestra, and any number of other cultural events in Manhattan.

It appears that tuition costs for this branch of the college cover even the price of tickets. The idea is that a school must not assume that its students will become automatically involved with art because it is physically close to where art is. Fairleigh Dickinson provides tickets for major events for all students. Since the students have paid for them, they get there. It's a great idea, even though Dr. Sammartino winces at its being called "forced exposure." It's precisely that —and I'm all for it.

EMILY GENAUER

Bibliography

BOOKS

1. Black, Robert. *The Art of Jacob Epstein.* New York: The World Publishing Co., 1942.
2. Buckle, Richard. *Jacob Epstein—Sculptor.* New York: The World Publishing Co., 1963.
3. Dieren, Bernard Van. *Epstein.* London: John Lane Ltd. 1920
4. Epstein, Jacob. *An Autobiography.* New York: E. P. Dutton & Co., Inc., 1955.
5. Epstein, Jacob. *Let There Be Sculpture.* New York: G. P. Putnam's Sons, 1940.
6. Epstein, Kathleen. *Epstein Drawings.* New York: The World Publishing Co., 1962.
7. Hapgood, Hutchins. *The Spirit of the Ghetto.* Cambridge: Harvard University Press, 1967.
8. Haskell, Arnold L. *The Sculptor Speaks*. London: William Heinemann Ltd., 1931.
9. Powell, L. B. *Jacob Epstein.* London: Chapman & Hall Ltd., 1932.
10. Wellington, Herbert. *Seventy-Five Drawings by Epstein.* London: J. Saville & Co.
11. Charles Scribner's Sons, 1925. *Jacob Epstein.* New York. (One of the Series of Contemporary British Artists: Edited by Albert Rutherston.)

Catalogues:

Epstein: Arts Council Memorial Exhibition, 1961.

Epstein: Edinburgh Festival Society Memorial Exhibition, 1961.

PERIODICALS AND NEWSPAPERS

Althaus, P. F. "Time: after; photography in the Sculptor's Studio." *Camera* (English Edition), XLV (March 1966), 30–39.

"A Modern Coventry Arises." *N.Y. Times Magazine* (May 6, 1962), 26–27.

"An Epstein Triumph: Mrs. Godfrey Phillips" (anon. rev.). *The Art Digest*, III (Mid-January 1929), cover, 6.

"A New Epstein: Paul Robeson" (anon. rev.). *The Art Digest,* IV (September 1928), 4.

Beavan, J. "Epstein: Victor in a Thirty Year War." *N.Y. Times Magazine* (Nov. 6, 1955), p. 26–27.

Bowness, A. "Tribute to Epstein as Battler for Modern Sculpture." *Arts Magazine*, XXXIV (February 1960), 16–17.
Brookner, A. "Exhibition of Works at the Tate." Burlington Magazine, CIII (December 1961), 523.
Bunting, J. "Reflections on Epstein's Madonna for the Convent of the Holy Child Jesus in Cavendish Square, London." *Liturgical Arts*, XXIII (February 1955), 43–44, 52–53.
Burr, J. "Exhibition at the Mercury Gallery." *Apollo* (new series) LXXXIV (October 1966), 333.
Carter, H. Review of *Let There Be Sculpture*, by Arnold L. Haskell. *Apollo*, XXXIII (February 1941), 51.
Cohn, D. L. "Jacob Epstein." *Atlantic Monthly*, CLXIV (December 1939), 751–758.
Connolly, C. "Sculptor Paints: Exhibition of Series of Illustrations to the Old Testament." *Architectural Review*, London, LXXI (March 1932), 101.
"Consummatum Est" (anon. rev.). *Apollo,* XXVI (December 1937), 363–364.
"Consummatum Est" (anon. rev.). *Art Digest*, XII (November 1, 1937), 15.
"Controversy Over the Epstein Theory in Sculpture" (anon. rev.). *Current Opinion*, LXVIII (June 1920), 826, 827.
Cournos, John. "Jacob Epstein: Artist-Philosopher." *International Studio*, LXXI (August 1920), 173–178.
Cournos, J. "Sculpture of Jacob Epstein." *Fortnightly Review*, London, CVII (June 1917), 1010–1019.
"Drawings and Bronzes by Jacob Epstein" (anon. rev.). *Apollo*, VIII (December 1928), 376–377.
Earp, T. W. "Jacob Epstein at the Leicester Galleries." *Apollo*, XXI (April 1935), 226–227.
"Epstein Answers His Critics" (anon. rev.). *Current History*, L (August 1939), 51–52.
"Epstein at the Leicester Galleries" (anon. rev.). *Apollo*, XVII (June 1933), 277–278.
"Epstein's Critics" (anon. rev.). *Burlington Magazine*, CI (November 1959), 369.
"Epstein's Consummatum Est" (anon. rev.). *Apollo*, XXVI (December 1937), 363–364.
"Epstein's Fighting Saint: Concluding Sir Basil Spence's Cathedral Out of the Ashes." *London Sunday Times*, magazine section (May 27, 1962), 26.
"Epstein's Latest—a Wrong Thing Well Done: Consummatum Est" (anon. rev.). *Art Digest,* XII (December 15, 1937), 17.
"Epstein's Recent Portraiture at the Leicester Galleries" (anon. rev.). *Apollo*, LVIII (July 1953), 3.
"Epstein's 'Risen Christ' Sensation of Art World." *N.Y. Call* (March 3, 1920).
"Epstein's Sympathy: Haile Selassie" (anon. rev.). *Art Digest XI* (December 15, 1936), 21.
"Epstein's Works Given To Israel." *N.Y. Times* (August 25, 1961).
"Exhibition at Crystal Gallery" (anon. rev.). *Art News*, LX (May 1961), 15.
"Exhibition at James Graham" (anon. rev.). *Art News*, LVII (April 1958), 14.
"Exhibition at New Arts Center Gallery" (anon. rev.). *Art News* LIX (November 1960), 14.
"Exhibition at The Tate Gallery" (anon. rev.). *Apollo*, LVI (November 1952), 136.
"Exhibition at The Tate Gallery" (anon. rev.). *Studio*, CLXXXIX (December 1952), 91.
"Exhibition at Washington Irving Gallery" (anon. rev.). *Art News*, LXV (December 1966), 10.
"Exhibition Leicester Galleries" (anon. rev.). London Studio XV (Studio CXV), (January 1938), 30 +.
"Exhibition Leicester Gallery" (anon. rev.). *Apollo*, XL (July 1944), 2–3.
"Exhibition Leicester Galleries" (anon. rev.). *Studio*, CXXXIII (May 1947), 133.

"Exhibition, Marie Sterner Galleries" (anon. rev.). *Art News*, XXXVIII (January 6, 1940), 13.

"Exhibition of Drawings, 'Les Fleurs de Mal' at Tooth's Galleries" (anon. rev.). *Apollo*, XXIX (January 1939), 29.

"Exhibition, Tooth's Galleries" (anon. rev.). *Apollo*, XXV (January 1937), 48.

"Exhibition at the Washington Irving Gallery" (anon. rev.). *Art News*, LXV (Summer 1966), 11.

Farr, D. Review of *Jacob Epstein Sculptor* by R. Buckle. *Apollo*, (New Series), LXXIX (April 1964), 346–347.

"Flower Pieces at the Leicester Galleries" (anon. rev.). *Apollo*, XXXII (December 1940), 164.

Fried, M. "Epstein Amid the Moderns." *Arts Magazine,* XXXVI (January 1962), 50–52.

Fry, Roger. "Mr. Epstein's Sculpture." *Dial*, LXXVI (June 1924), 502–506.

Furst, H. "Jacob Epstein's Night Group on the Underground Railway Offices." *Apollo*, X (July 1929), 66.

Furst, H. "Madonna and Child: Bronze Group." *Apollo*, XI (June 1930), 484–485.

Furst, H. "Series of Drawings." *Apollo*, XII (July 1930), 80.

Gadfly, Dorothy. "Gill and Epstein." *The American Magazine of Art*, XXVII (June 1934), 325–333.

Gaunt, W. "Jacob Epstein and the Old Testament." *London Studio*, III (*Studio*, CIII) (May 1932), 290–291.

Genauer, Emily. "Remember Jacob Epstein?" *N.Y. World Telegram* (March 5, 1947), 29, 33.

Golding, Louis. "Persons and Personages, Michaelangelo of Today." *Living Age,* CCCXLVII (November 1939), 244–247.

Golding, Louis. "Jacob Epstein." *T'ien Hsia,* VII (November 1938), 331–341 (*Shanghai Literary Monthly*).

Gordon-Stables, L. "Exhibition, Knoedler Galleries." *Art News*, XXVIII (June 7, 1930), 15.

Haskell, Arnold L. "Epstein's 'Behold the Man.'" *London Studio,* IX (*Studio* CIX) (May 1935), 272–273.

"Illustrations to the Old Testament by Epstein at the Redfern Gallery" (anon. rev.). *Apollo*, XV (March 1932), 133–135.

Irwin, David. "Review of Epstein Drawings." *Burlington Magazine,* CV (February 1963), 82.

Irwin, D. Review of *Jacob Epstein. Sculptor*, by R. Buckle. *Burlington Magazine*, CVI (September 1964), 431–432.

"It is Finished: Consummatum Est" (anon. rev.). *Life*, III (November 15, 1937). 88–92.

"Jacob Epstein, Sculptor: Lillian Shelley, Augustus John, Portrait Busts by Jacob Epstein" (anon. rev.). *American Art News,* XV (May 26, 1917), 3.

"Jew on Jewry" (anon. rev.). *Art Digest, VI* (April 15, 1932), 19.

Kramer, Hilton. "Homage to Sir Jacob." *Reporter,* XXI (October 1, 1959), 38–40.

Kramer, Hilton. "Sir Jacob Epstein at the Modern Museum." *N.Y. Times* (October 29, 1966).

Kuh, Katherine. "Jacob Epstein: A True Romantic." *Saturday Review* (March 25, 1967), 48–49.

Kuh, Katherine. "The Art that History Shaped." *Saturday Review* (January 29, 1966), 17–24.

McCance, William. "Consummatum Est: 1937." *The News Chronicle,* London (October 28, 1937).

"Masque de Meum" (anon. rev.). *Chicago Art Institute Newsletter* (December 1921–December 1923), 125.
"Miriam, Bronze Statuette" (anon. rev.). *Architectural Review,* LV (March 1924), 107.
Nicolson, Benedict. "Editorial: Epstein's Critics." *Burlington Magazine,* CI (November 1959), 369.
O'Connor, J. "Bronze Head of G. B. Shaw." *Carnegie Magazine,* XXII (October 1948), 77.
"Orchids: Design for Steuben Glass." (anon. rev.). *American Artist,* XVIII (June 1954), 52; *Studio,* CXLIX (May 1955), 17.
"Paintings at Leicester Gallery." (anon. rev.). *Studio,* CXXIX (March 1945), 89.
Payne, Elizabeth H. "A Portrait Head of Paul Robeson." Smith College Museum of Art Bulletin, XIV (May 1933), 11–13.
Remington, Preston. "Jacob Epstein: A Study in Treatment of Surface." *Metropolitan Museum of Art Bulletin,* No. 19, (July 1924), 165–166.
"Retrospective at the Tate Gallery" (anon. rev.). *Art News,* LI (June 1952), 102.
"Retrospective Exhibition at the Tate" (anon. rev.). *Burlington Magazine,* XCIV (October 1952), 304.
Richards, L. "Epstein's Bronze Mask: Marchesa Casati." *Oberlin College Bulletin* VII, (No. 2. 1949), 46–49.
Savage, G. "Art for Investment." *Studio,* CLXII (July 1961), 36.
Sayre, A. H. "Epstein in Watercolor and in Bronze: Exhibition, Gallery of René Gimpel." *Art News,* XXXIV (April 11, 1936), 9.
"Sculptor Speaks: Jacob Epstein to Arnold L. Haskell; a Series of Conversations on Art" (anon. rev.). *American Magazine of Art,* XXIV (June 1932), 466–468; *Art News,* XXX (May 14, 1932), 12; *Burlington Magazine,* XLII (May 1933), 249.
"Sculptors of Today" (anon. rev.). *Aalantic Monthly,* CLXVI (November 1940), 592–603.
"Sell Eight Epsteins" (anon. rev.). *The Art Digest,* II (December 1, 1927), 1, 4.
Shipp, H. "Epstein at the Leicester Galleries." *Apollo,* LXXI (June 1960), 164.
"Show at Weintraub Gallery" (anon. rev.). *Art News,* LXV (January 1967), 12.
"Sir Jacob" (anon. rev.). *Time,* LXIII (January 11, 1954), 54.
"Sir Jacob Epstein Dies; Controversial Sculptor." *N. Y. Herald Tribune* (August 22, 1959).
"Sir Jacob Epstein, 78, is Dead After Stormy Career as Sculptor." *N. Y. Times* (August 22, 1959), pp. 1 and 17.
Sorrell, M. "Epstein." *Apollo,* LI (February 1950), 36–38.
Souchal, F. Review of *Jacob Epstein, Sculptor,* by Buekle. *La Gazette des Beaux Arts* (Series 6) LXIII (May 1964), 373–374.
"Spurned Sculptor Triumphs." (anon. rev.). *Life,* XXXIII (November 3, 1952), 65–66.
Stechow, W. "Three Works by Jacob Epstein." *Oberlin College—Allen Memorial Art Museum Bulletin,* XXV, No. 1 (Fall 1967), 19–25.
Stone, M. "Portrait." *Artist,* XXXVIII (December 1949), 81.
Sutton, Denys. "Retrospective at The Tate Gallery." *Art News,* LI (June 1952), 102.
Sutton, Denys. "The Significance of Epstein." *Country Life* (London) CXII (Oct. 17, 1952), 1194.
Tittle, W. "Is It Art?" *World's Work,* LV (February 1928), 408–4151.
"Ti-Yi" (anon. rev.). *Los Angeles County Museum of Art Bulletin,* VI (No. 3 Supplement 1954), 33.
"Two Bronze Heads: G. B. Shaw and A. Einstein" (anon. rev.). *Baltimore Museum News Record* XII (March 1949), 3–6.
"Two Heads, Shaw and Albert Einstein, Loaned to The Baltimore Museum of Art" (anon. rev.). *Pictures on Exhibit,* XI (April 1949), 56–57.

Vincent, C. "In Search of a Likeness: Some European Portrait Sculpture." *Metropolitan Museum of Art Bulletin* (new series) XXIV (April 1966), 250–251.
"Volcanic Knight" (anon. rev.). *Time,* LXXIV (August 31, 1959), 44.
"Water-Colours of Epping Forest and the Portrait Bust of Professor Albert Einstein" (anon. rev.). *Apollo,* XIX (January 1934), 47–48.
Wellington, Hubert. "Sir Jacob Epstein." *Goya,* XXXII (September 1959), 88–91.
Whittet, G. S. "Exhibition at The Leicester Galleries." *Studio,* CLX (September 1960), 160.
Whittet, G. S. "Show in The Tate Gallery." *Studio,* CLXIII (January 1962), 34–35.
"Will Epstein's Madonna and Child Cause American Sensation" (anon. rev.). *The Art Digest* II (November 1, 1927), 7.
Winn, Godfrey. "The Day of The Century for Coventry." *London Daily Express* (May 25, 1962), 5.

Catalogue of the Collection

Portraits are printed in the chronological order of their completion. They are listed in this index alphabetically by the first letter in the identification plaque, to make it easy for the viewer to find the matching illustration and accompanying description.

STONE CARVINGS

CHIMERA 1932
CONSUMMATUM EST 1936
ELEMENTAL MAN 1932
FEMALE FIGURE 1913
FLENITE RELIEF 1913
MRS. CHADBURN 1909
SUNFLOWER 1910
WOMAN POSSESSED 1932

DRAWINGS

PROFILE OF WOMAN 1906
STUDY FOR "MATERNITY" 1910
WOMAN RESTING ON ARMS 1906
MATERNITY 1910
PHILOSOPHER 1907
MAN THE DREAMER 1911
STANDING NUDE 1911
VORTICIST FIGURE 1913
ROCK DRILL REFLECTIONS 1915
ROCK DRILL STUDY 1915
STUDY FOR ROCK DRILL 1915
VORTICIST COMPOSITION 1915
ARMY NURSE 1919
RECUMBENT NEGRESS 1925
RECLINING NUDE 1925
SUNITA ASLEEP 1928
SUNITA RECLINING 1928
SUNITA RELAXED 1928
STUDY FOR "NIGHT" 1928
SPIRIT MOVING ON THE WATERS 1930
STUDY FOR "GENESIS" 1931
PIETA 1932
JACKIE—*First Portrait* 1935
JACKIE—*Second Portrait* 1937
INDIAN MOTHER AND CHILD 1932
JACKIE—*Third Portrait* 1940
JACKIE—*Fourth Portrait* 1942
SLAVE HOLD 1941
LA FONTAINE DE SANG 1939
NEGRO CHILD 1940
CHADRACK, MESCHAK AND ABEDNEGO 1933
CALAMUS SKETCH 1901

WATER COLORS

SUNITA DREAMING 1928
SUNITA RESTING 1928
MYSTERY OF EPPING FOREST 1933
GOD IN PEONIES 1933
PROFUSION OF COLOR 1933
NUDE RECLINING 1925
REGAL LILIES 1933
SONG OF SOLOMON 1931
THREE WISE MEN 1932
CALAMUS ILLUSTRATION 1901
CALAMUS ILLUSTRATION II 1901

OIL PAINTING

MEUM

BRONZES

ADMIRAL LORD FISHER	Ca. 1915
AUGUSTUS JOHN	1916
ANGEL OF ANNUNCIATION	1923
ANNABEL FREUD WITH BONNET	1953
BABY AWAKE	Ca. 1904
BABY WITH ARMS	1949
BERNARD VAN DIEREN	1916
BETTY PETERS	1939
BETTY PETERS RECLINING	1939
CHRIST CHILD	1925
DAISY DUNN	1927
DEIRDRE *First Portrait*	1941
DEIRDRE *Third Portrait*	1942
DOLORES	1923
DR. CHAIM WEIZMANN	1933
DR. FREDERICK MALLON	1954
DR. KLEMPERER	1957
ESTHER WITH FLOWER	1949
EUPHEMIA LAMB	1911
FALL OF LUCIFER	1944
FIELD-MARSHAL SMUTS	1955
GEORGE BERNARD SHAW	1934
GERMAINE BRAS	1930
GIRL FROM BAKU	1944
HAILE SELASSIE	1936
HELENE	1919
HEROIC TORSO	1954
IAN	1942
INFANT BACCHUS	1956
JACOB KRAMER	1921
JOAN GREENWOOD	1948
JOSEPH CONRAD	1924
KATHLEEN	1921
KATHLEEN *Fifth*	1935
KATHLEEN *Sixth*	1941
KATHLEEN *Seventh*	1948
KITTY *Third Portrait*	1957
LEDA *Fifth Portrait*	1944
LITTLE PRINCE OF BARODA	1951
LOUISE—BERENICE	1938
LUCIAN FREUD	1947
MADONNA	1927
MADONNA AND CHILD	1927
MAN OF ARAN	1933
MARY	1931
MIRIAM PLICHTE	1921
MRS. EPSTEIN, MANTILLA	1918
MRS. EPSTEIN *Second*	1916
MRS. GODFREY PHILLIPS	1928
MEUM MASK	1918
MURIEL	1948
NAN SEATED	1911
NEPTUNE	1946
OLD ITALIAN WOMAN	1908
OLIVE	1934
PANDIT NEHRU	1949
PAUL ROBESON	1928
PEGGY JEAN ASLEEP	1920
PEGGY JEAN LAUGHING	1921
PEGGY JEAN SICK CHILD	1928
PRINCESS DE BRAGANZA	1944
PRINCESS DESTA	1949
RAGAMUFFIN	1940
RECLINING GODDESS	1931
RESURRECTION	1941
ROMILLY JOHN	1908
SELF PORTRAIT—HAND	
SELF PORTRAIT IN A CAP	1912
SELF PORTRAIT WITH BEARD	1920
SHEILA	1924
SIR RABINDRANATH TAGORE	1926
ST. MICHAEL AND THE DEVIL	1956
TABITHA	1957
TANYA	1937
THE SWIMMER	1939
TIN HAT	1916
TI-YI	1938
TWO SISTERS	1950, 1953
WILLIAM BLAKE	1956
WINSTON CHURCHILL	1946
WYNNE GODLEY	1956
YEHUDI MENUHIN	1943

Plates

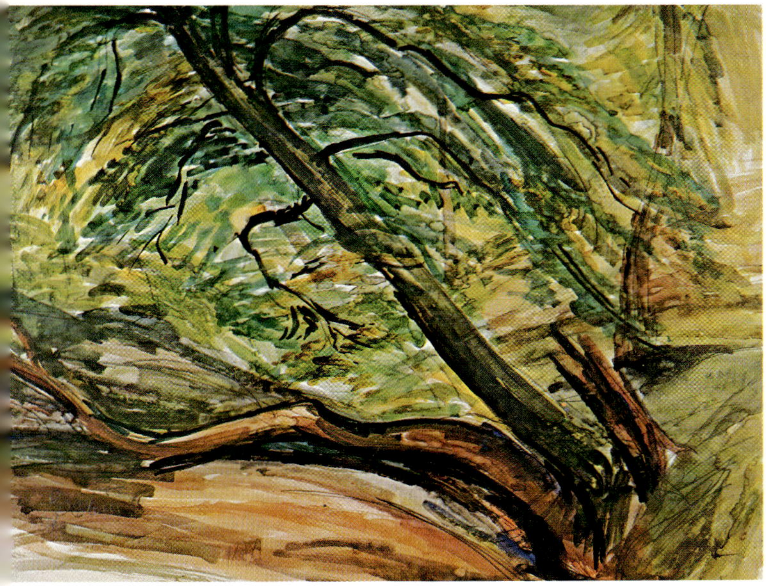

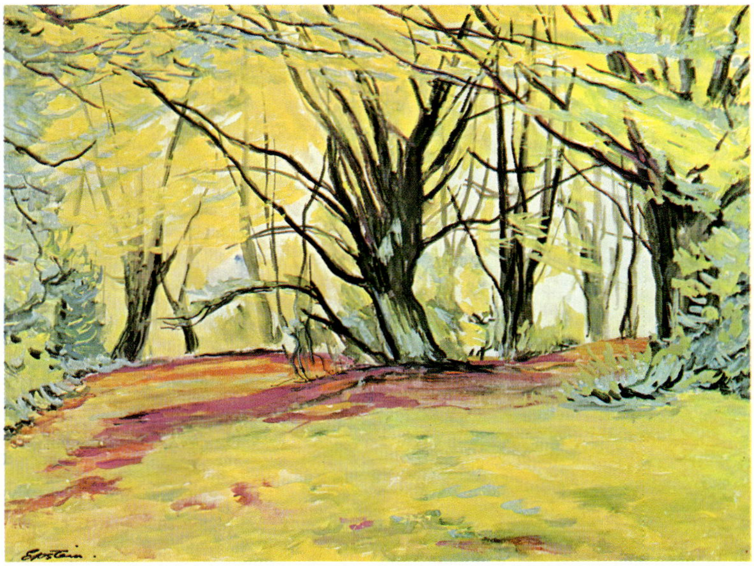

EPPING FOREST, 1926—*Water Color*

For many years Epstein lived at Epping Forest at the edge of Monk's Wood, which is only three miles from Chasing Square in London. There, he was inspired to paint landscapes and flowers in countless numbers.

The technique used for the series of flowers is repeated here. The long, parallel strokes which create the forms of trees seem alive with movement. These are neither abstract nor realistic illustrations of Epping Forest but expressionist landscapes which evoke the happiness Epstein was able to draw from these picturesque surroundings.

SPRING IN EPPING FOREST, 1933—*Water Color*

Sunlight dominates this picture. It is so strong that it even obscures parts of trees. Epstein uses red to keep the ground from merging with the upper zone of the composition. Here the brilliance of his coloring is blinding.

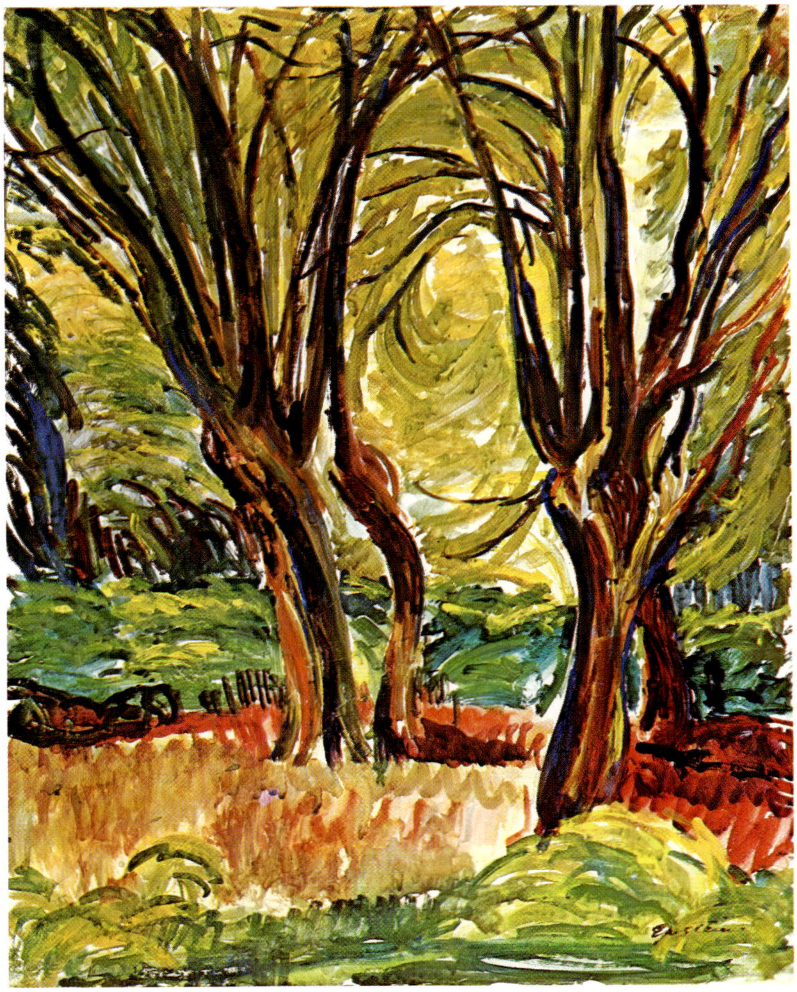

SUMMER IN EPPING FOREST, 1933—*Water Color*

Epstein differentiates earth and sky more by stroke than color. The circular streaks of "air" are set in motion by the branches of the trees. The ground strokes are shorter and straighter. The composition focuses on the yellow sun framed by trees enlivened by their variety of color.

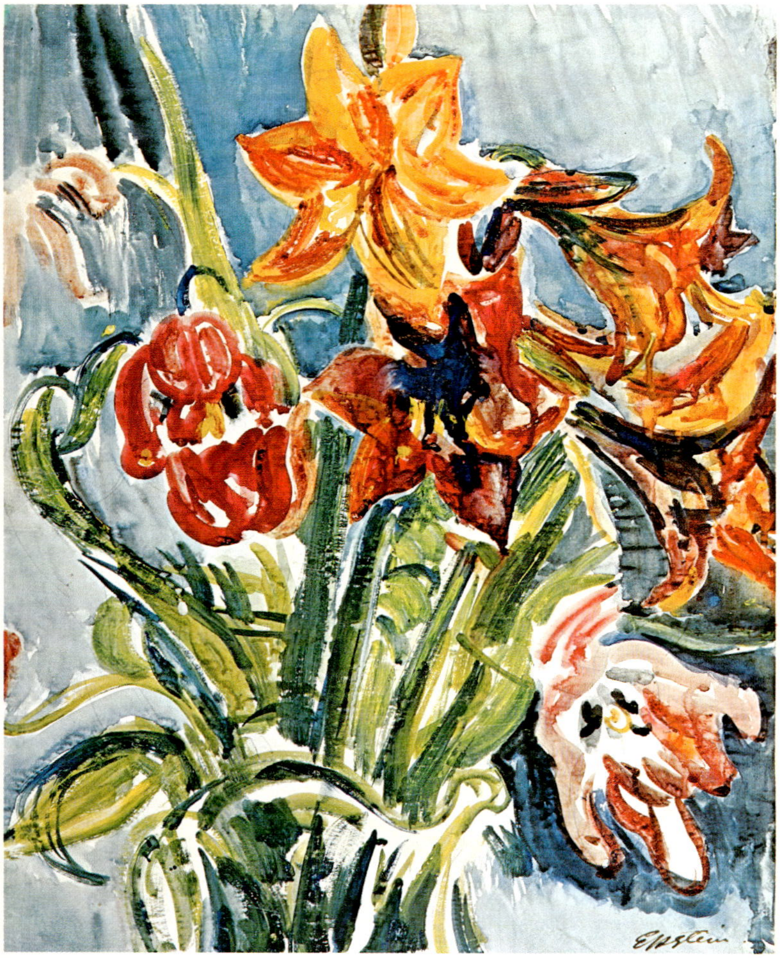

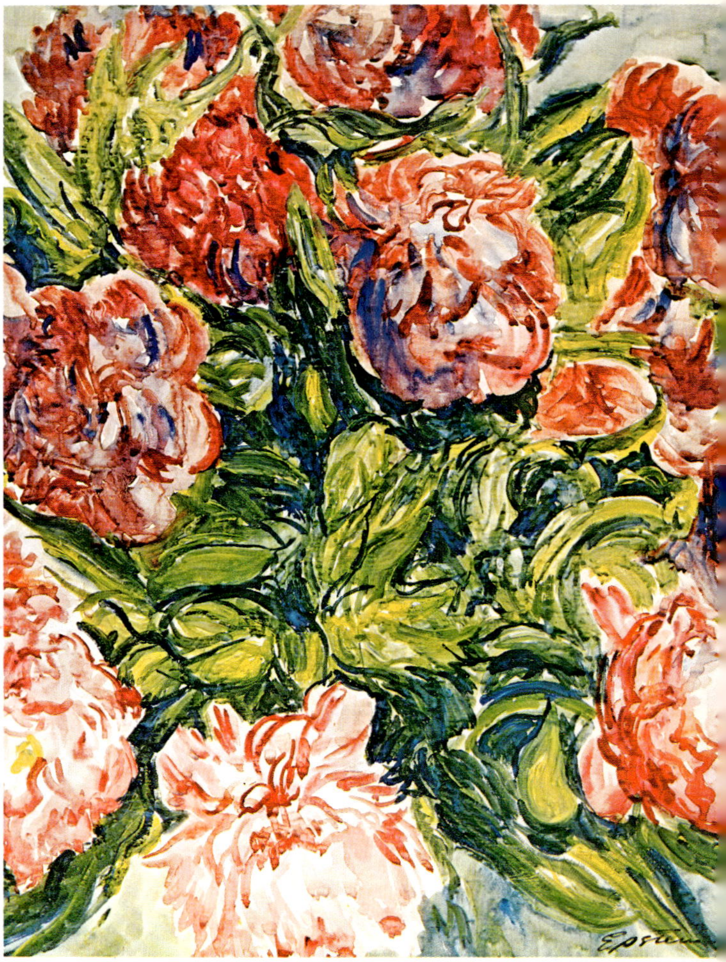

TULIPS—TIGER LILIES, 1933—*Water Color*
Against the cool blue background, the fiery-colored flowers seem to droop into the viewer's space.

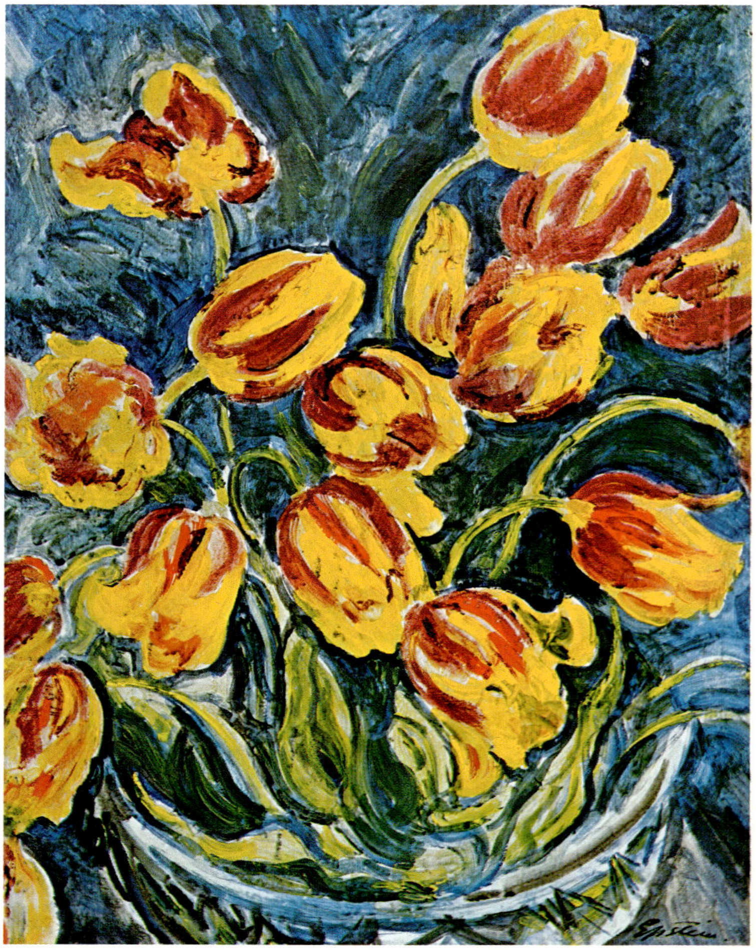

TULIPS, 1933—*Water Color*
Here, the darkness of the blue background gives the water color a mysterious, nocturnal atmosphere.

PEONIES, 1933—*Water Color*

The short, circular strokes of warm red create three-dimensional flowers which stand out against the flatter leaves.

REPOSE, 1928—*Water Color*

The mass of the body is increased by its contrast to the neutral ground. Epstein avoids having the figure float in space by letting the model's arm extend across the pillows.

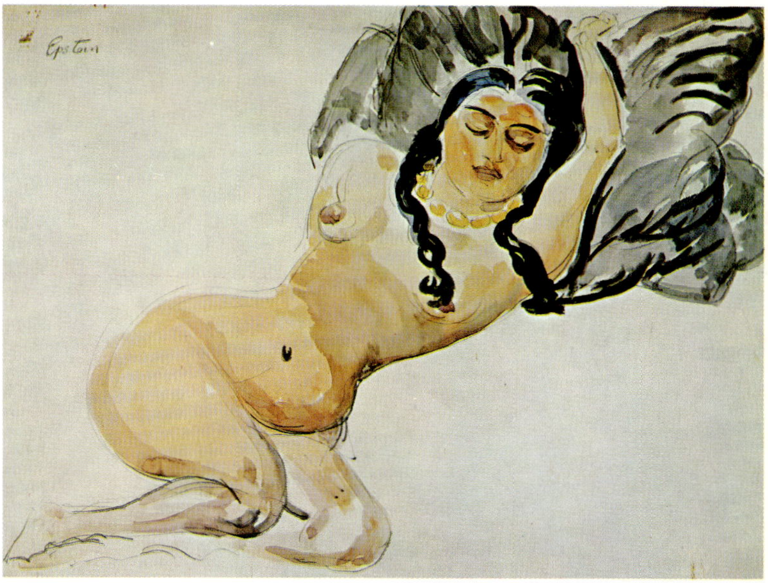

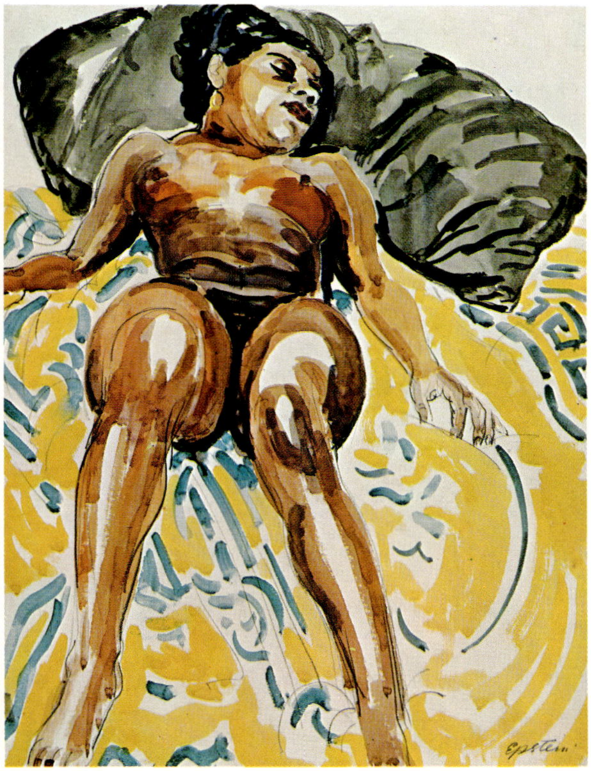

BETTY PETERS, 1945—*Water Color*

In this daring composition Epstein combines the bold foreshortening of a sleeping figure and the two-dimensional pattern of a bedspread. The confident, broad strokes of blue and yellow vibrate over the surface as they swirl in and around the recumbent nude.

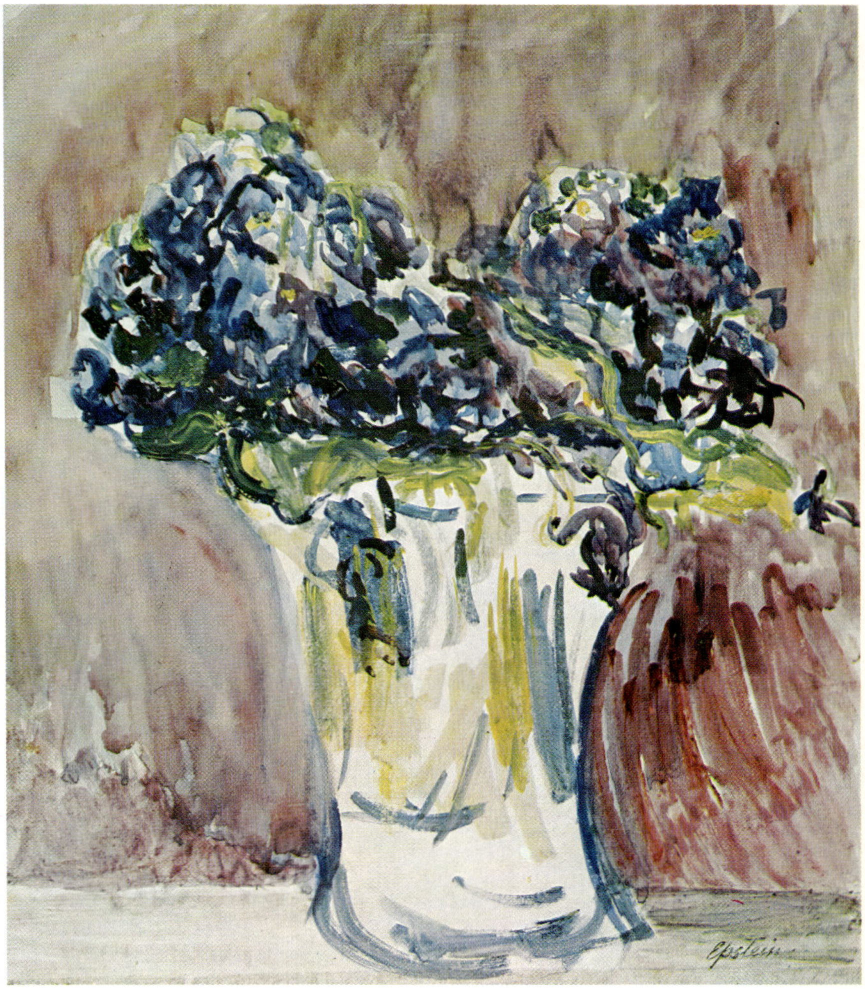

VIOLETS IN VASE, 1933. h. 17″ x w. 15″

Unlike his achievements in the water colors of large flowers, the natural delicacy of these violets is obscured by the heavy-handed wash used in the background and in the vase.

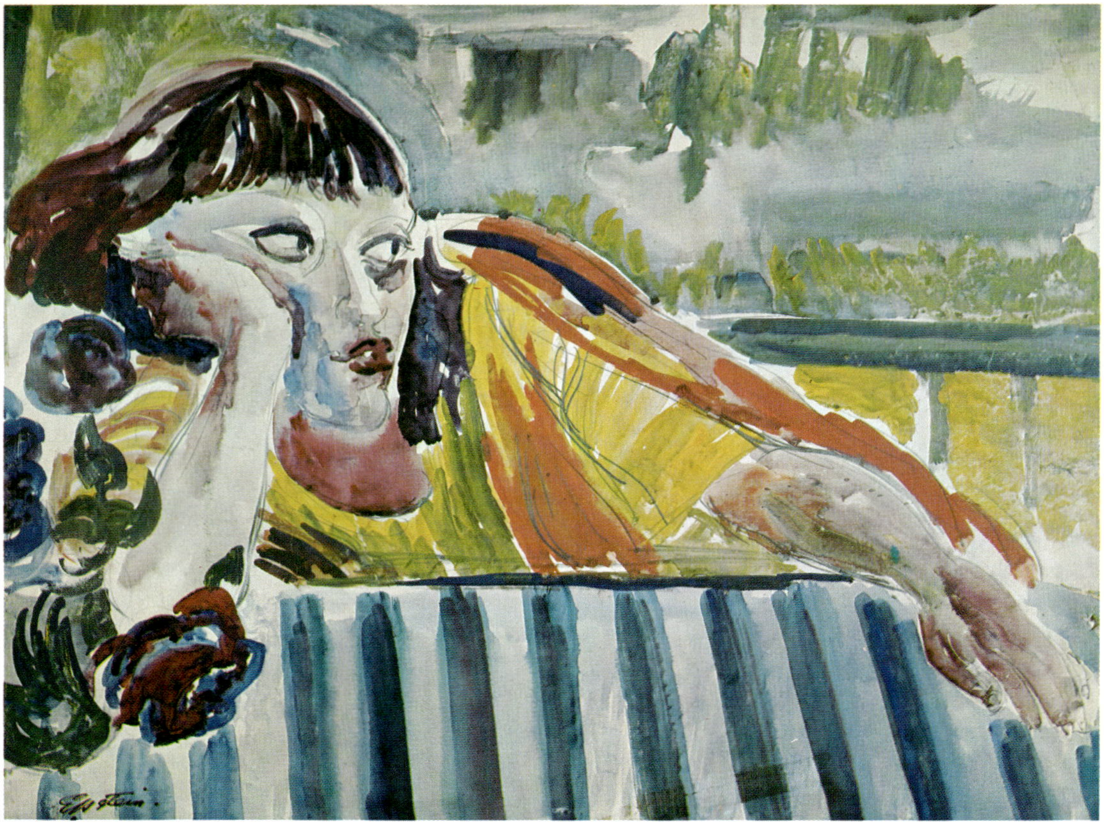

MRS. EPSTEIN, c. 1935. h. 18″ x w. 23″

The movement of this composition clearly reads from left to right—from the windswept hair to the extended left arm. The vivid colors splash boldly across the picture. The background is impressionist in technique while the foreground is expressionist.

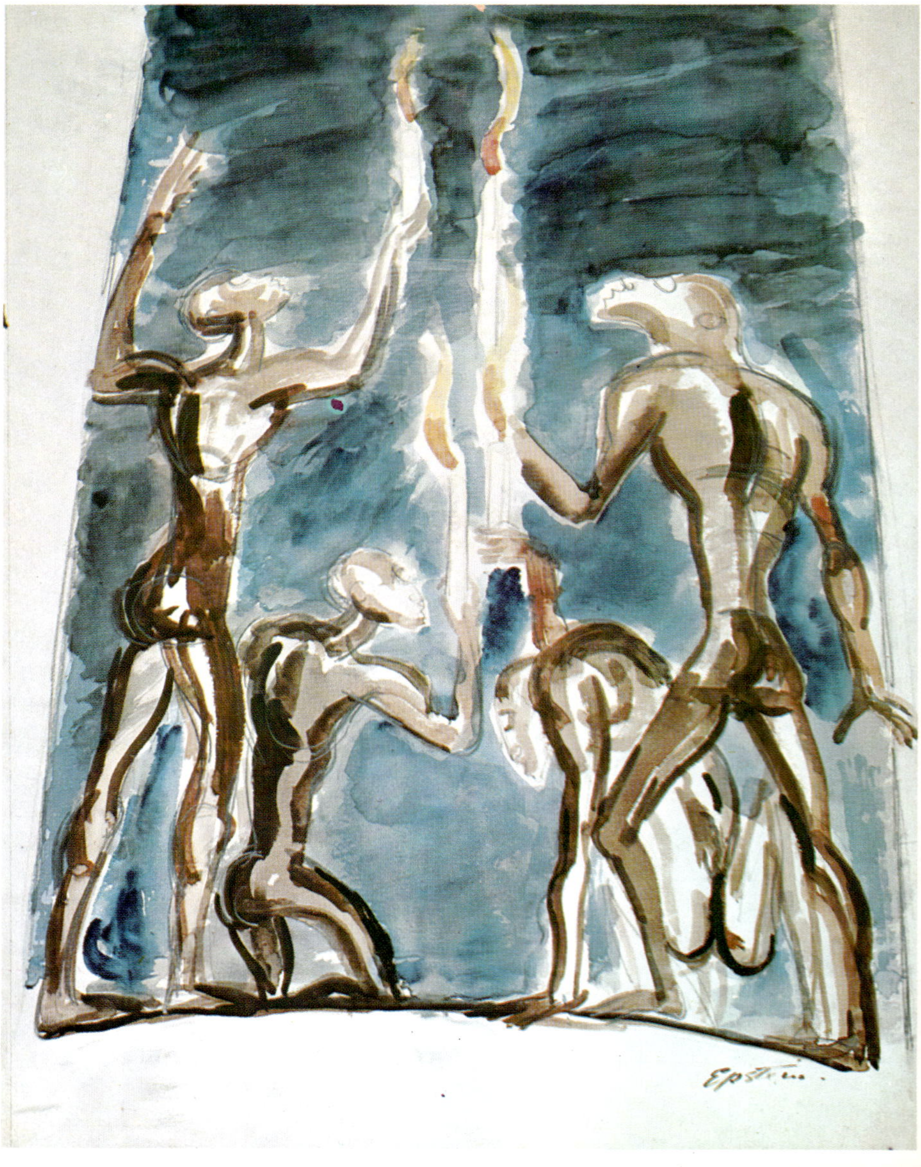

THE FIRE WORSHIPPERS, c. 1940. h. 22″ x w. 17″

This unusual scene shows four dark brown figures bearing torches in a blue darkness. Epstein confines the water color to an area shaped like a truncated triangle. Yet this does not prevent him from letting one of the rightmost figures' hands extend beyond the frame. Although the two upright figures seem to stand in the foreground, the torches of the kneeling figures seem to be well in front of the other two torches. The tension created almost splits the composition in two. The influence of African sculpture is seen in the mask-like faces.

DAISY DUNN, 1927. h. 18½″ w. 18¾″ d. 11½″

The American revue *Florence Mills Blackbirds,* the first all-Negro musical, appeared in London in 1925. Daisy Dunn, an original member of the cast, seems to be deeply involved in the rhythm and blues of the music that surrounds her in Epstein's sculpture. The head nods forward with its fleshy features lost in the world of jazz.

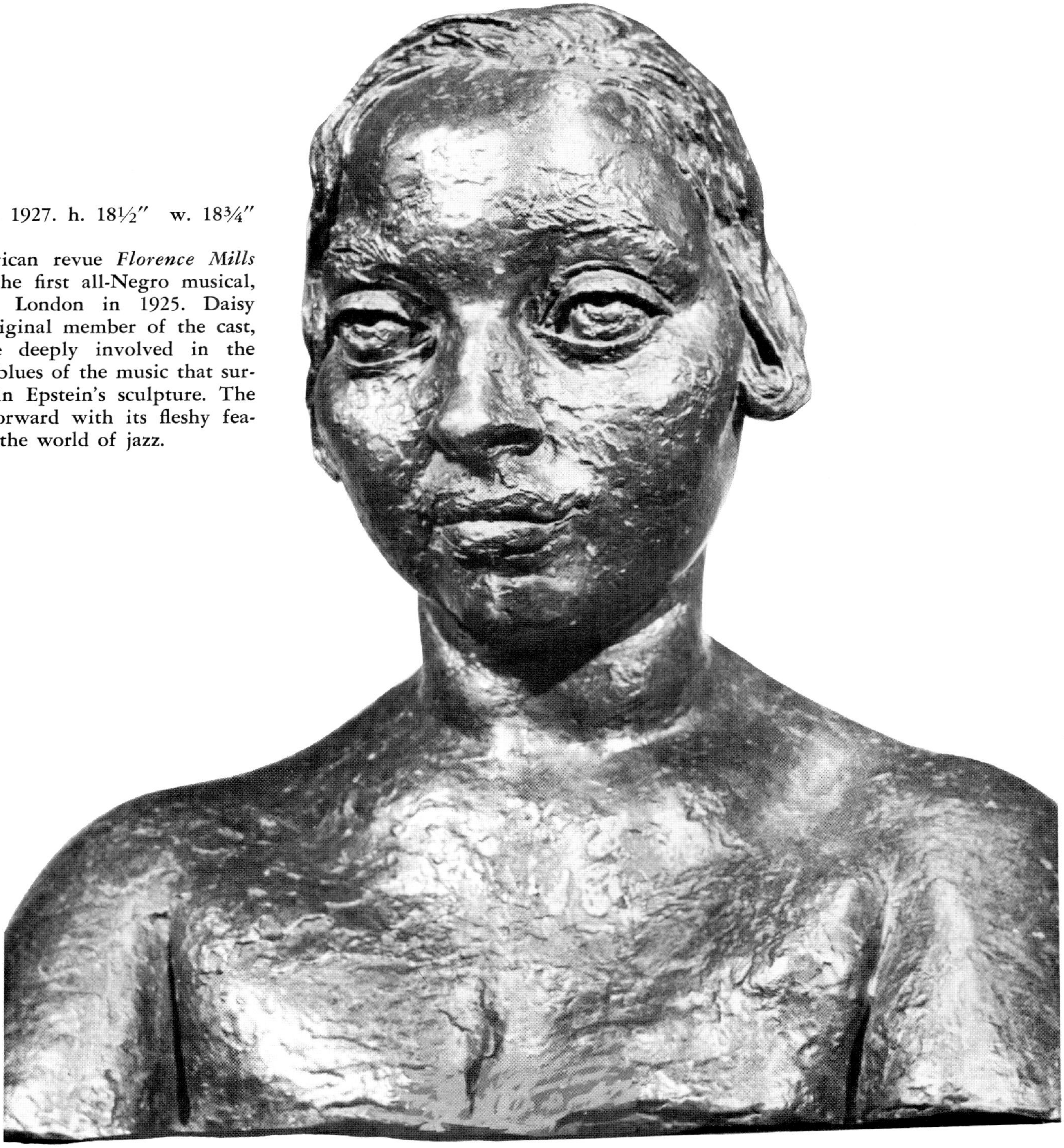

MRS. GODFREY PHILLIPS, 1928. h. 18″ w. 17½″ d. 12″

The sweeping upturned collar and cap-like hair frame the gaunt features of the wife of the director of the Leicester Gallery where Epstein held sixteen exhibitions. Textures range from flesh to the veil-like blouse to the starched collar of the jacket. The vertical lines of the cropped hair arrest the movement of the collar.

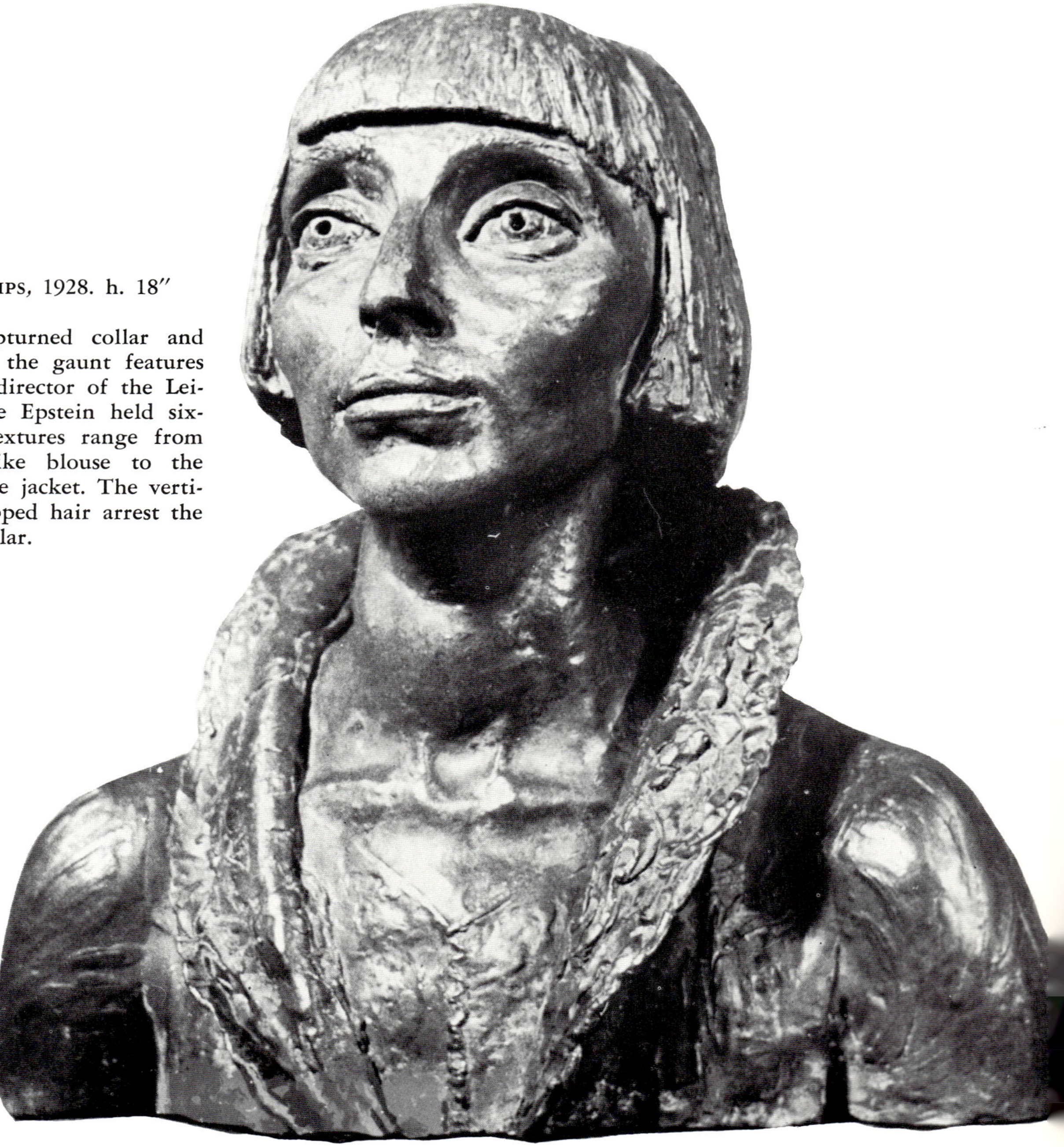

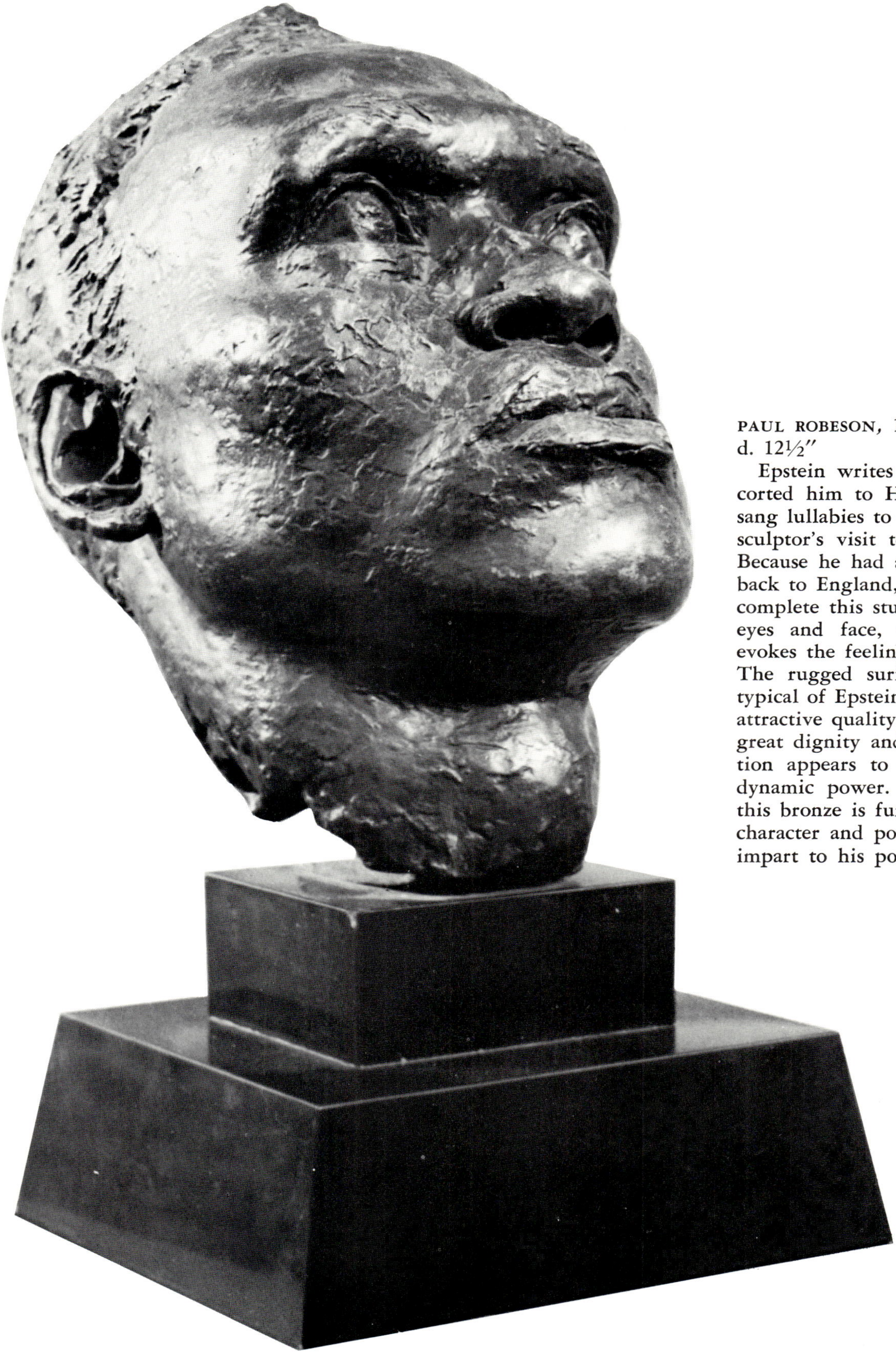

PAUL ROBESON, 1928. h. 12″ w. 9″ d. 12½″

Epstein writes that Paul Robeson escorted him to Harlem dance halls and sang lullabies to Peggy Jean during the sculptor's visit to New York in 1927. Because he had already booked passage back to England, Epstein was unable to complete this study. But with upturned eyes and face, the powerful portrait evokes the feeling of a Negro spiritual. The rugged surface of this bronze is typical of Epstein and has a particularly attractive quality. It adds to the already great dignity and vitality, and in addition appears to create a personage of dynamic power. The surface finish on this bronze is further illustrative of the character and power that Epstein could impart to his portraits.

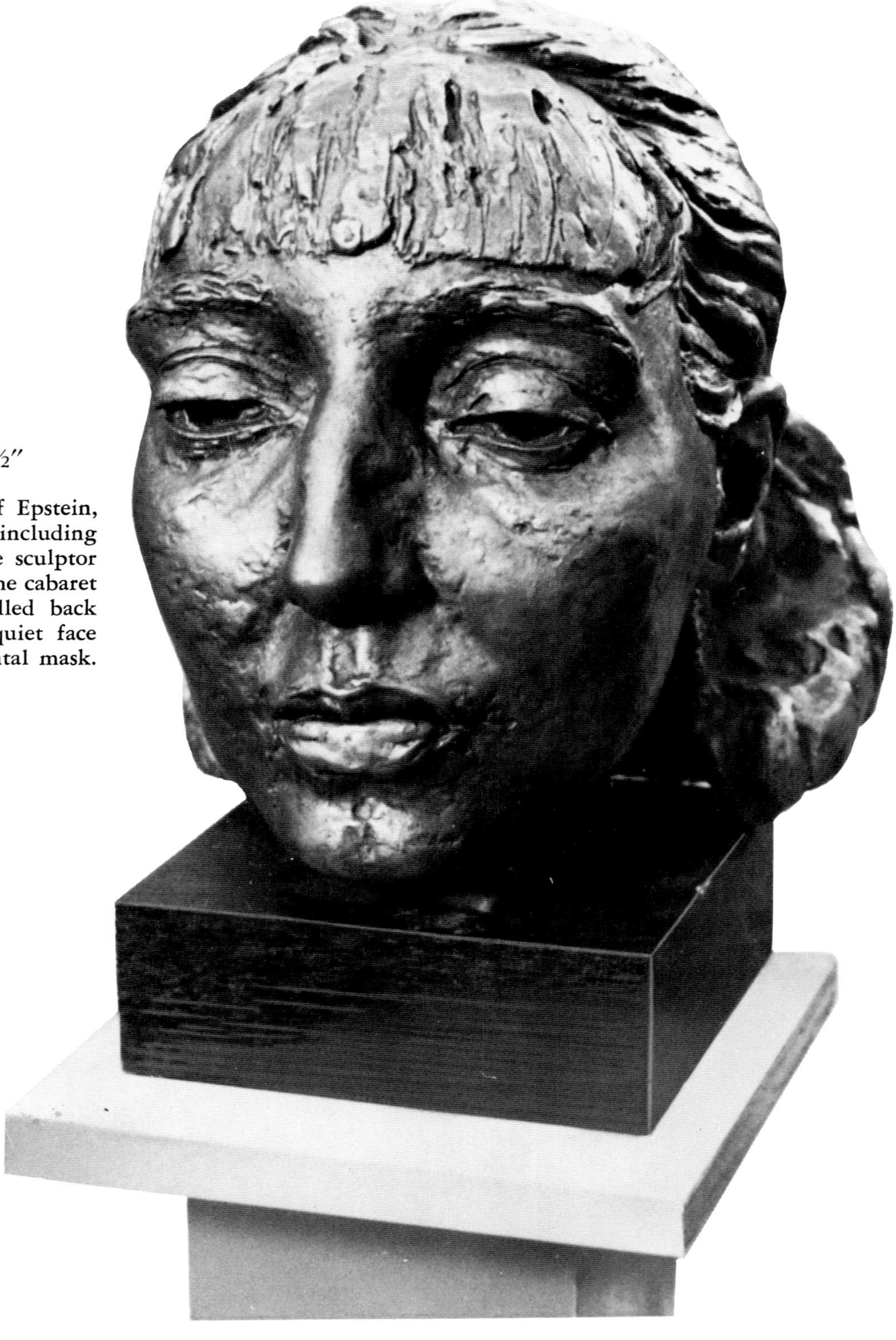

DOLORES, 1923. h. 9½″ w. 8½″ d. 10¾″

Dolores, a favorite model of Epstein, was the subject of five studies including this Fourth Portrait. Here, the sculptor finally captures the essence of the cabaret singer. The wavy hair is pulled back behind her ears to reveal a quiet face styled in the form of an Oriental mask.

ANGEL OF ANNUNCIATION (torso, 62½″) 1923.

This unfinished Angel Torso bears a woman's head modeled after the Parsee pianist Flrose Rastounji and a man's body. Such representation of holy persons goes back to Leonardo's St. John and to the Sistine Ignatius of Michelangelo.

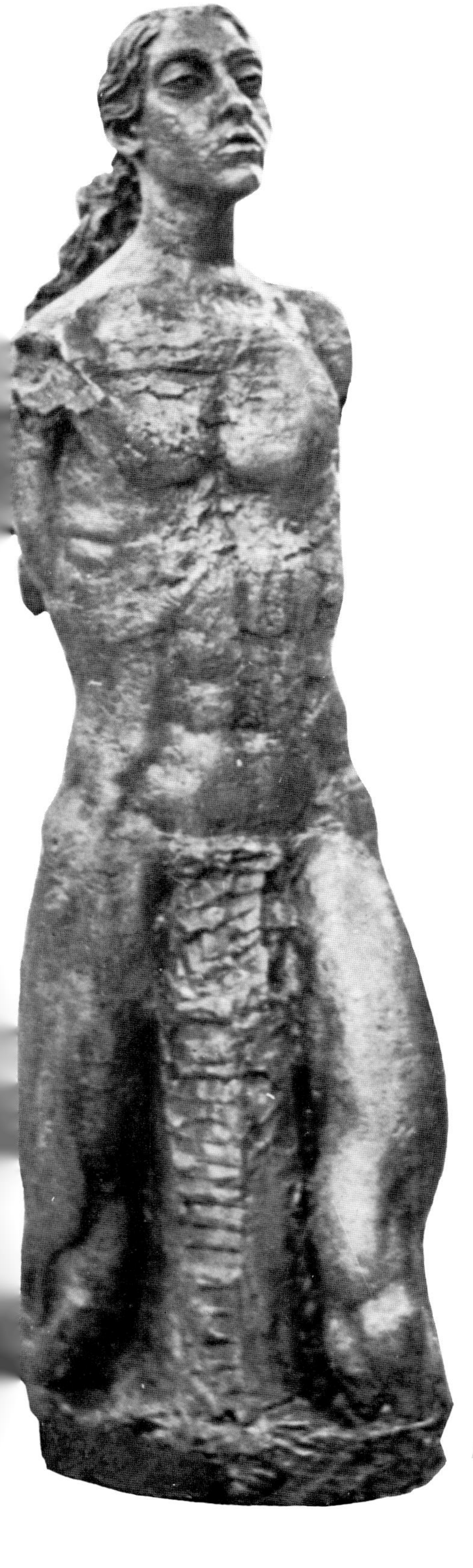

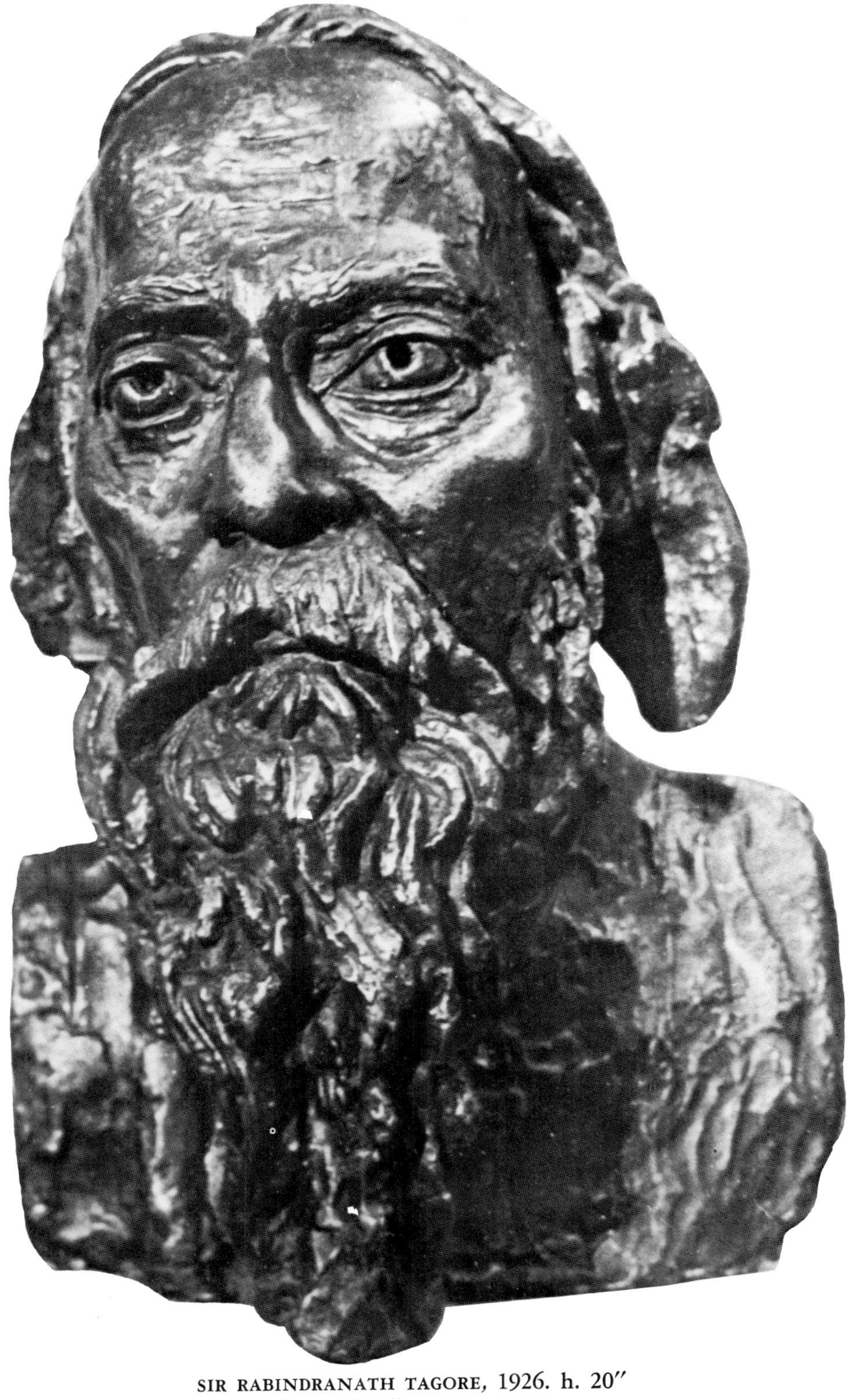

SIR RABINDRANATH TAGORE, 1926. h. 20″ w. 13¼″ d. 11½″

The intense expression and bold modeling combine in this over-lifesize portrait to achieve monumental grandeur. Epstein admits that resting the bust on the beard was an unconscious bit of symbolism. He found the Nobel prizewinner cold, commanding, and uninspiring. (Tagore founded the Vasva-Bharati, the International Institution in Bengal, besides writing poems in English and Bengali, many of which he set to music.)

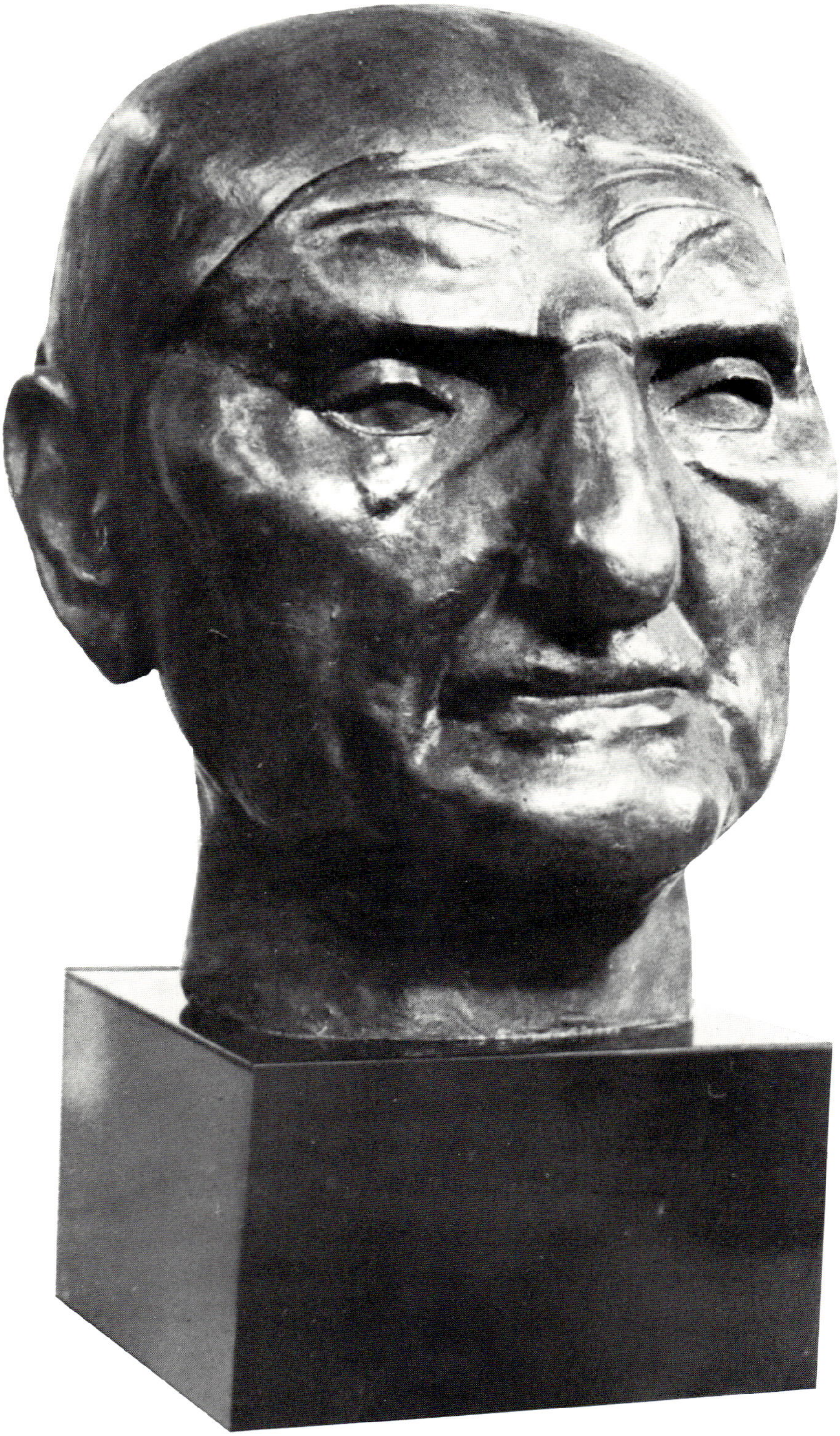

OLD ITALIAN WOMAN, 1907–08. h. 11½″ w. 8″ d. 10″

This portrait and *Romilly John* are the only surviving works of Epstein's early London period. The aged model forms an interesting contrast to the smooth soft flesh of the baby's hands. The hair, parted in the middle and brought back into a bun, is cap-like. Epstein does not attempt to idealize her face.

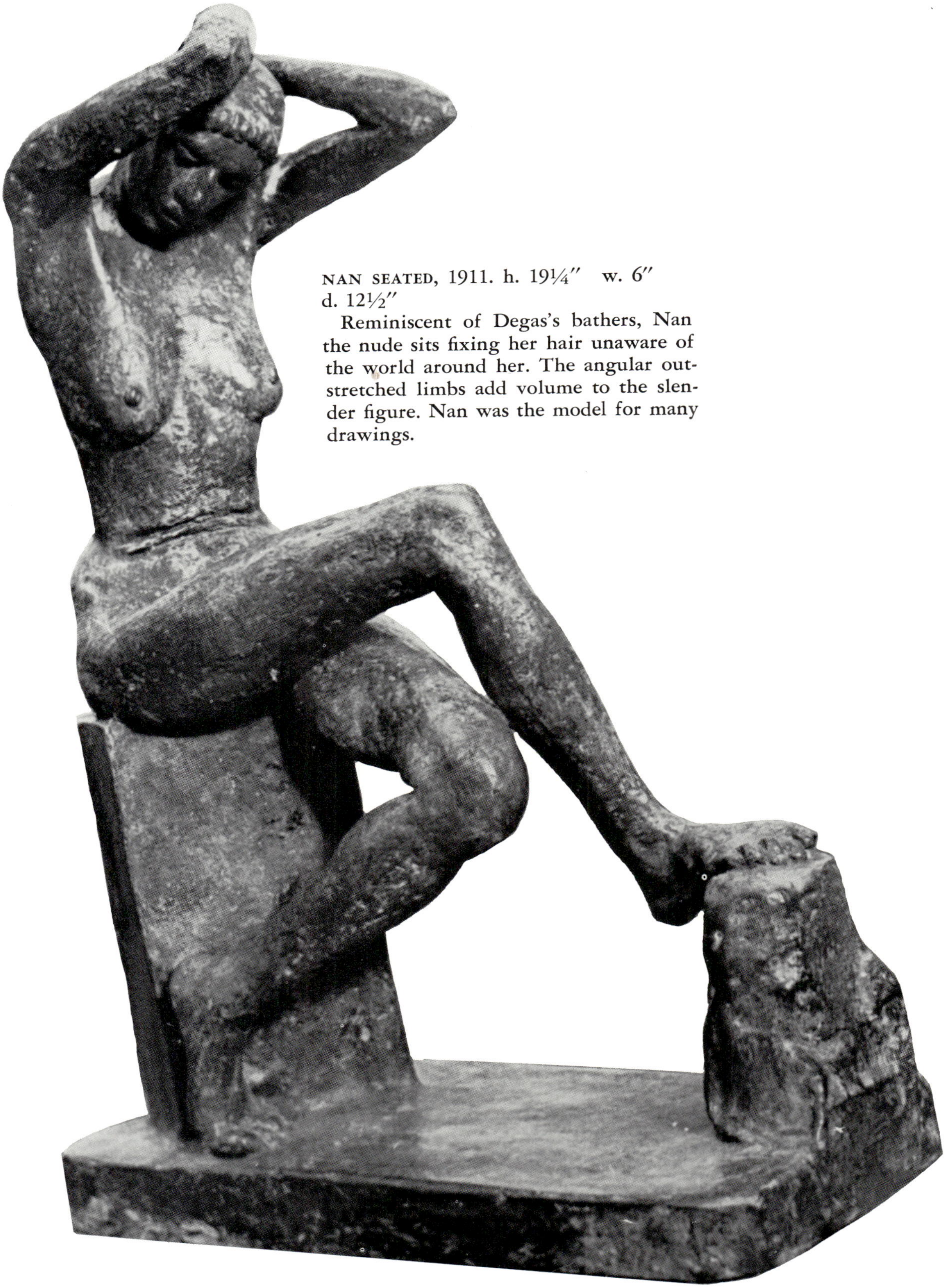

NAN SEATED, 1911. h. 19¼″ w. 6″ d. 12½″

Reminiscent of Degas's bathers, Nan the nude sits fixing her hair unaware of the world around her. The angular outstretched limbs add volume to the slender figure. Nan was the model for many drawings.

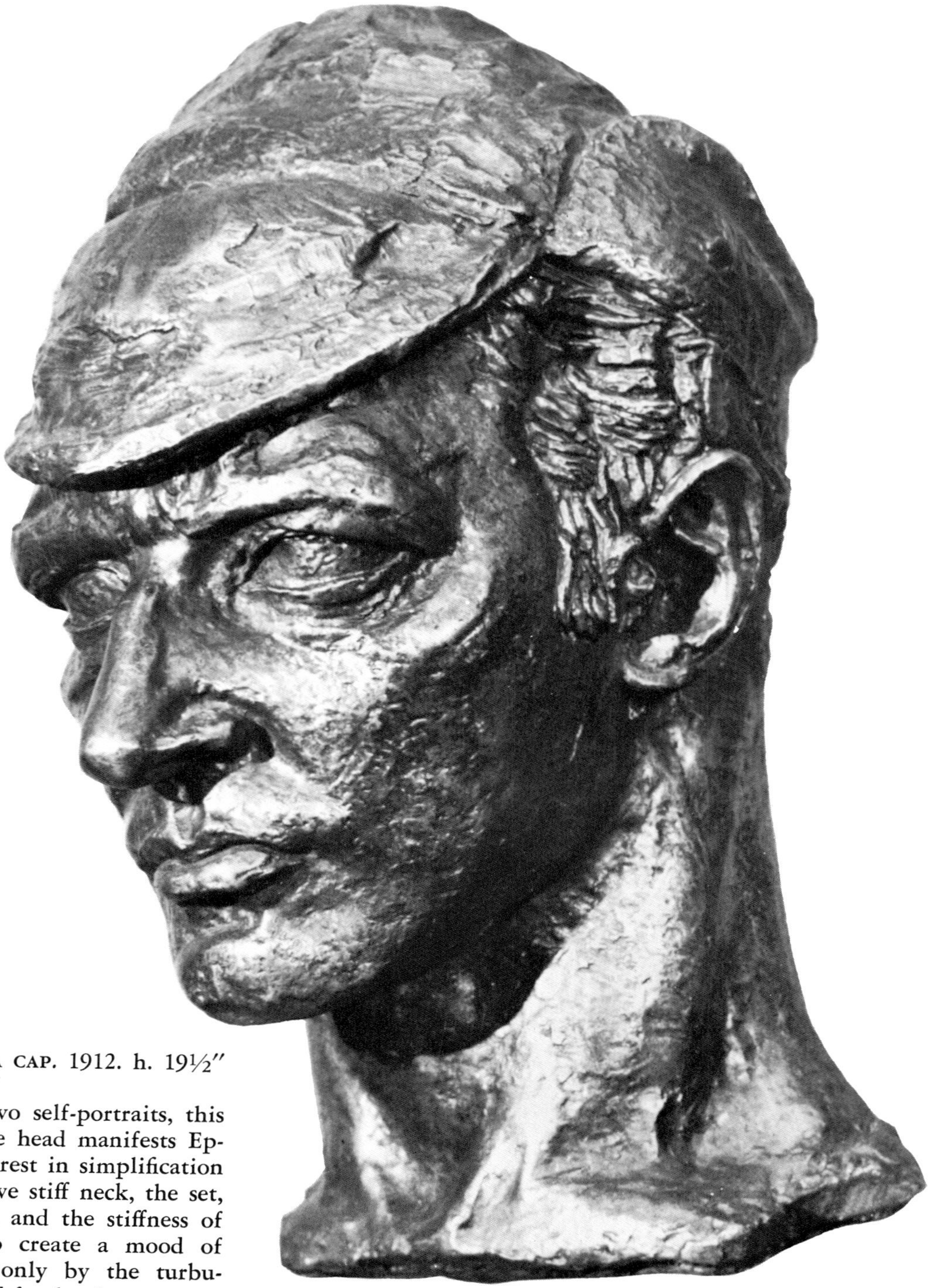

SELF PORTRAIT IN A CAP. 1912. h. 19½″ w. 11¾″ d. 14½″

The earlier of two self-portraits, this greater than lifesize head manifests Epstein's constant interest in simplification of form. The massive stiff neck, the set, angular lower face, and the stiffness of the workman's cap create a mood of defiance tempered only by the turbulence of the eyes and forehead.

EUPHEMIA LAMB, 1911. h. 14½″ w. 15½″ d. 9½″

This delicately composed bust, untraditional in being cut off just below the shoulders, is a fine example of Epstein's early work in which he concentrated on simple unified forms. Epstein writes of this period: ". . . I had the desire to train myself in a more intensive method of working . . . I began a series of studies from the model, which were as exact as I could make them. I worked with great care, and followed the forms of the model by quarter inches, . . . not letting up on any detail of construction of plan, but always keeping the final composition in view." (*An Autobiography*, p. 42)

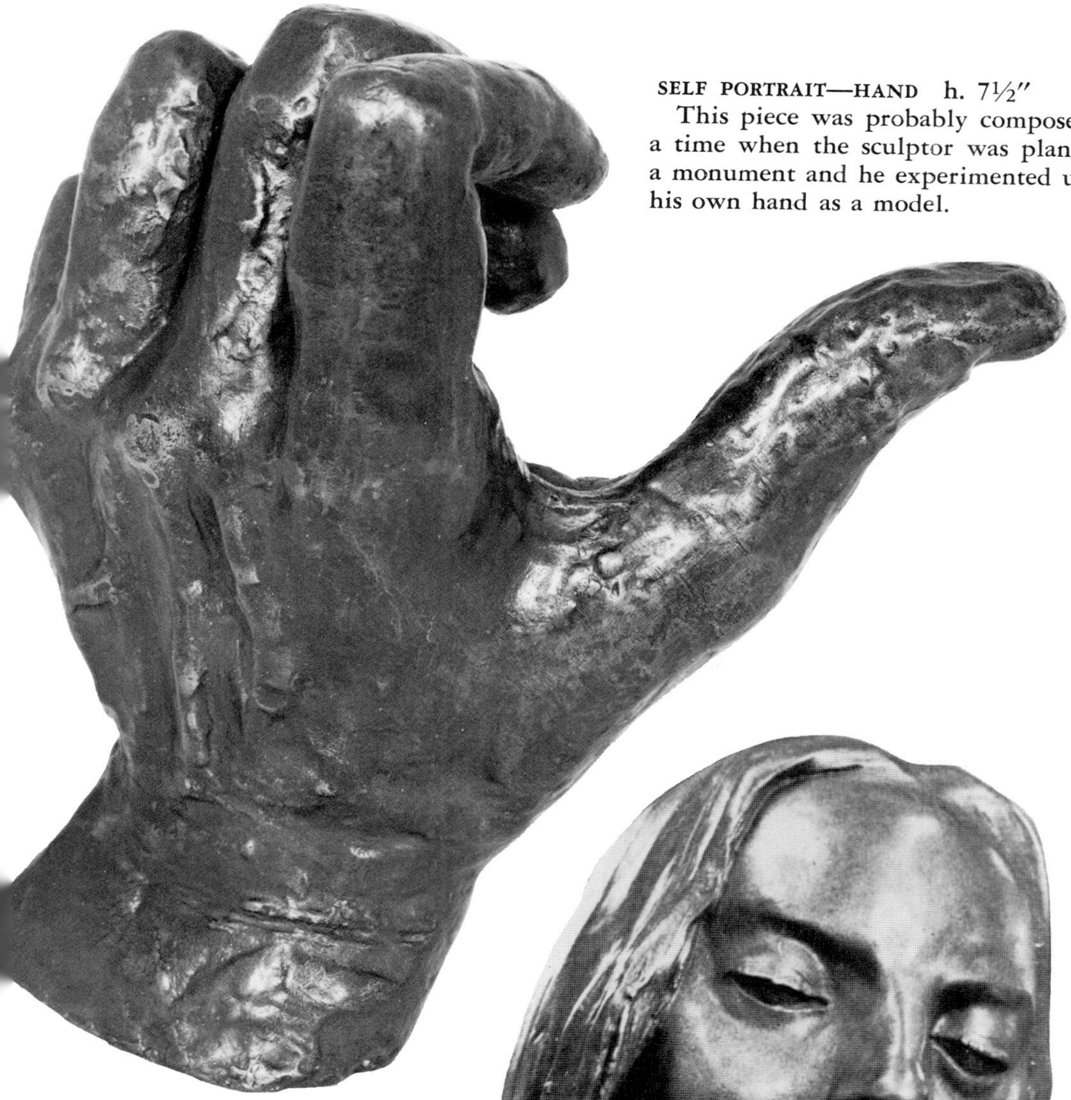

SELF PORTRAIT—HAND h. 7½″
This piece was probably composed at a time when the sculptor was planning a monument and he experimented using his own hand as a model.

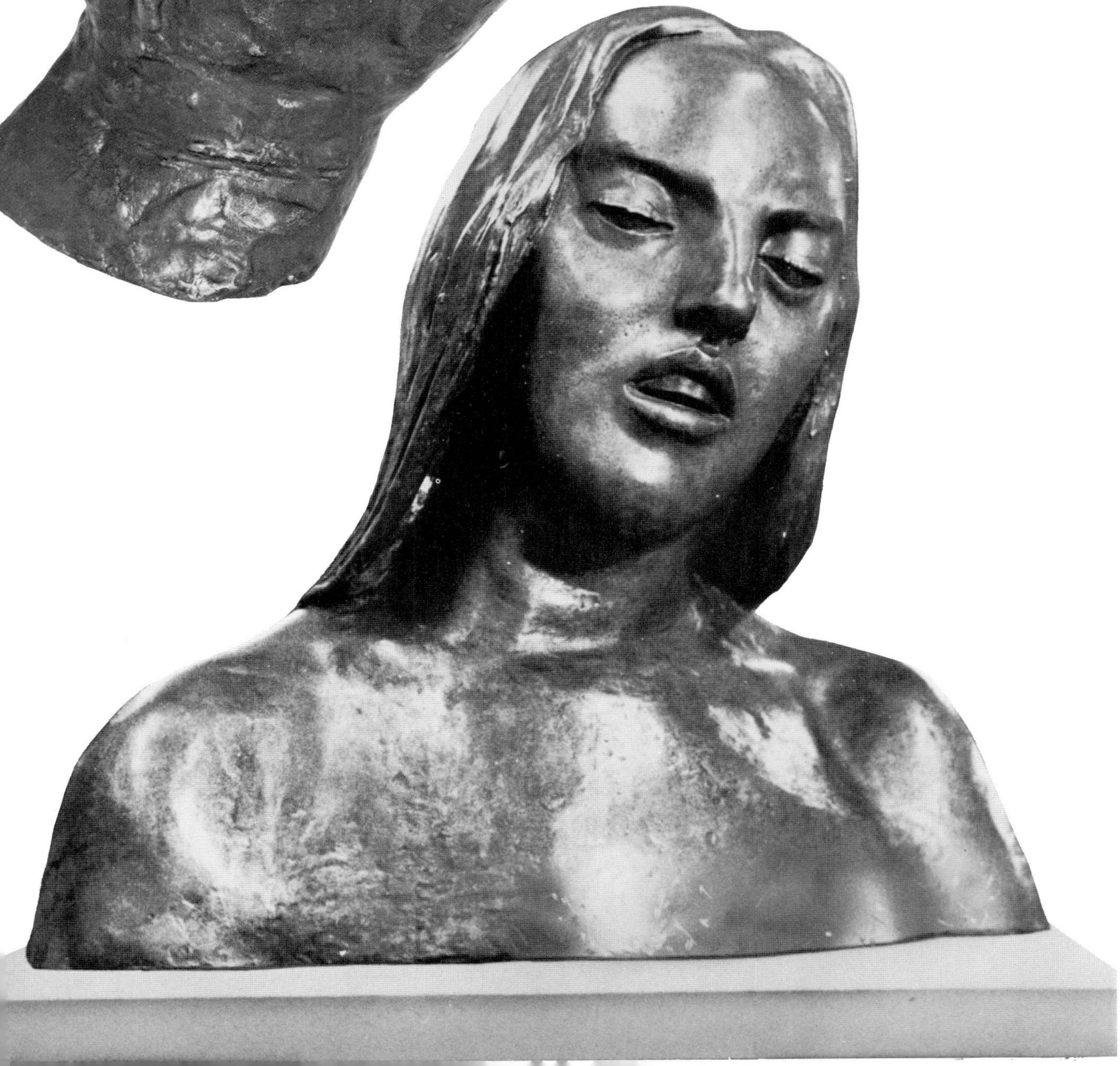

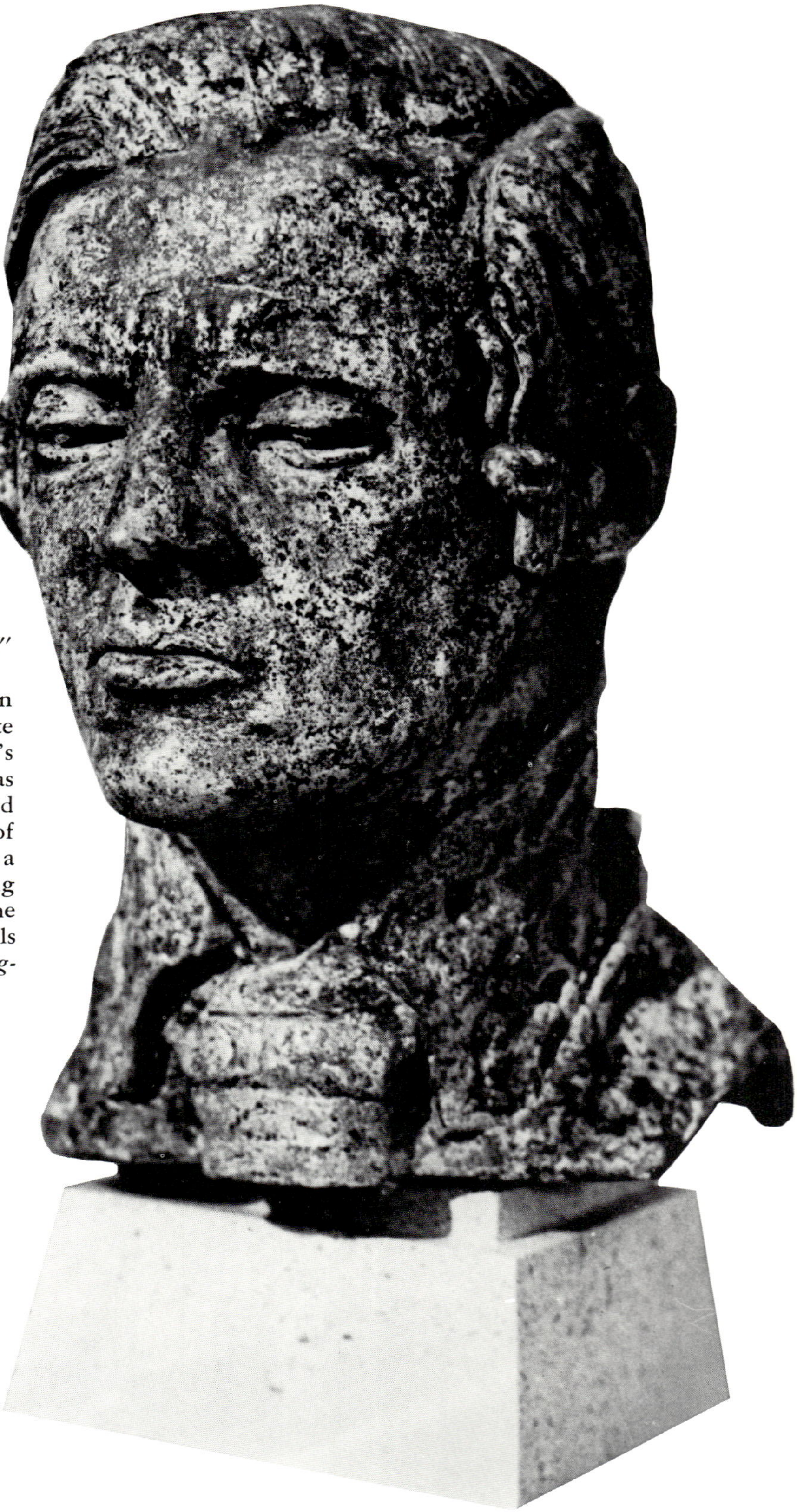

BERNARD VAN DIEREN, 1916. h. 12¾″ w. 7½″ d. 10¼″

This is the first of three heads Epstein made of the Dutch composer who wrote a book in 1920 in defense of Epstein's sculpture. Epstein said of him: "He was strikingly handsome and the head I did of him resembled superficially one of Napoleon's generals; but there was a quality of force allied to something mystical, far different, and beyond the vulgar good looks of the dandy generals of the First Empire . . . " (*Autobiography*, p. 78)

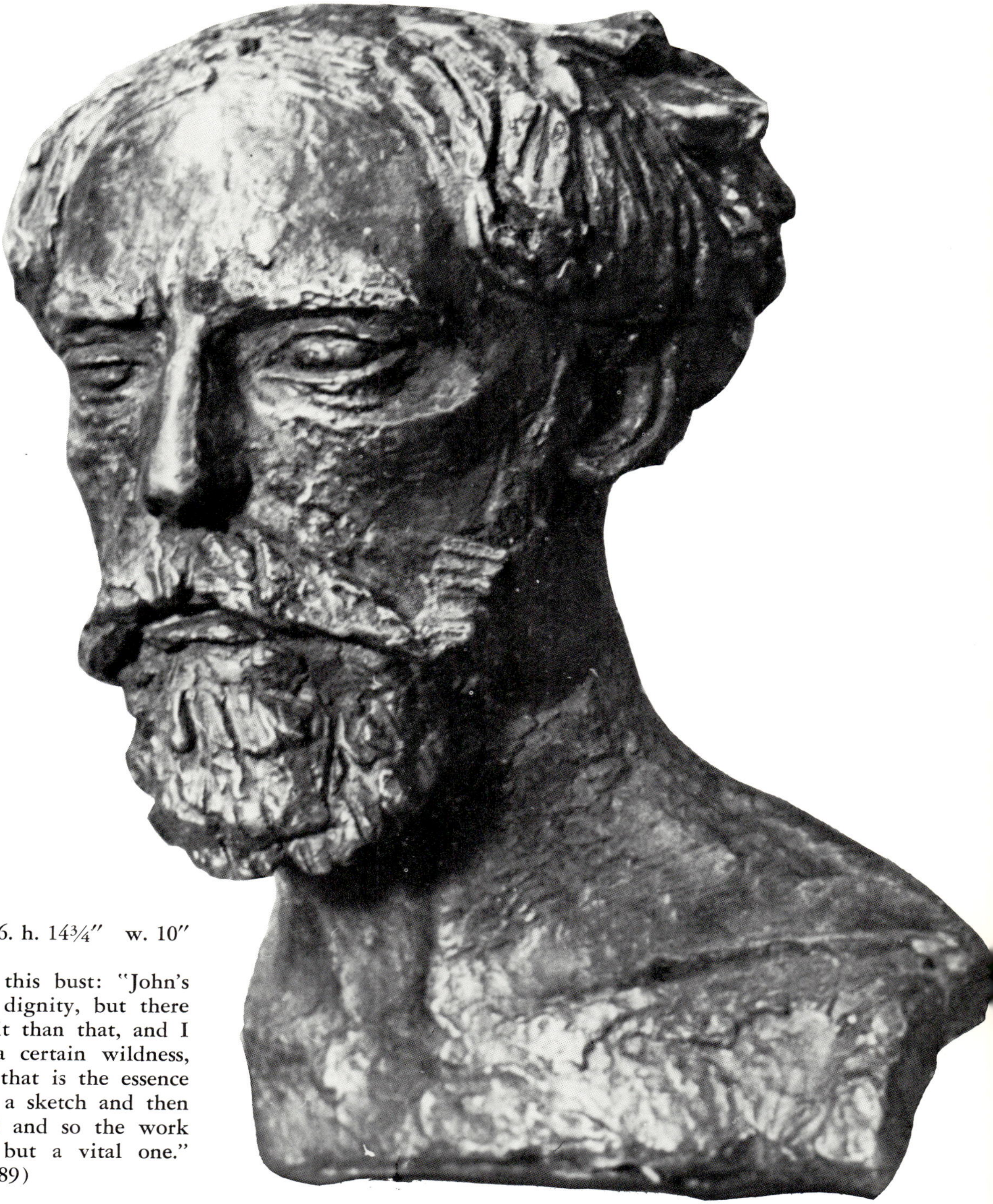

AUGUSTUS JOHN, 1916. h. 14¾″ w. 10″ d. 10″

Epstein writes of this bust: "John's head had plenty of dignity, but there was much more to it than that, and I wanted to capture a certain wildness, an untamed quality that is the essence of the man. I made a sketch and then something interfered and so the work remained a sketch, but a vital one." (*Autobiography,* p. 89)

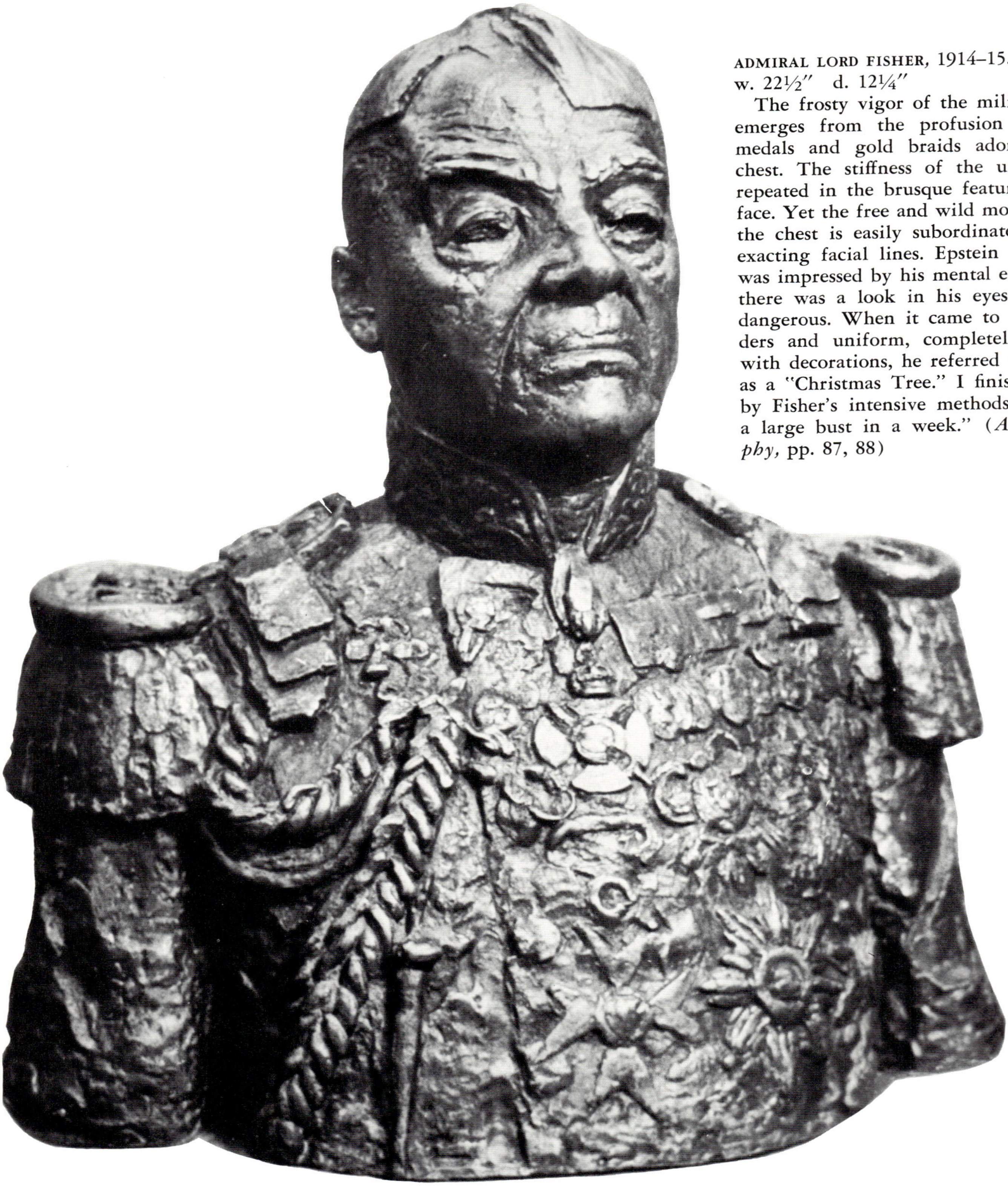

ADMIRAL LORD FISHER, 1914–15. h. 23½″ w. 22½″ d. 12¼″

The frosty vigor of the military man emerges from the profusion of brass medals and gold braids adorning his chest. The stiffness of the uniform is repeated in the brusque features of the face. Yet the free and wild modelling of the chest is easily subordinated by the exacting facial lines. Epstein wrote: "I was impressed by his mental energy and there was a look in his eyes that was dangerous. When it came to his shoulders and uniform, completely covered with decorations, he referred to himself as a "Christmas Tree." I finished aided by Fisher's intensive methods of work, a large bust in a week." (*Autobiography,* pp. 87, 88)

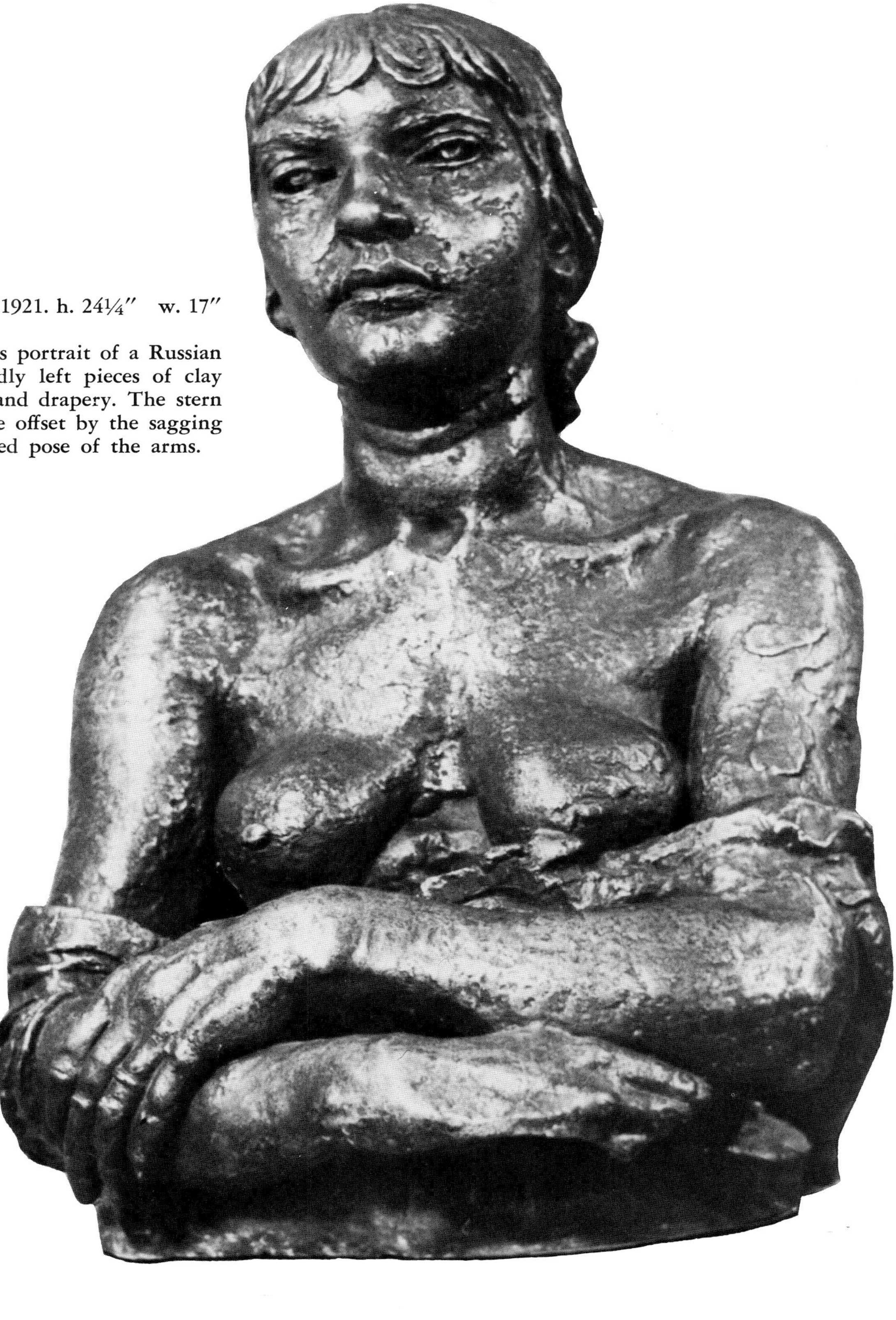

MIRIAM PLICHTE, 1921. h. 24¼″ w. 17″ d. 15½″

In this sensuous portrait of a Russian girl, Epstein boldly left pieces of clay on the left arm and drapery. The stern facial features are offset by the sagging breasts and relaxed pose of the arms.

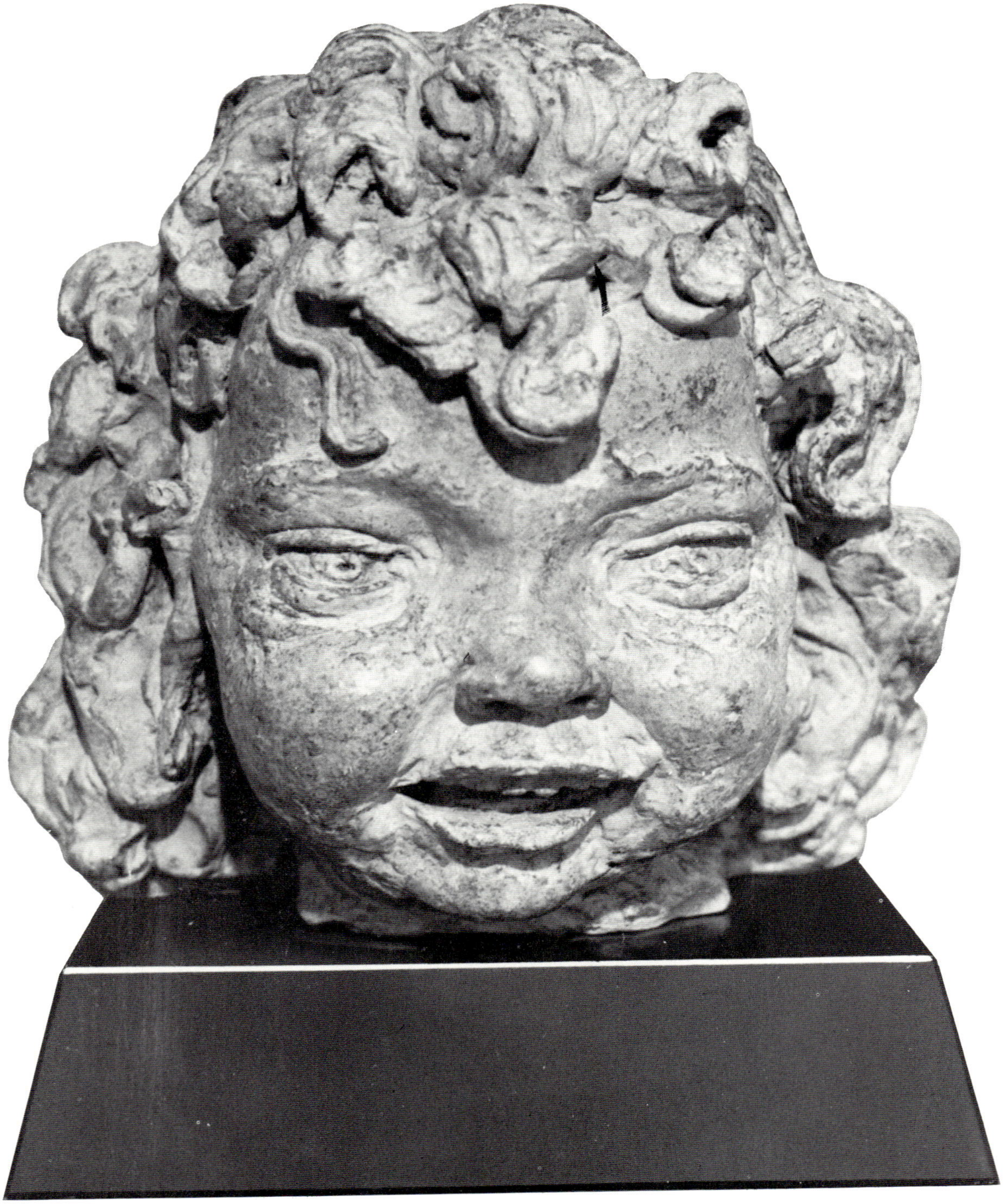

PEGGY JEAN LAUGHING, 1921. h. 9½″ w. 8½″ d. 9½″

This is the ninth portrait of Peggy Jean. The richly modeled curly hair encircles the chubby face that displays an expression halfway between wonder and merriment.

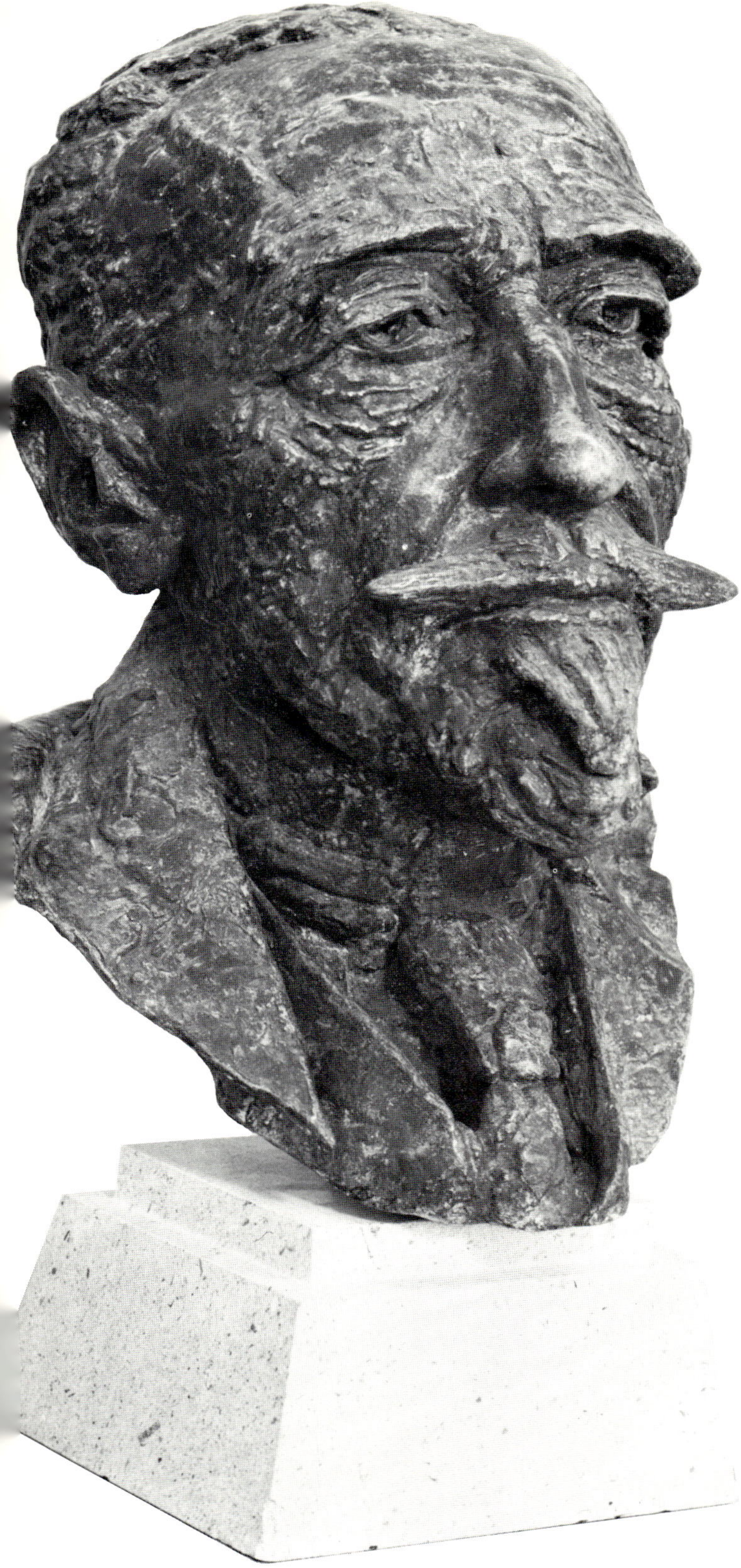

JOSEPH CONRAD, 1924. h. 15″ w. 10½″ d. 11¼″

Epstein spent three weeks with Conrad. In his autobiography, Epstein recalls: "Conrad had a demon expression in the left eye, while his right eye was smothered by a drooping lid, but the eyes glowed with a great intensity of feeling. The drooping, weary lids intensified the impression of brooding thought. The whole head revealed the man who had suffered much.

"His clothes were immaculately conventional, and his collar enclosed his neck like an Iron Maiden's vise or garroter's grip. He was worried if his hair and beard were not trim and neat as became a sea captain."

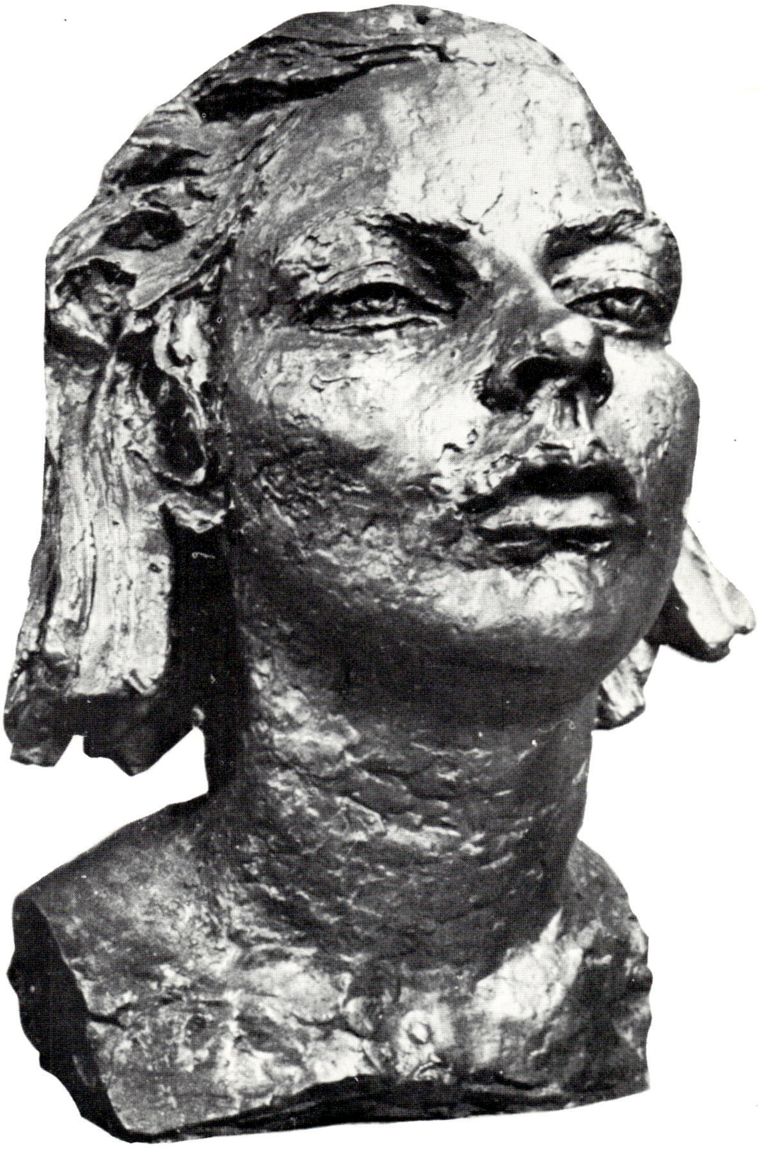

SHEILA, 1924. h. 14″ w. 10″ d. 10″

A girl named Sheila was the model for this head whose profile is full of movement. The smooth face contrasts with the roughly furrowed hair.

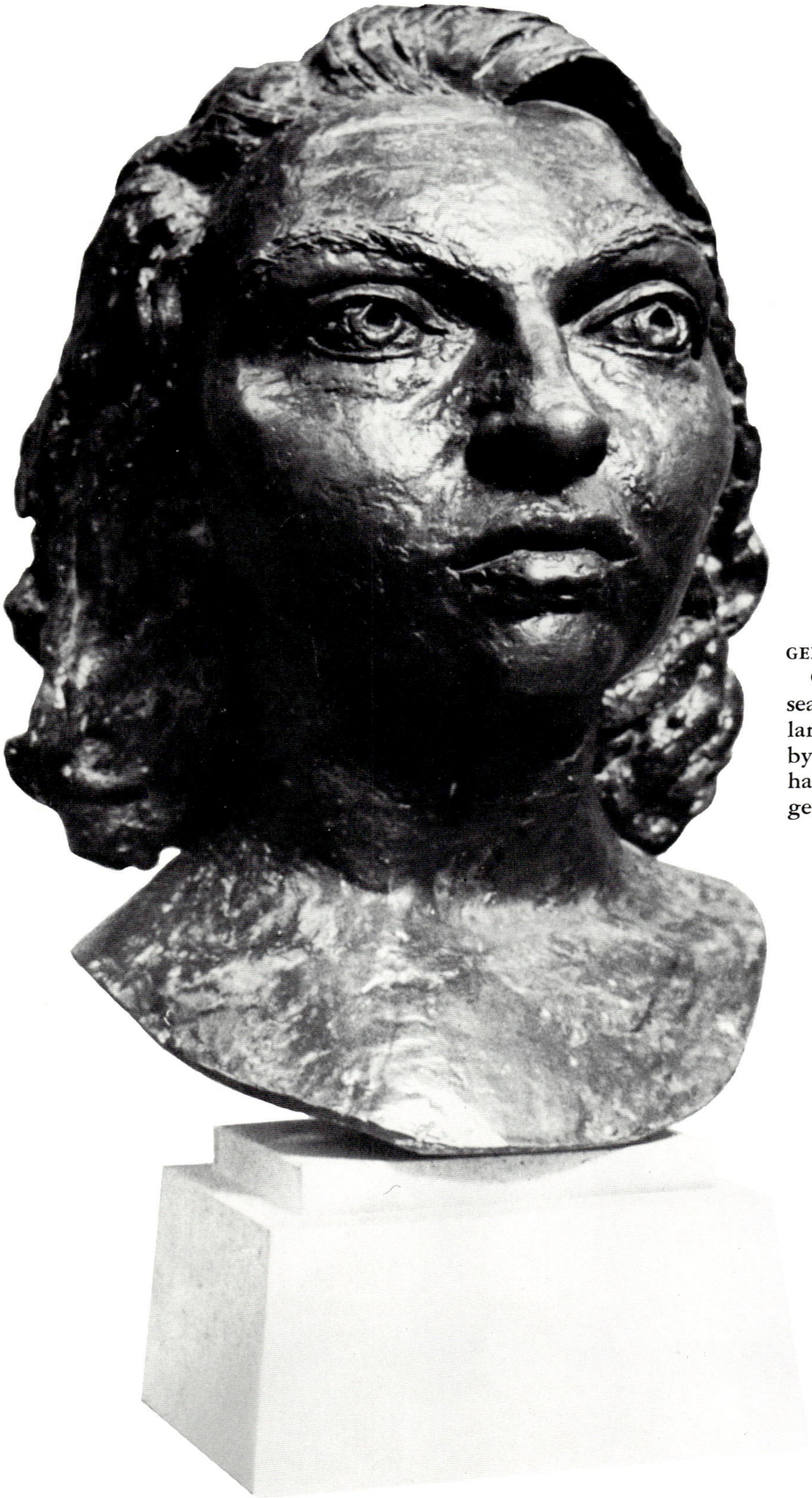

GERMAINE BRAS, 1930. h. 15¼″
Of hardy, peasant stock, the French seamstress Germaine Bras is portrayed larger than life. The head is dominated by the sheer size of the features. The hard lines of the face are softened by the gently swept back hair.

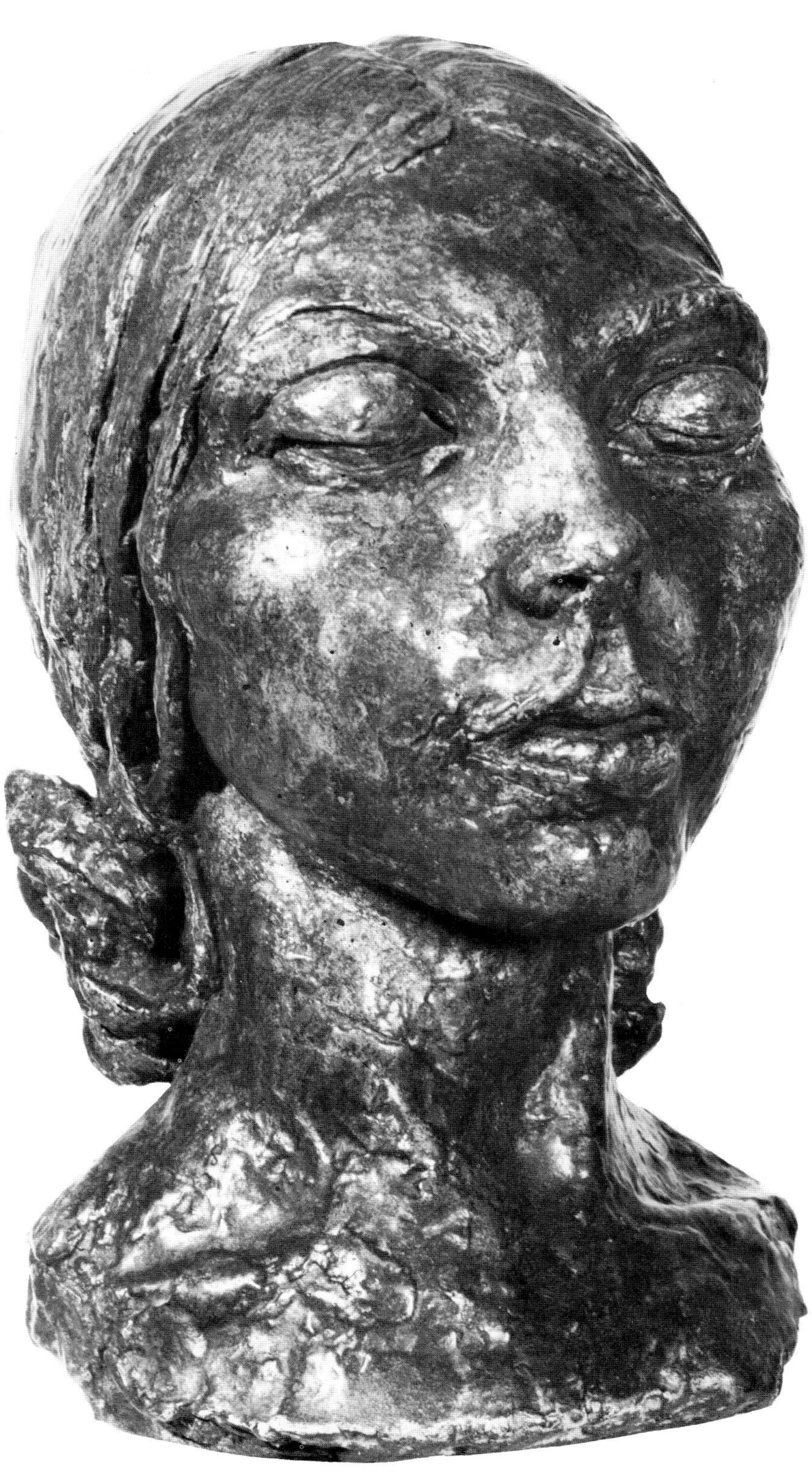

MARY, 1931. h. 14½″ w. 8½″ d. 9½″
The feeling of a person having a religious experience emanates from Epstein's Mary. Much of the face falls back in a position of responsiveness, with the eyes closed and the lips unconsciously open.

OLIVE, 1934. h. 13¾″ w. 7½″ d. 11¼″

One can sense the youthful blush o this Negro girl, her head bowed in in nocent modesty. The shape of the hai provides a graceful covering for he head. Olive was brought to Epstein' studio by her parents as a prospectiv model.

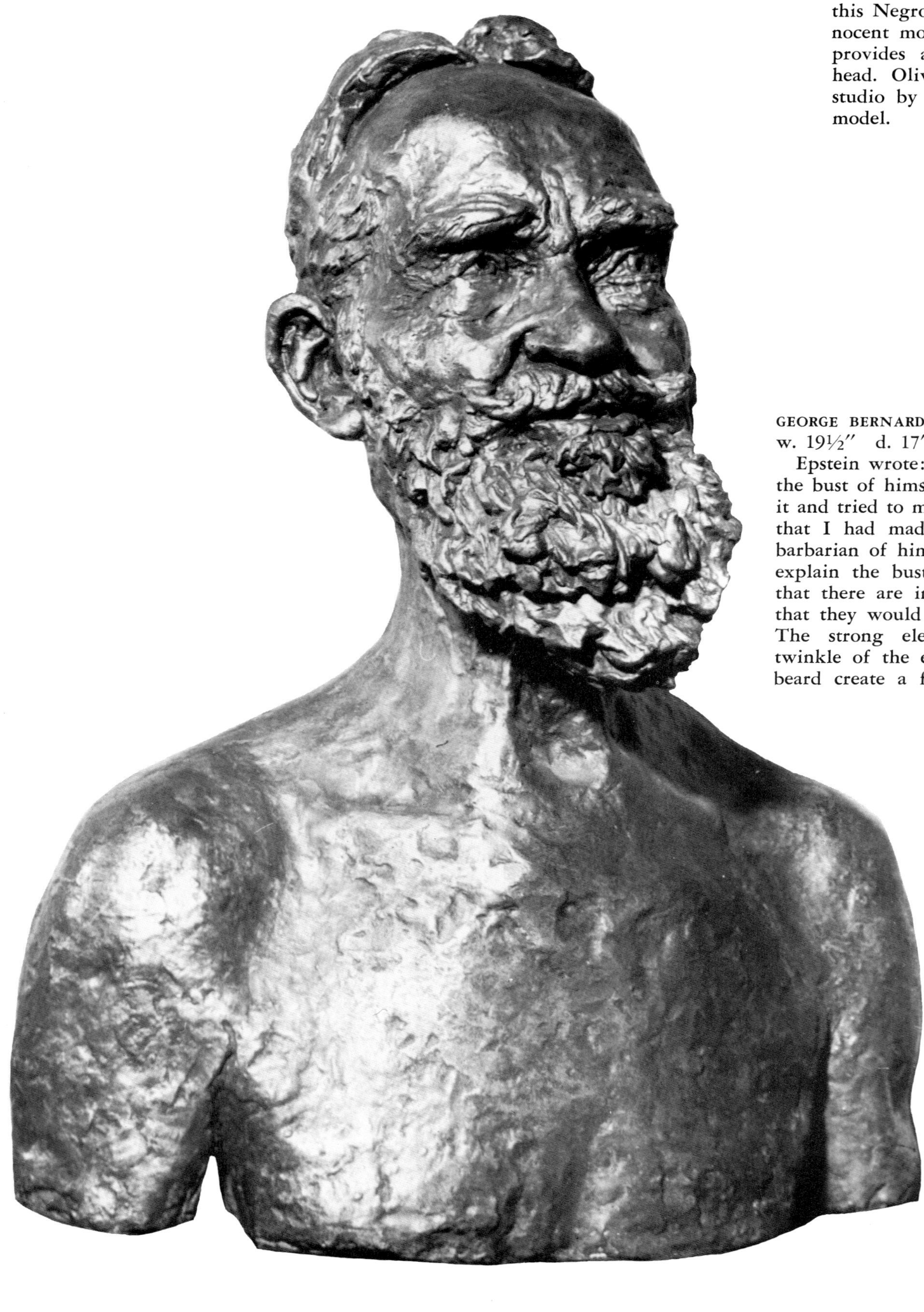

GEORGE BERNARD SHAW, 1934. h. 25¼″ w. 19½″ d. 17″

Epstein wrote: "Shaw was puzzled by the bust of himself and often looked at it and tried to make it out. He believed that I had made a kind of primitive barbarian of him. . . . I never tried to explain the bust to him, and I think that there are in it elements so subtle that they would be difficult to explain. The strong element of humor, the twinkle of the eyes, the mustache and beard create a feeling of intensity."

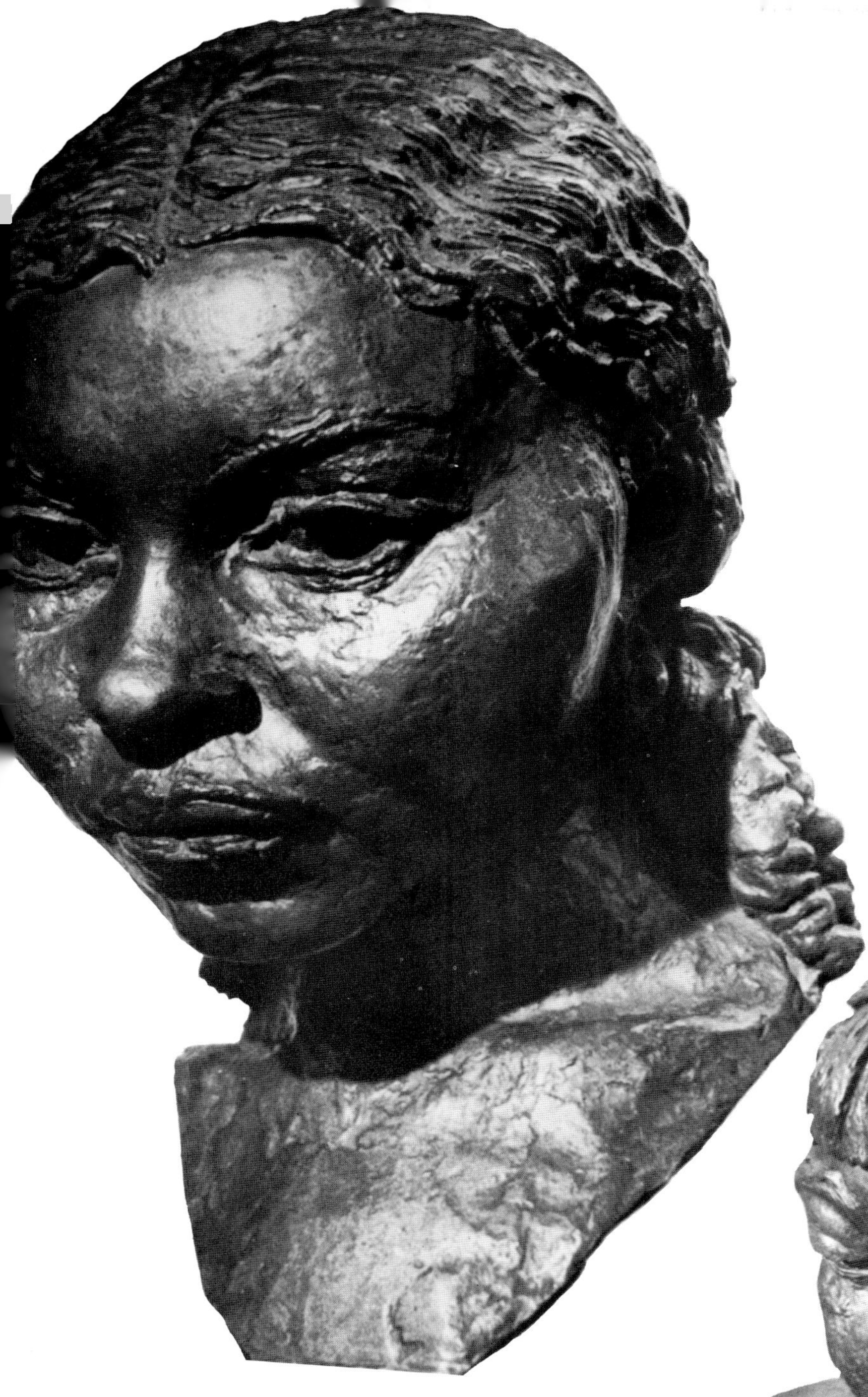

PEGGY JEAN SICK CHILD, 1928. h. 14¼″ w. 9¼″ d. 22¼″

This sensitive and subtle portrait of ten-year-old Peggy Jean, known as "The Sick Child," was modeled when Epstein returned to London in 1928. The outstretched arms form a necessary base for the bronze as the child leans forward with half-shut eyes. Epstein's capability of expression is so complete that he is able to impart to the bronze the innocence of childhood. An interesting anecdote concerning this sculpture is that a doctor, upon seeing it, was immediately able to diagnose the child's illness as an eye infection.

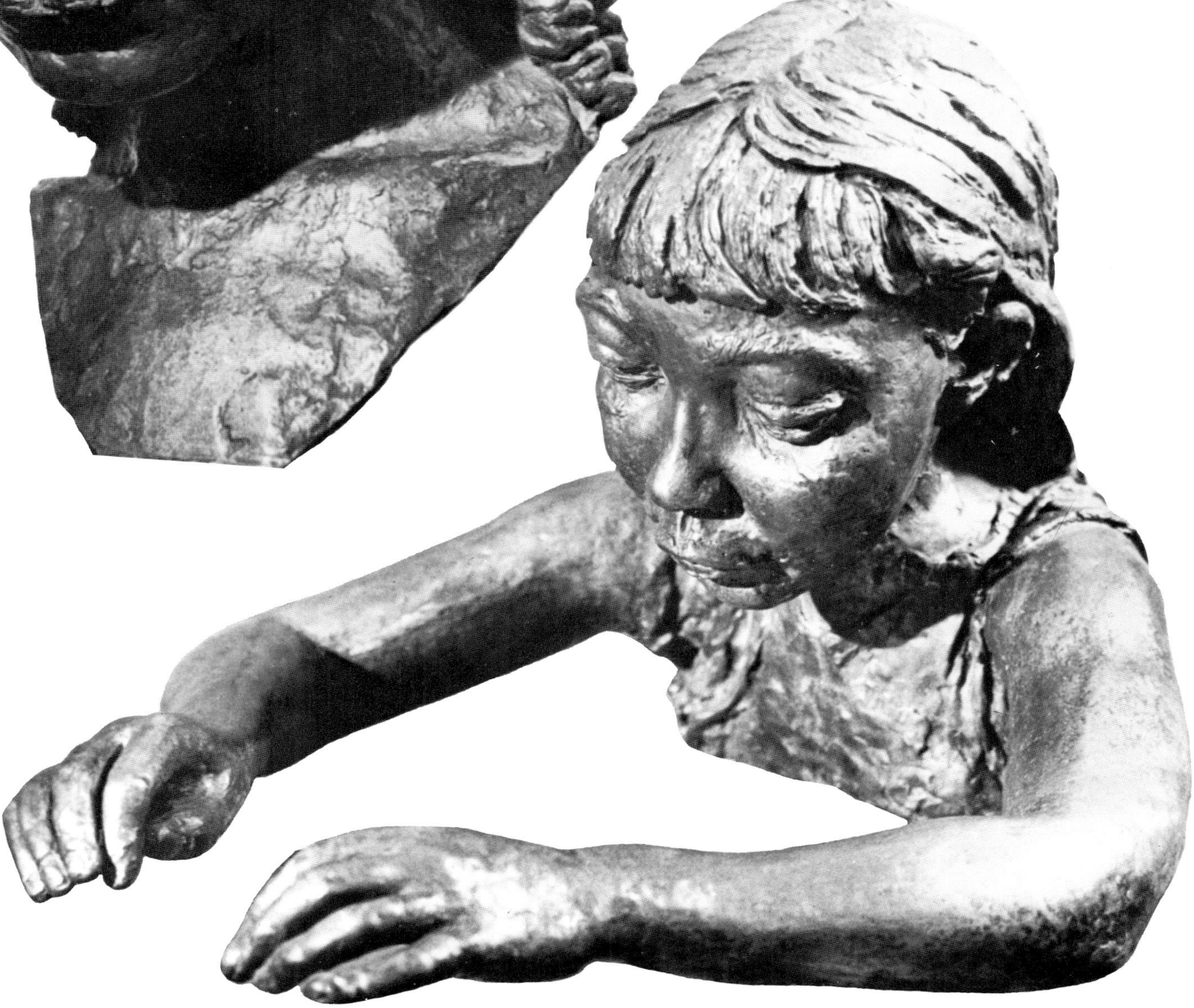

WINSTON CHURCHILL, 1946. 12″

Epstein wrote in his autobiography: "The Ministry of Information were naturally eager for me to work from Churchill but the opportunity did not come until after the war when he was living opposite me. He arrived at my studio complete with secretary, and a plain-clothesman who planted himself at the door intending to remain on guard throughout the sitting. I offered this gentleman a chair whereupon Churchill abruptly dismissed him. Lighting his cigar, with his secretary seated behind me ready for dictation, we were all set for a fair start. After an hour this secretary was dismissed and a second appeared for further dictation to the accompaniment of a second cigar. After three somewhat restless sittings, Churchill decided to stay at Chartwell where he gave me three further sittings. Unfortunately it was winter and the light far from ideal and I felt that I had made no more than an interesting character study. . . ."

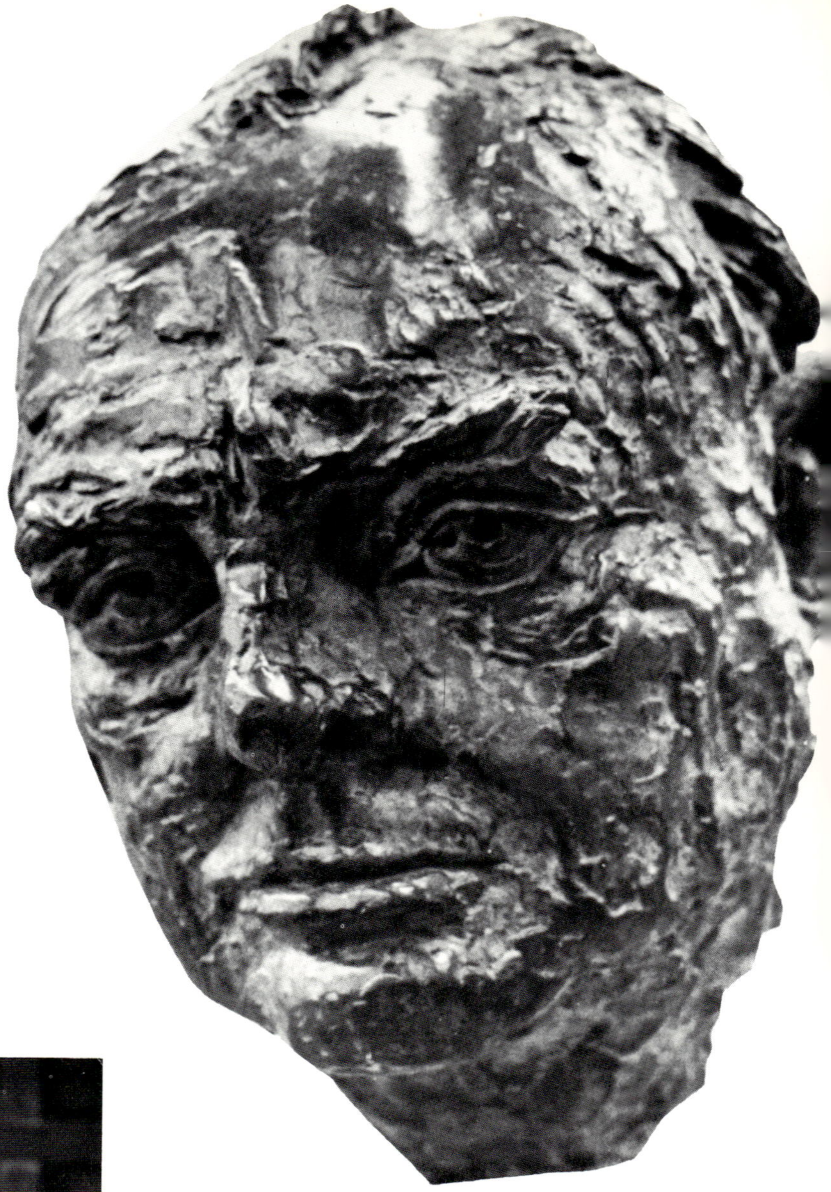

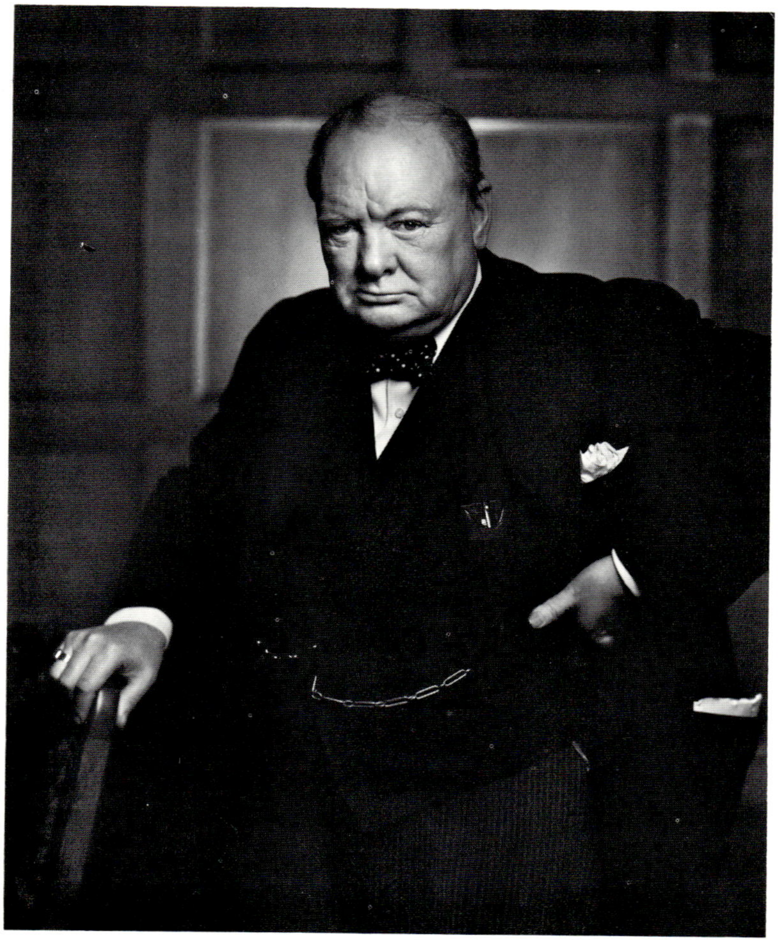

It is interesting to compare Churchill as portrayed by Epstein with Churchill as photographed by Yousuf Karsh, one of the world's leading photographers. (*Copyright, Karsh of Ottawa*)

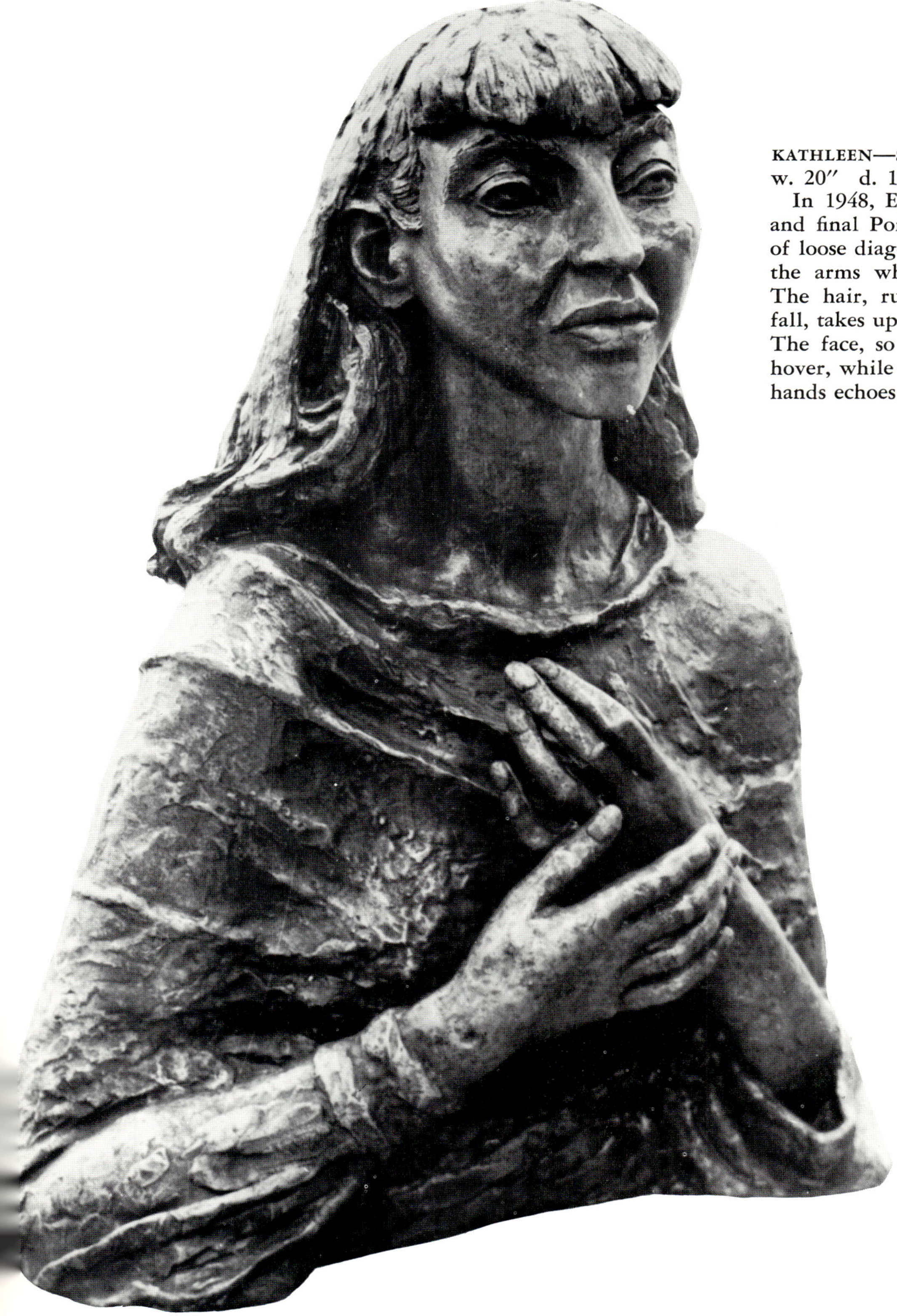

KATHLEEN—SEVENTH, 1948. h. 30″ w. 20″ d. 14½″

In 1948, Epstein modeled his seventh and final Portrait of Kathleen. Patterns of loose diagonal folds are reinforced by the arms which fold across her chest. The hair, rushing down like a waterfall, takes up the rhythm of the drapery. The face, so sharply outlined, seems to hover, while the tenuous position of the hands echoes this feeling.

MURIEL, 1948. h. 10″ w. 8½″ d. 8½″
Here we feel a simplicity in the very nature of Muriel herself, although the head is somewhat complex. Epstein emphasizes the broad planes of the forehead and cheeks which are framed by chains of hair.

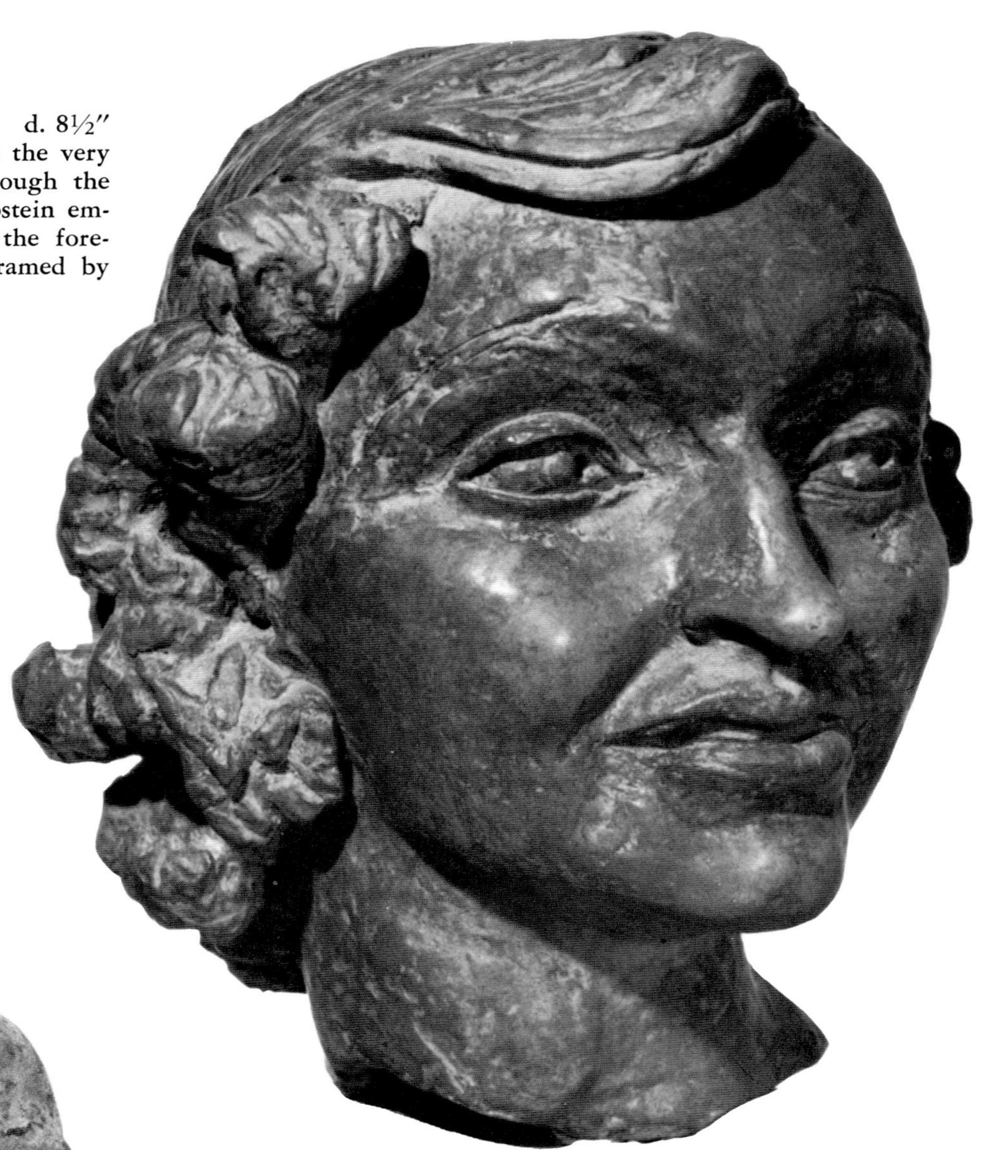

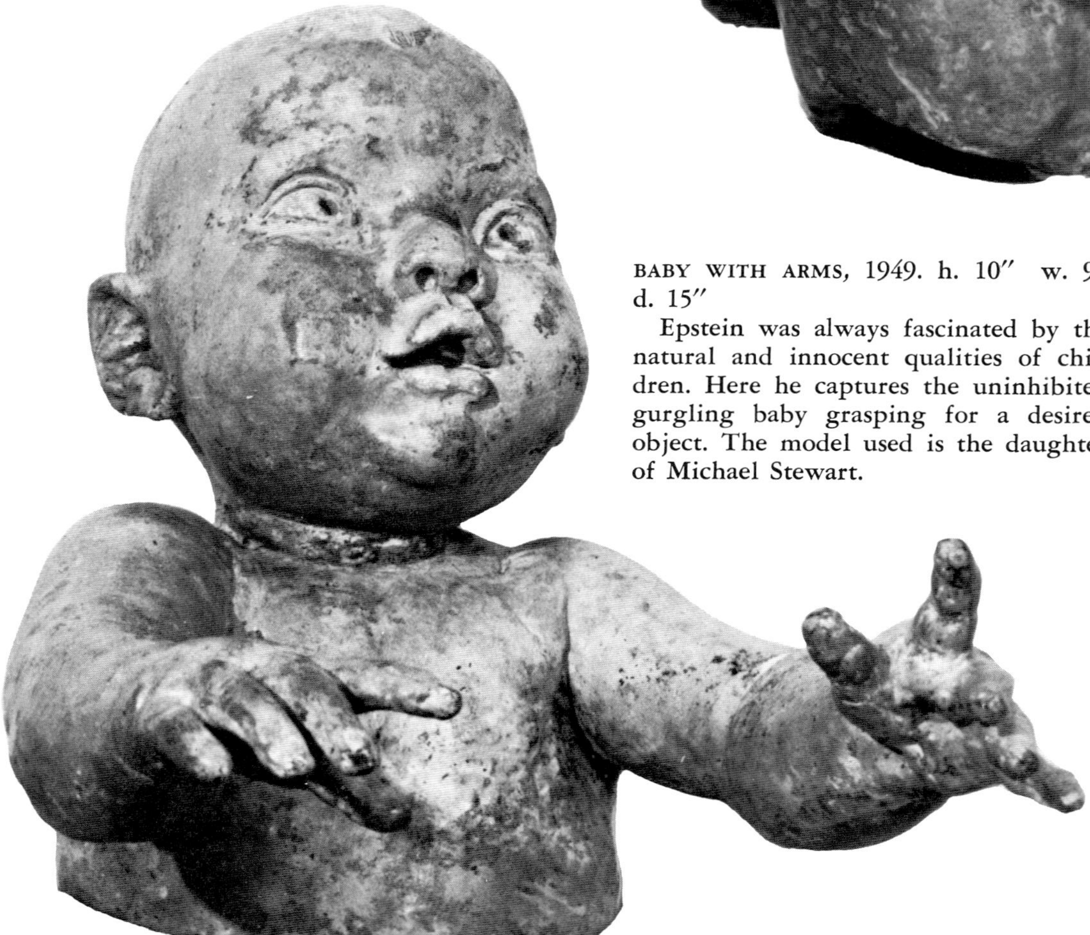

BABY WITH ARMS, 1949. h. 10″ w. 9″ d. 15″
Epstein was always fascinated by the natural and innocent qualities of children. Here he captures the uninhibited gurgling baby grasping for a desired object. The model used is the daughter of Michael Stewart.

ST. MICHAEL AND THE DEVIL, 1956.
h. 20½″ w. 11½″ d. 5½″

This bronze maquette was the study made for submission to the Cathedral Council; but without waiting for their approval, Epstein began the upper part of the monumental relief now adorning Coventry Cathedral. When the committee saw what was emerging they were quick to approve. In June 1960, ten months after his death, *St. Michael and the Devil* was unveiled by Lady Epstein.

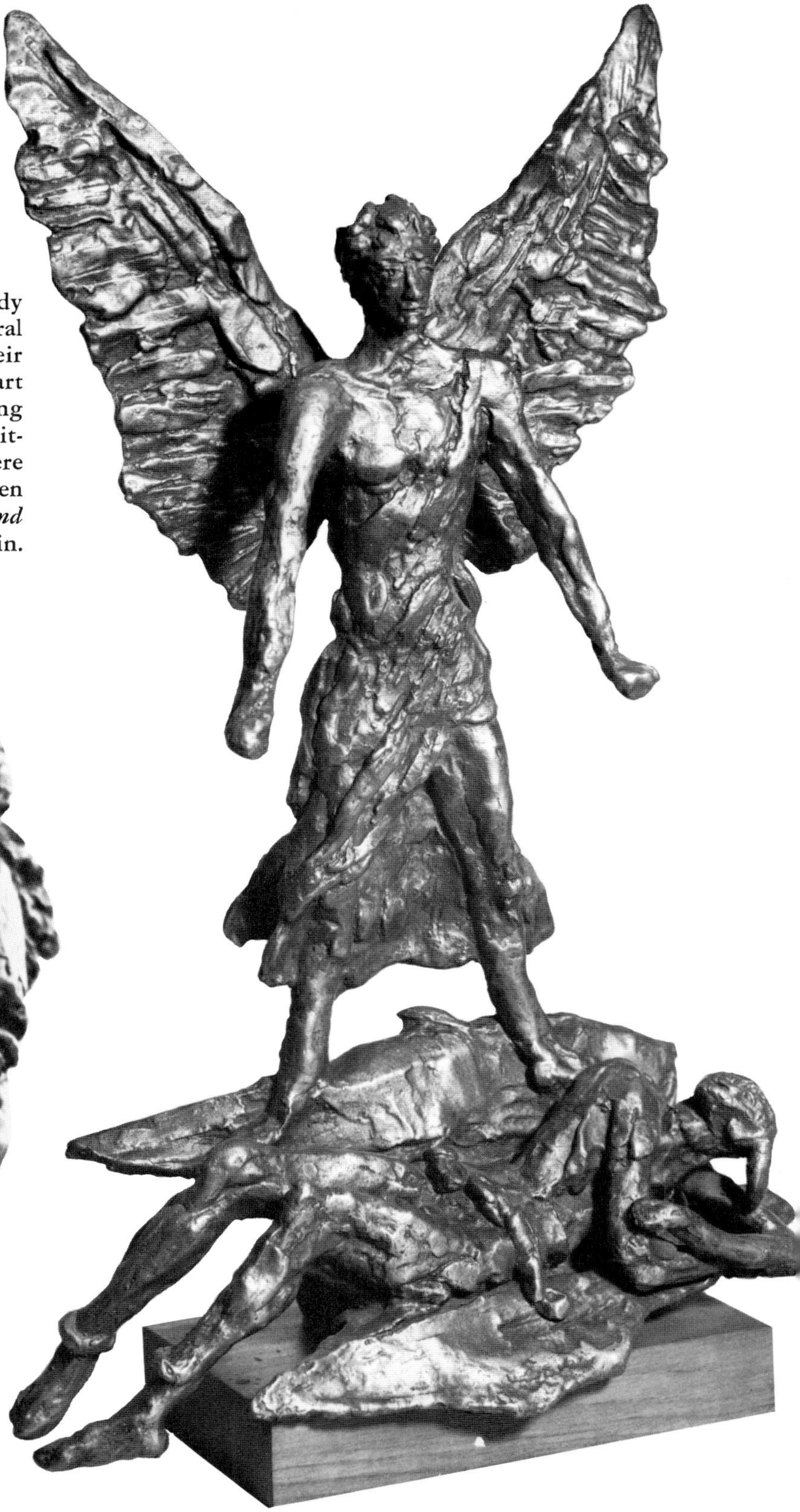

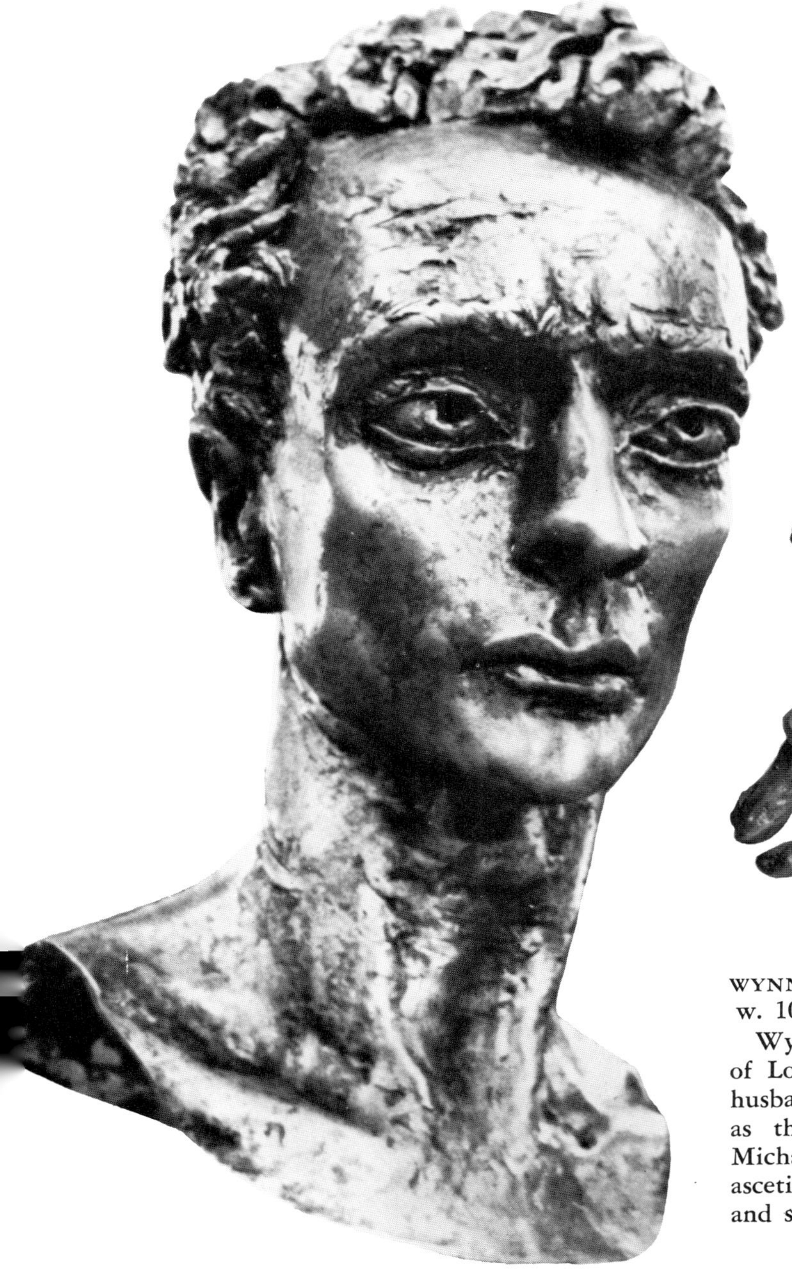

WYNNE GODLEY, 1956. h. 18½″
w. 10¼″ d. 12½″

Wynne Godley, the younger brother of Lord Kilbracker, was Kitty's second husband. Epstein chose his son-in-law as the model for the Coventry "St. Michael." The head is angular and ascetic. It seems to burn with concern and strength of purpose.

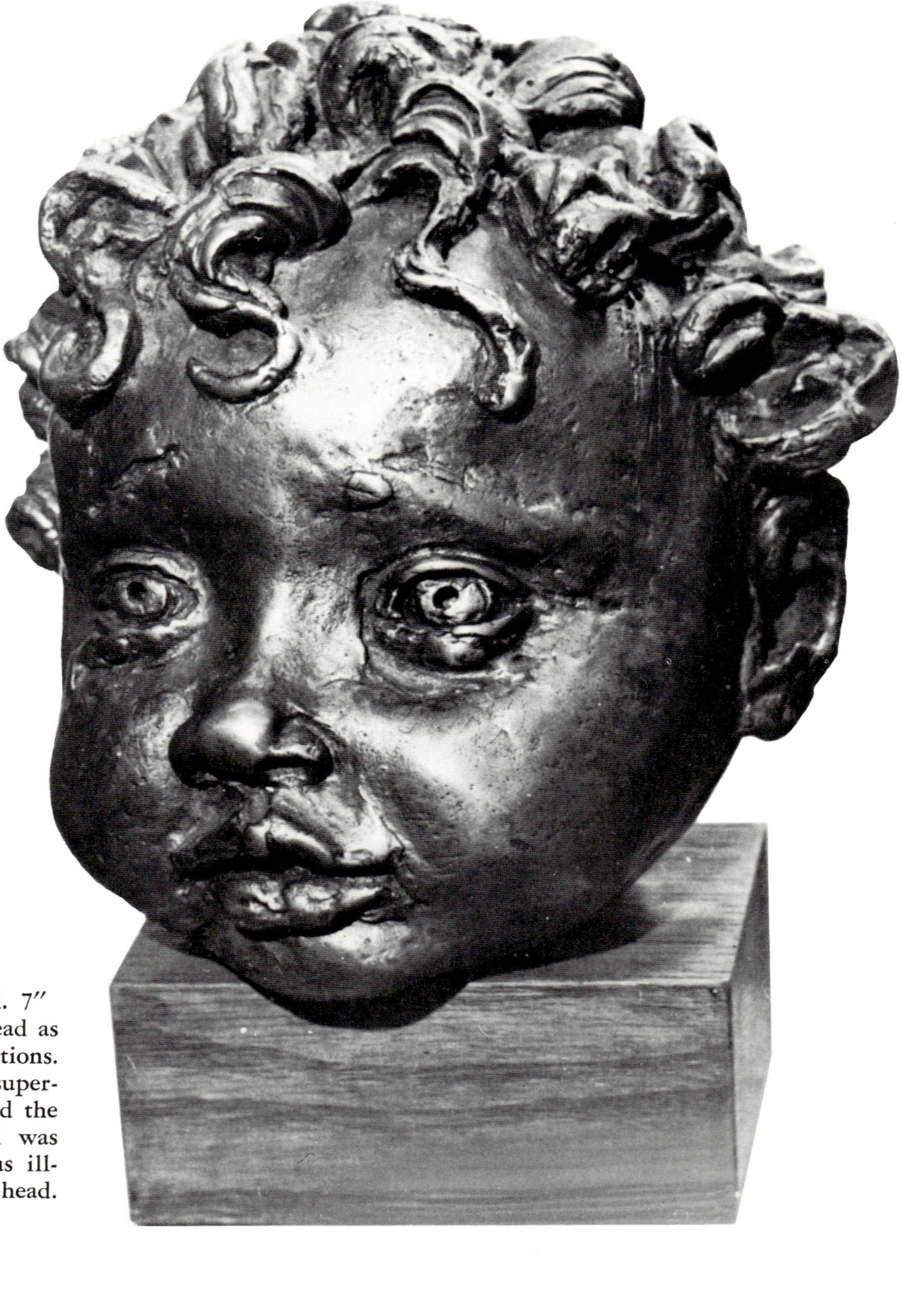

TABITHA, 1957. h. 9″ w. 6½″ d. 7″

In *Tabitha,* Epstein treats the head as a single surface with slight variations. Facial features appear somewhat superficial although they do exist around the eyes and mouth. Perhaps Epstein was imparting some of his own serious illness to this sad, curly-haired little head.

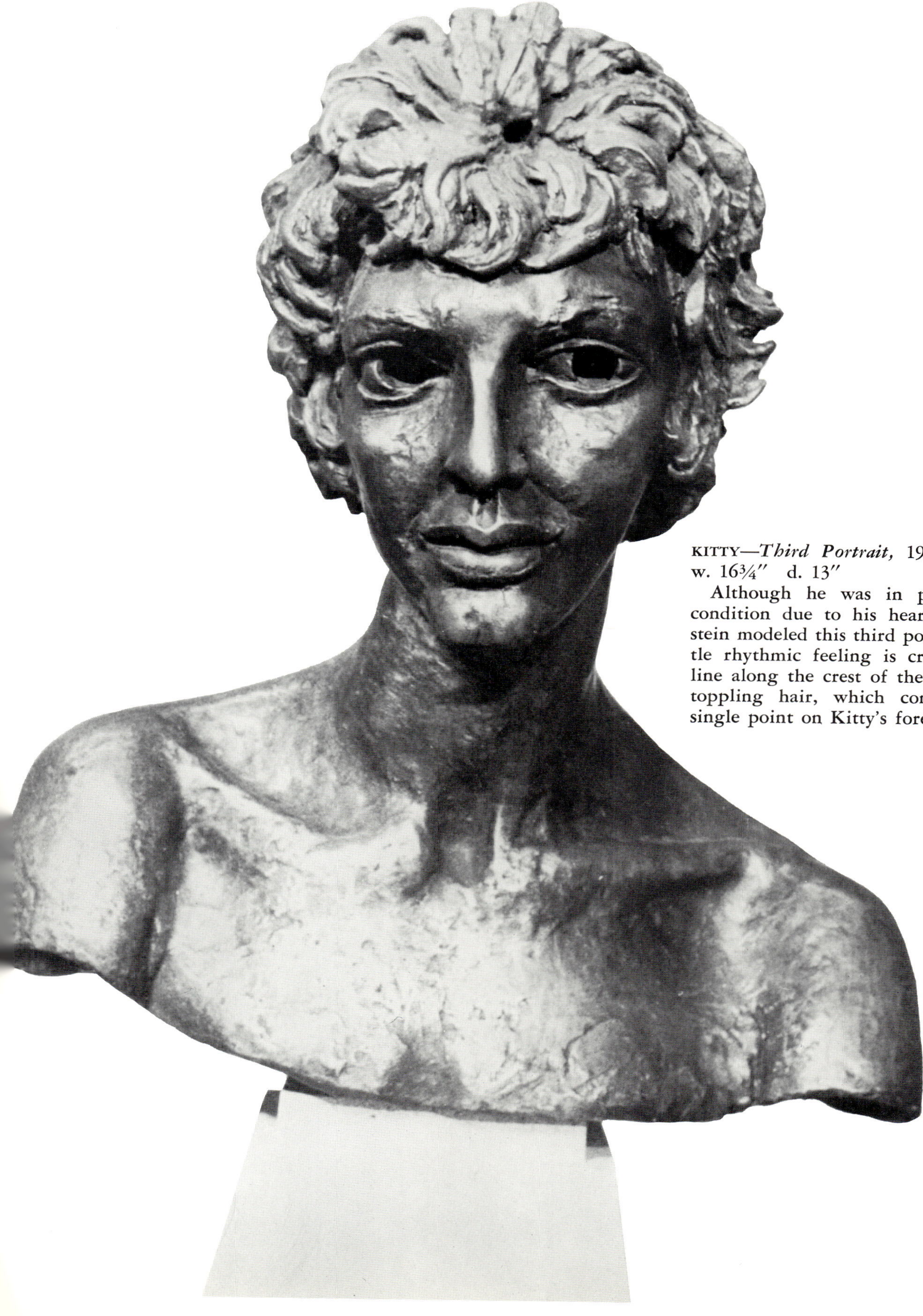

KITTY—*Third Portrait,* 1957. h. 19½″ w. 16¾″ d. 13″

Although he was in poor physical condition due to his heart attack, Epstein modeled this third portrait. A gentle rhythmic feeling is created by the line along the crest of the lips and the toppling hair, which converges at a single point on Kitty's forehead.

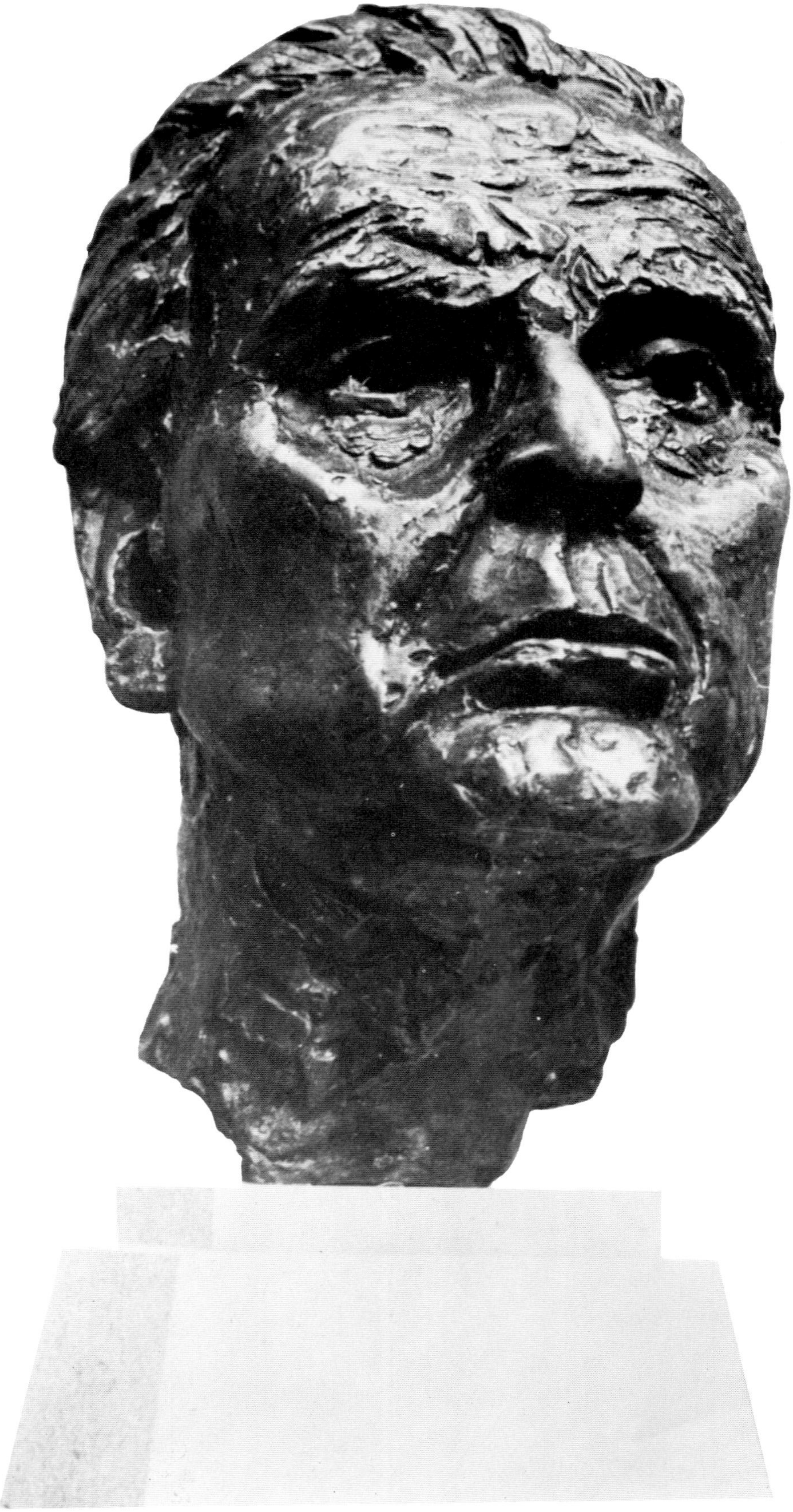

DR. KLEMPERER, 1957. h. 14¼″ w. 8¾″ d. 11¼″

An avid concert-goer, Epstein was emotionally moved by Dr. Otto Klemperer's first Beethoven cycle. The manager of the Royal Festival Hall, upon learning this, brought the conductor to sit. Here the sculptor has captured in a single head three distinct character expressions. The two profiles are completely different from the front view. He was able to present qualities seemingly inexpressible in non-living material.

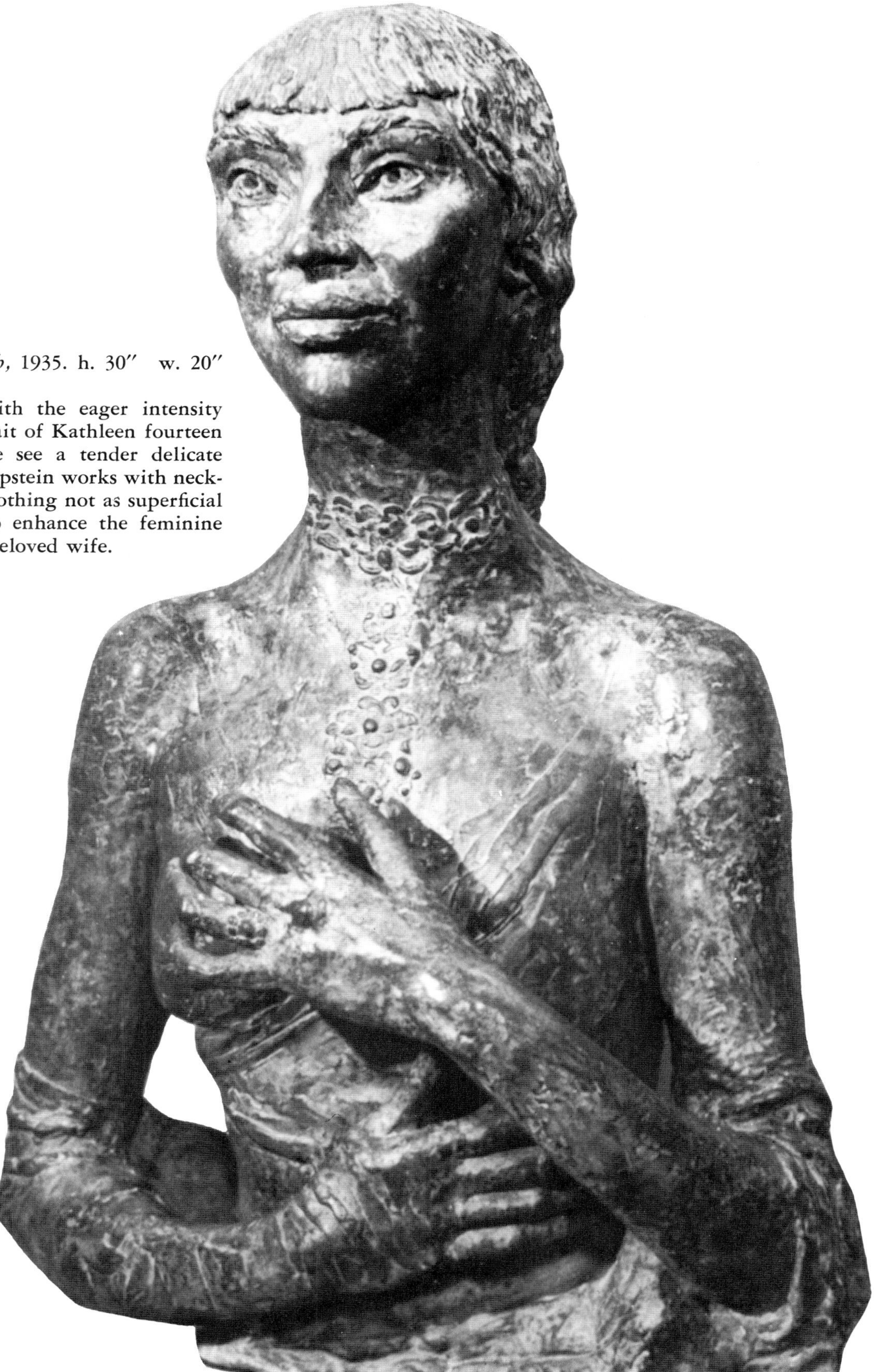

KATHLEEN—*Fifth,* 1935. h. 30″ w. 20″ d. 14½″

In contrast with the eager intensity of his first portrait of Kathleen fourteen years earlier, we see a tender delicate elegance. Here, Epstein works with necklace, ring, and clothing not as superficial additions, but to enhance the feminine qualities of his beloved wife.

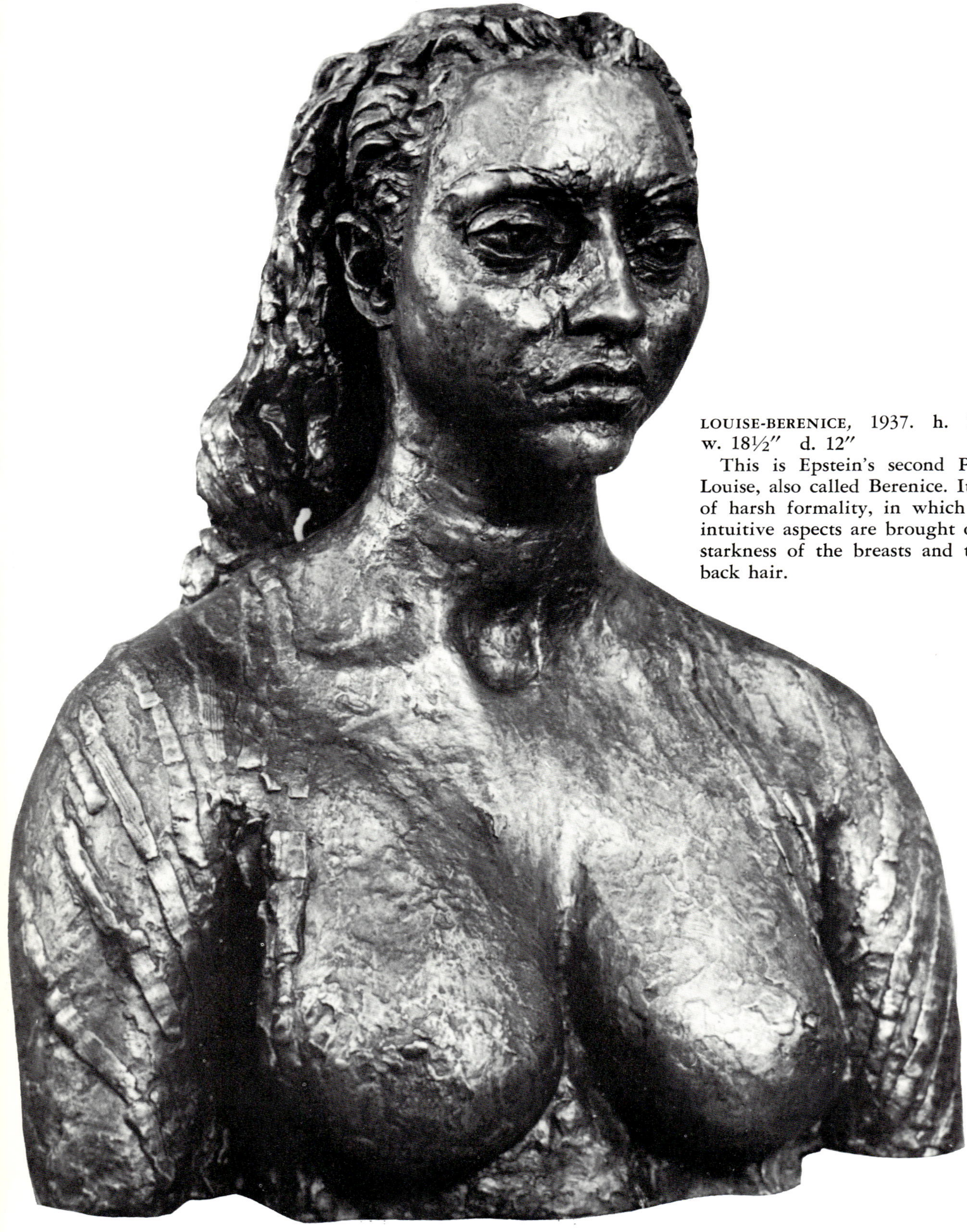

LOUISE-BERENICE, 1937. h. 22¼″ w. 18½″ d. 12″

This is Epstein's second Portrait of Louise, also called Berenice. It is a bust of harsh formality, in which primitive intuitive aspects are brought out by the starkness of the breasts and the swept-back hair.

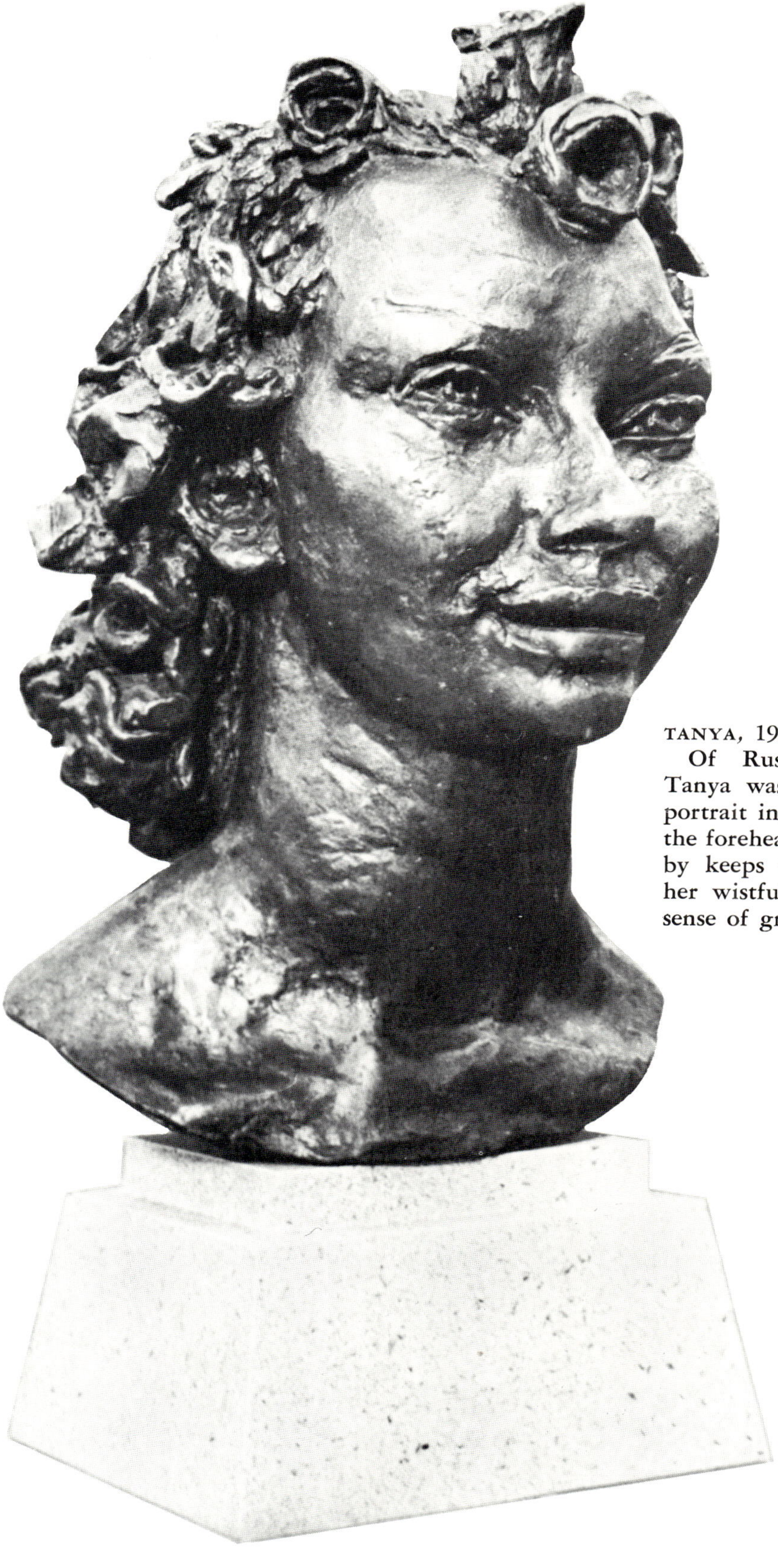

TANYA, 1937. h. 6¼″ w. 9″ d. 11″

Of Russian and Belgian descent, Tanya was the model for this curious portrait in which Epstein playfully tops the forehead with a thick curl. He thereby keeps the viewer's eye focused on her wistful expression. The hair has a sense of growth all its own.

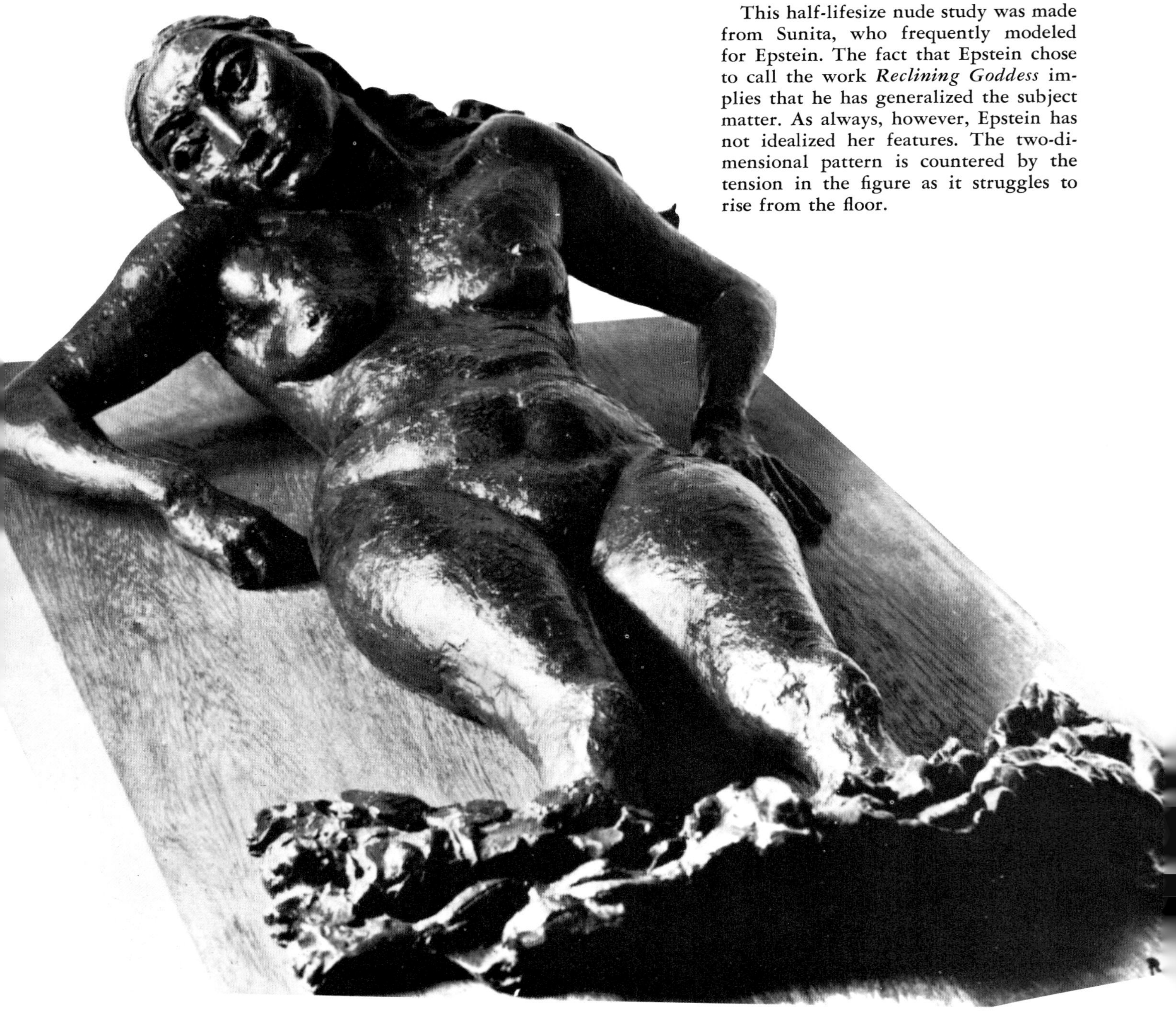

RECLINING GODDESS, 1931. h. 32″ w. 22½″ d. 10½″

This half-lifesize nude study was made from Sunita, who frequently modeled for Epstein. The fact that Epstein chose to call the work *Reclining Goddess* implies that he has generalized the subject matter. As always, however, Epstein has not idealized her features. The two-dimensional pattern is countered by the tension in the figure as it struggles to rise from the floor.

DR. CHAIM WEIZMANN, 1933. h. 18¼″ w. 23¼″ d. 11¼″

In this bust of Dr. Chaim Weizmann, one of the charter organizers founding the state of Israel, Epstein uses very impressionistic modeling. The sketchy mass is made alive by the scooped-out eyes, parted lips and flared nostrils.

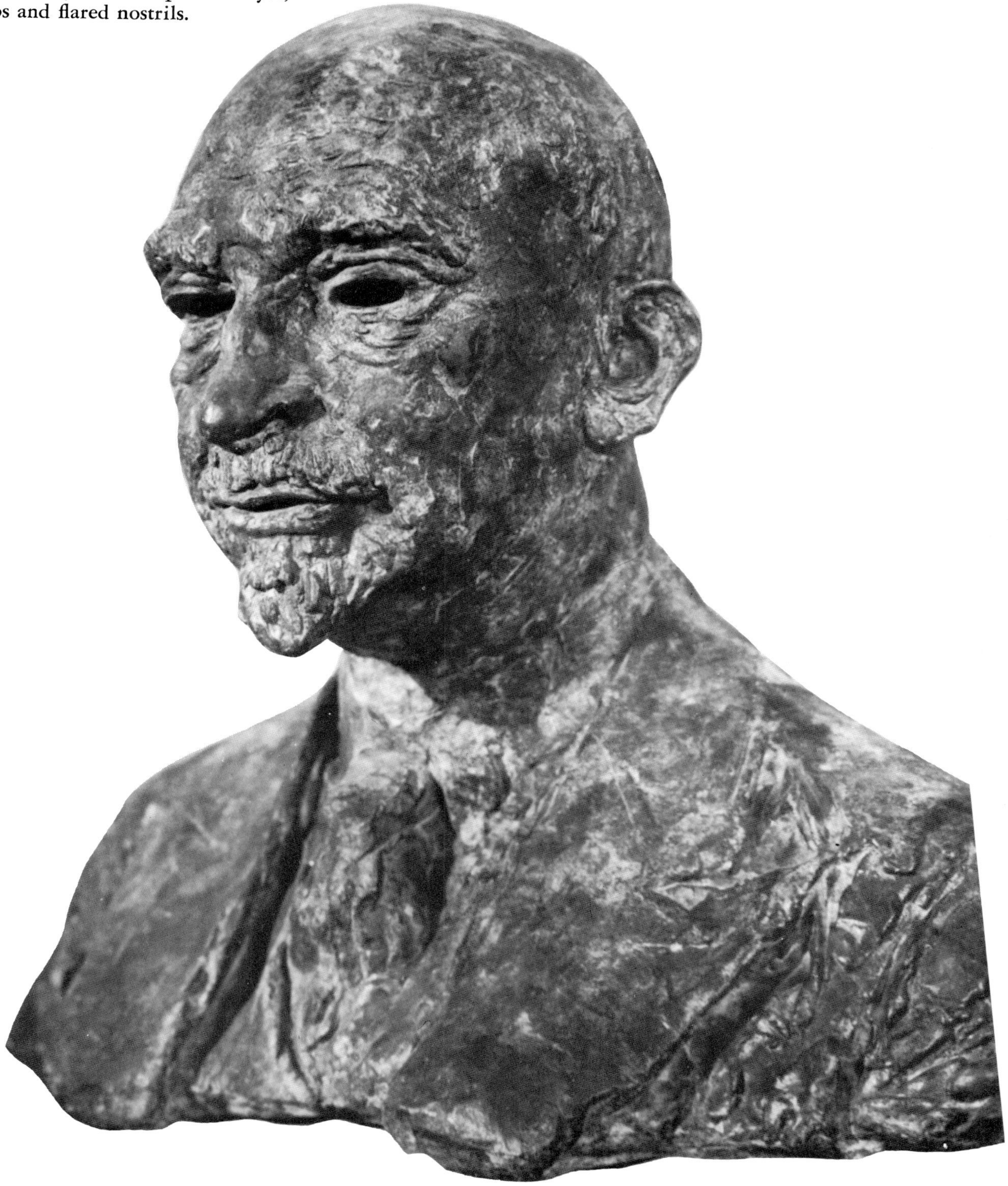

MAN OF ARAN, 1933. h. 17″ w. 9¾″ d. 10¾″

This Irish fisherman possesses a muscular face with massive jaw and chin. Crowning these rugged features is thick, wild curly hair. The model "Tiger" King was brought to Epstein by Robert Flaherty, the director of a film in which the Man of Aran was starring.

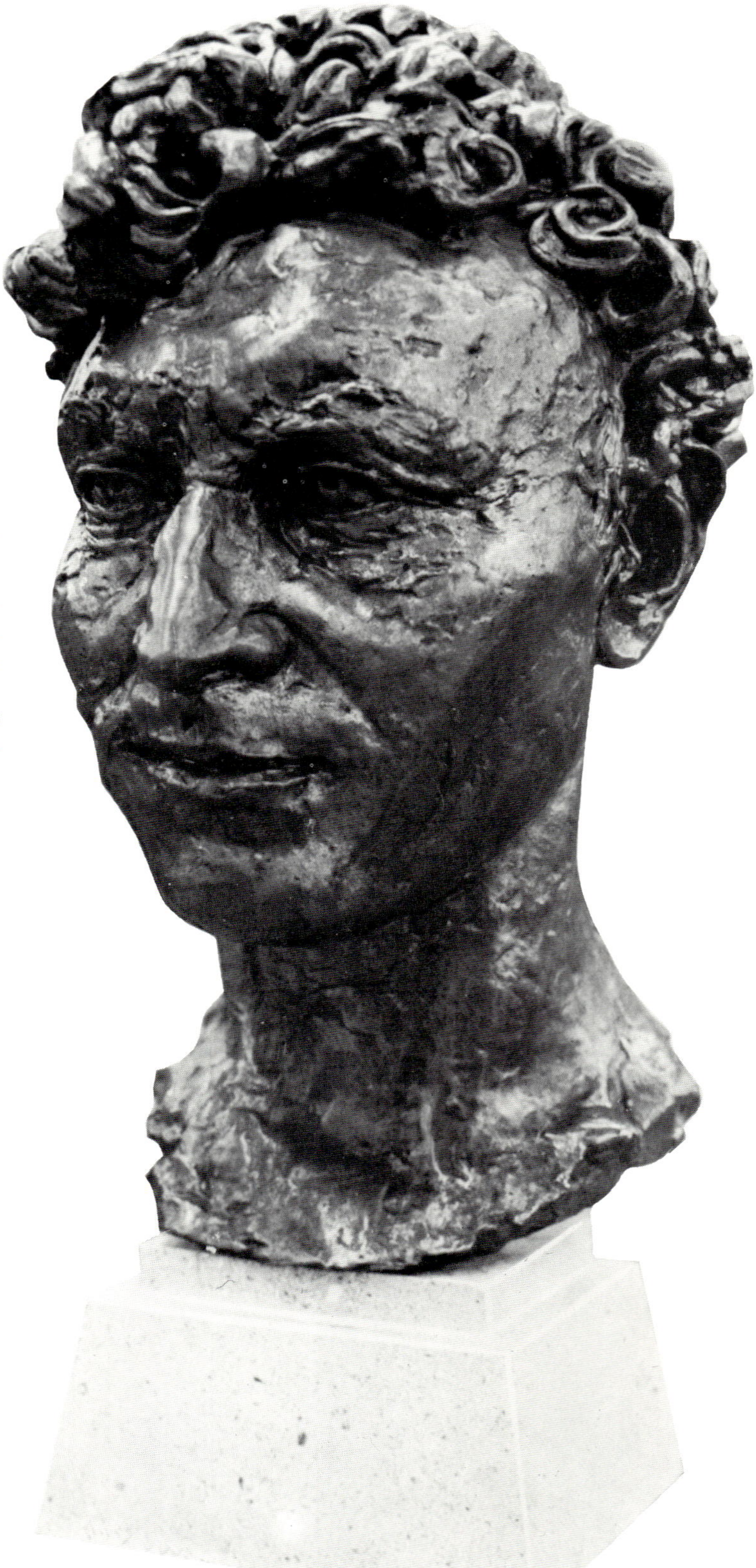

MADONNA AND CHRIST CHILD, 1927.
Madonna: h. 19″ w. 21″ d. 13″
Child: h. 11½″ w. 8″ d. 9″

The casts of the two heads represent but a part of the finished group now in Riverside Church, New York. Epstein has only slightly idealized the figures and he does this without any loss of religious feeling. He used not simply a particular mother and child but an Indian mother and child, Sunita and son Enver. The huge eyes of the Christ Child seem to be all-seeing, while still projecting his innocence. The Madonna's face exhibits the stoic acceptance of the future death of Christ. Epstein wrote: "The model was of that eternal Oriental type which seemed to me just right for a work of this religious character. When I had finished the head the model remarked that she could not possibly 'look as good as I had made her.' " She recognized that there was something eternal and divine in it and outside herself.

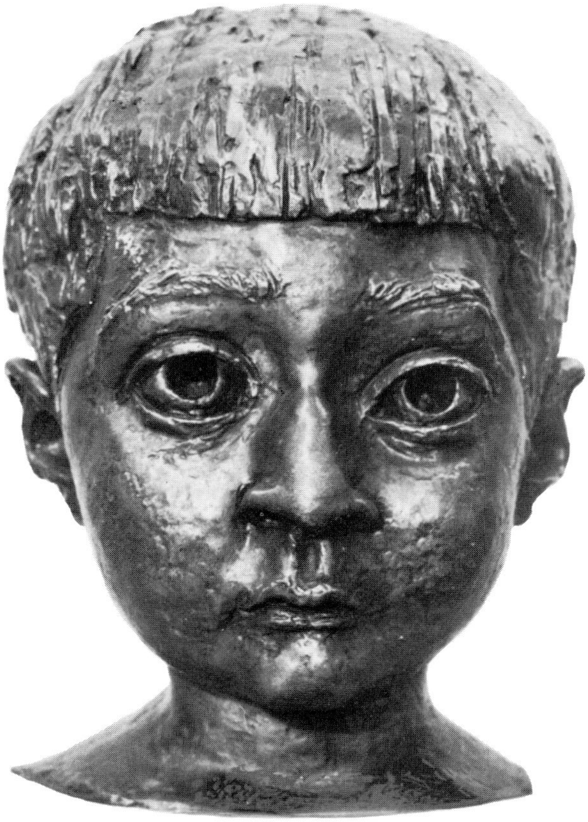

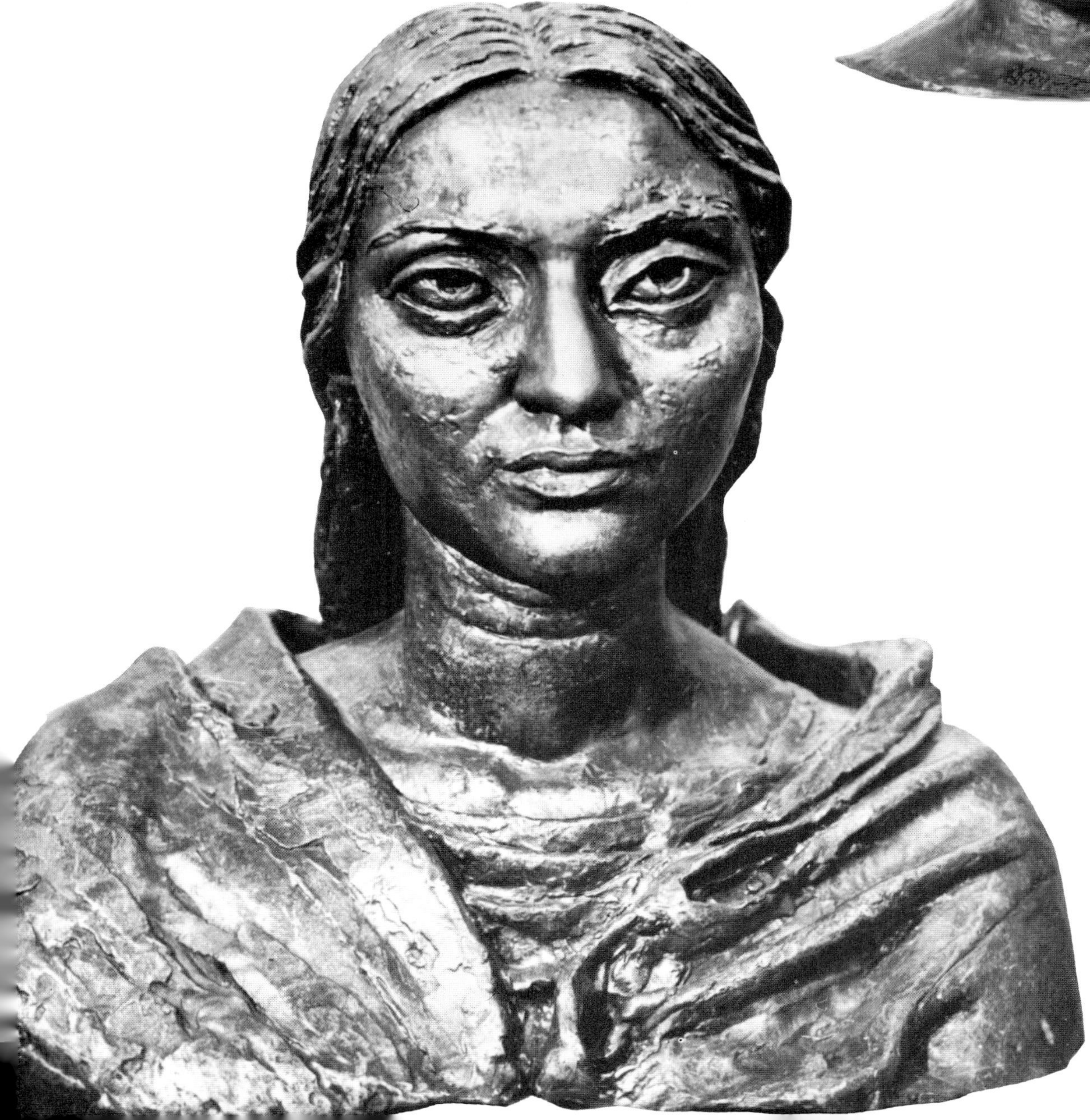

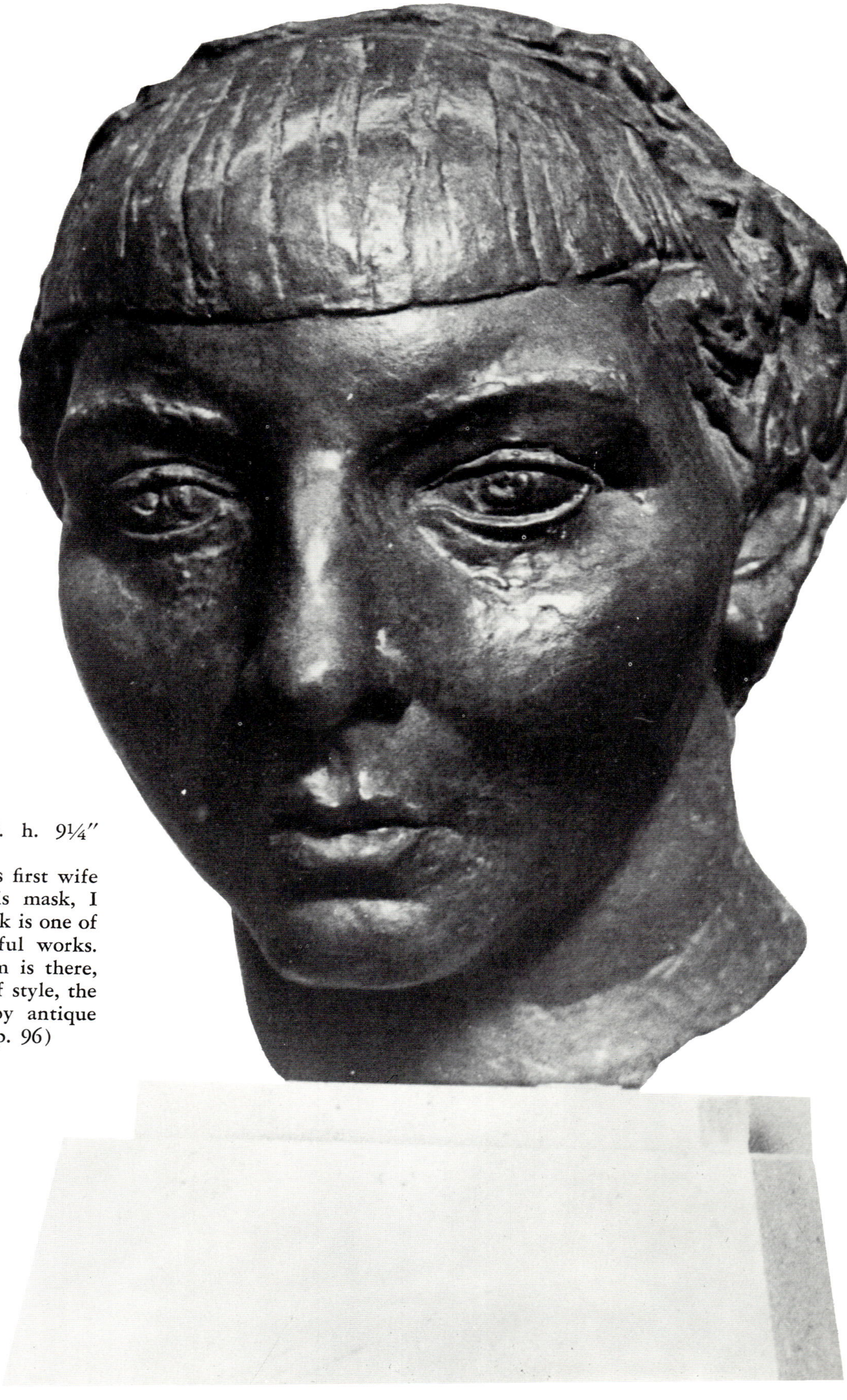

MRS. EPSTEIN—*Second,* 1916. h. 9¼″ w. 8¾″ d. 7¼″

Epstein made a mask of his first wife in 1916. He recalls: "In this mask, I immediately made what I think is one of my subtlest and most beautiful works. The serenity and inward calm is there, and from the point of view of style, the simplicity is that achieved by antique sculpture." (*Autobiography,* p. 96)

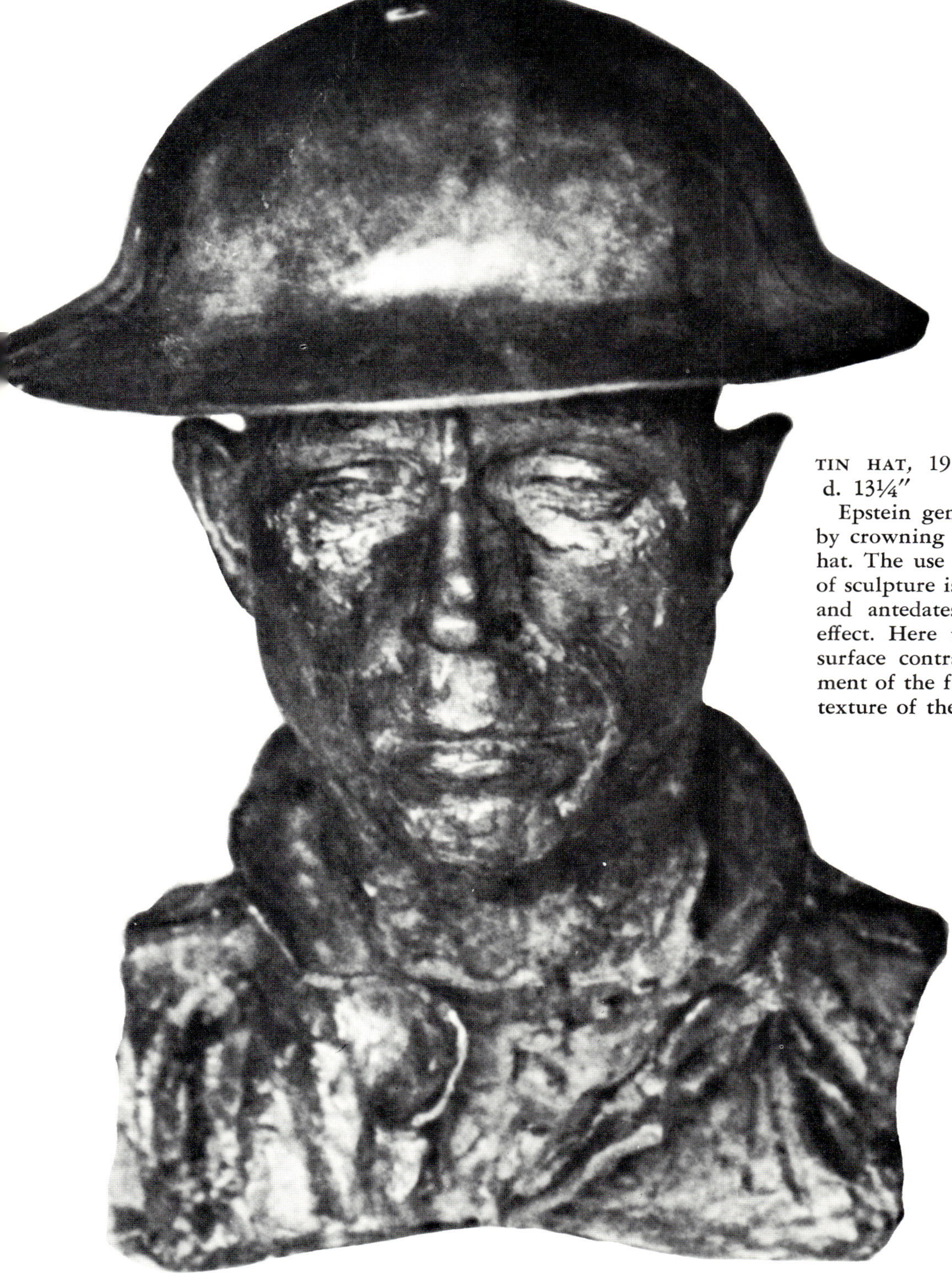

TIN HAT, 1916. h. 15¾″ w. 11″ d. 13¼″

Epstein generalizes the subject matter by crowning the soldier with a real tin hat. The use of a real object in a piece of sculpture is unusual in Epstein's work and antedates a now common artistic effect. Here the helmet's smooth, hard surface contrasts with the rough treatment of the face and the softly wrinkled texture of the shirt.

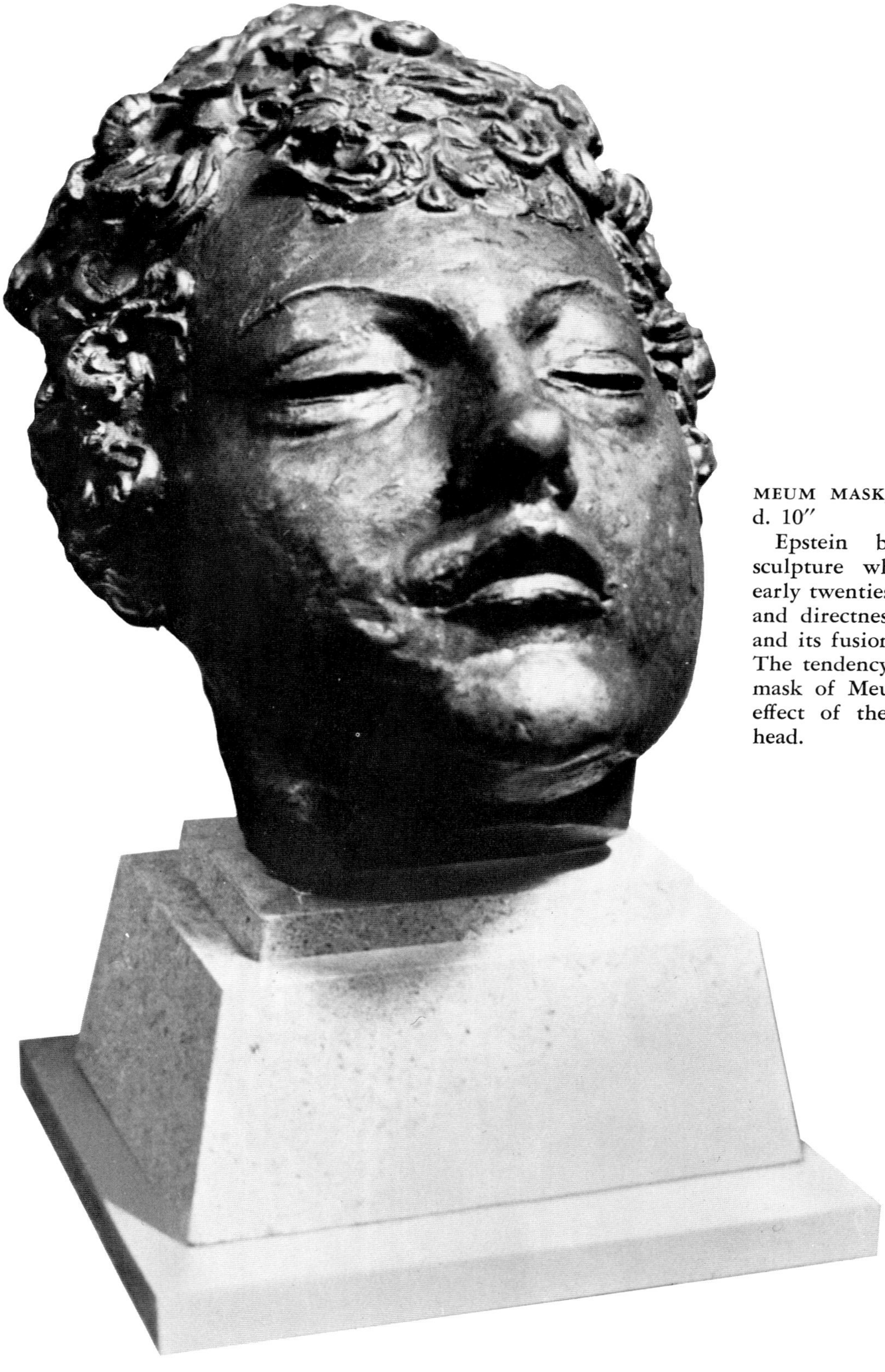

MEUM MASK, 1918. h. 11¾″ w. 7½″ d. 10″

Epstein began collecting African sculpture while in Paris during his early twenties. He admired its simplicity and directness, its architectural aspects, and its fusion of naturalism and design. The tendency toward abstraction in the mask of Meum heightens the dramatic effect of the closed eyes and angular head.

HELENE, 1919. h. 21½″ w. 16″ d. 14¼″

A half-caste and wife of the musician W. Yellin, Helene was the model for this lyrical and haunting bronze. Typical of Epstein are the pensive features and supple feeling of flesh. The classic calm of the head prevails as the tenderly posed hand clasps her dress, leaving an imaginary arm in space.

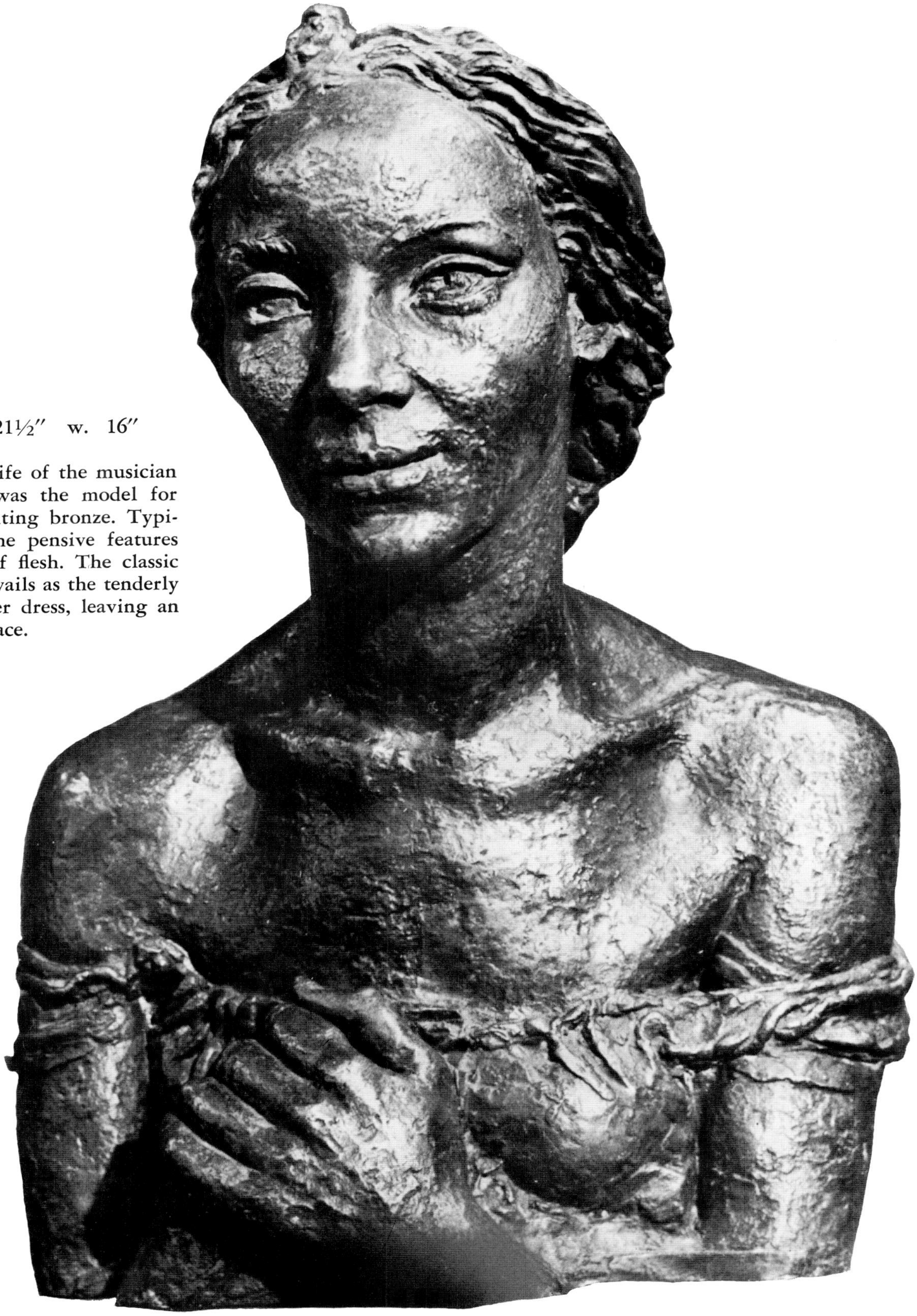

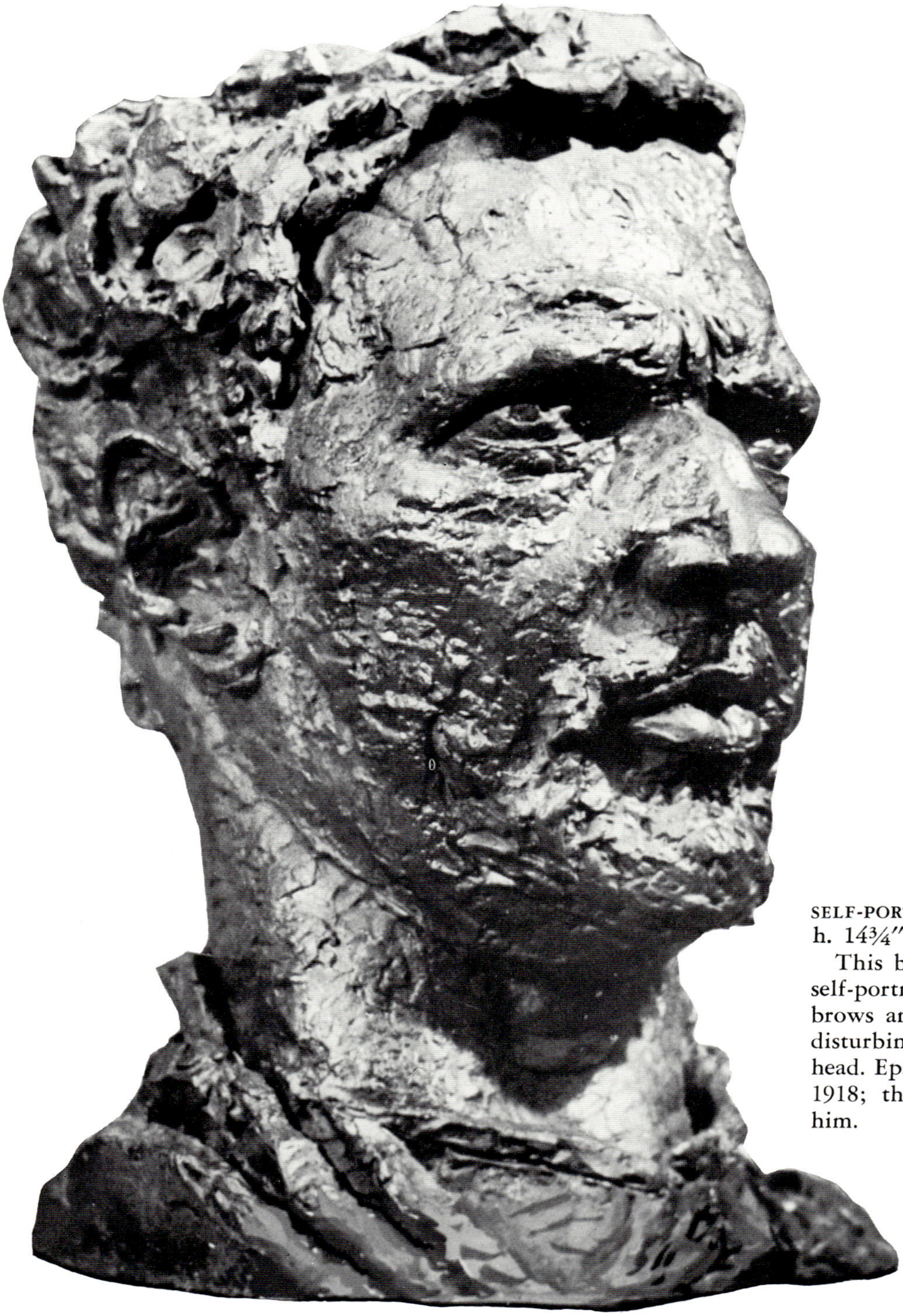

SELF-PORTRAIT WITH BEARD, 1920.
h. 14¾″ w. 9½″

This bronze was the second and final self-portrait made by Epstein. The knit brows and rough surface dramatize the disturbing mood which permeates the head. Epstein was in an army hospital in 1918; the effect of the war never left him.

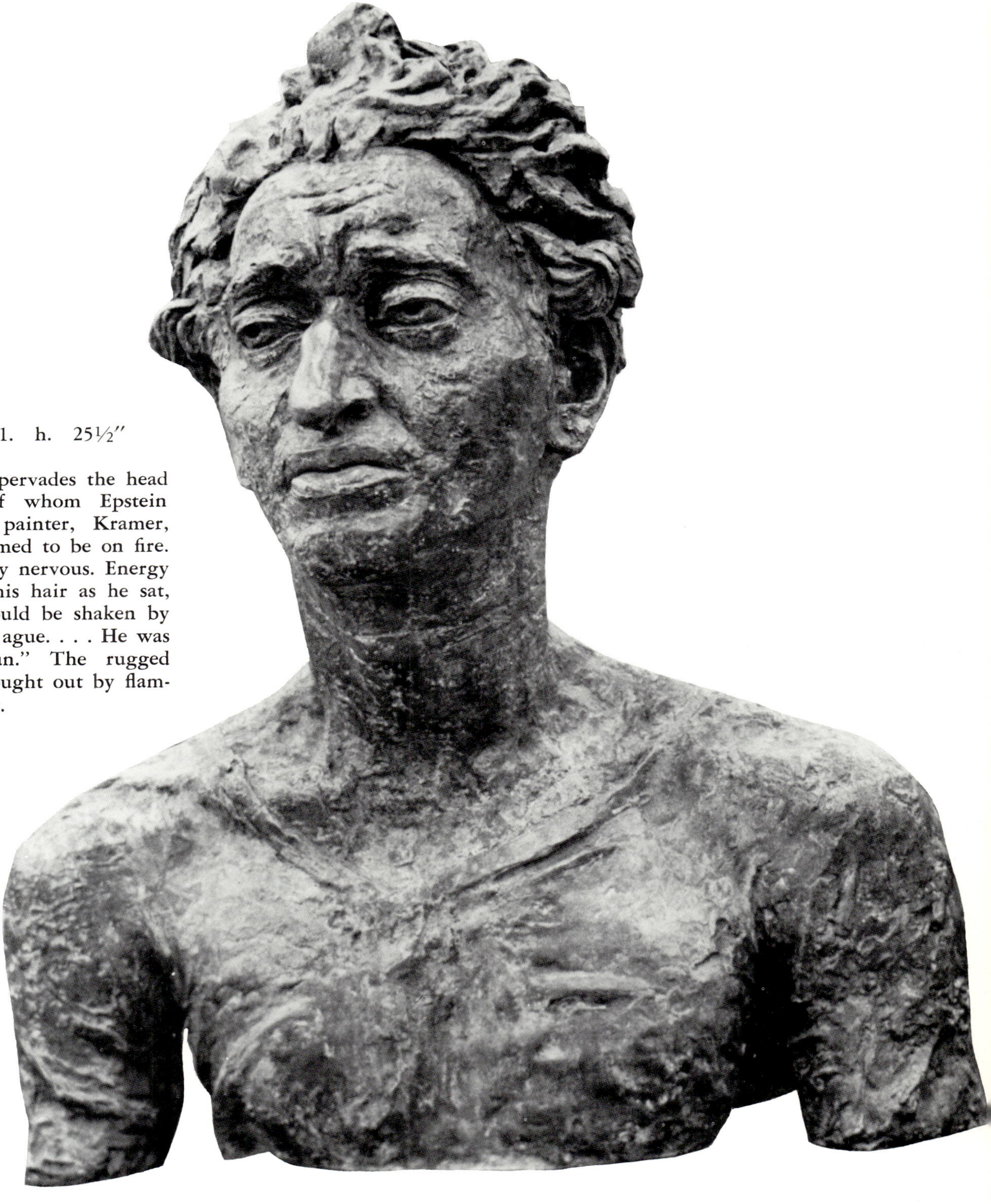

JACOB KRAMER, 1921. h. 25½″ w. 21½″ d. 13″

Restless movement pervades the head of Jacob Kramer of whom Epstein wrote: "The Leeds painter, Kramer, was a model who seemed to be on fire. He was extraordinarily nervous. Energy seemed to leap into his hair as he sat, and sometimes he would be shaken by queer tremblings like ague. . . . He was the typical Bohemian." The rugged facial features are brought out by flamboyant strokes of clay.

PEGGY JEAN ASLEEP, 1920. h. 10¼″ w. 11″ d. 15″

Epstein's first child Peggy Jean was born in October 1918. This is the Fourth Portrait of Peggy Jean, at Eighteen Months; it is one of at least ten studies done before she was three. Epstein writes: "To have a child to work from was delightful. The little Peggy Jean was a real source of inspiration. I never tired of watching her, and to watch her was, for me, to work from her. . . . To work from a child seemed to me the only work worth doing, and I was prepared to go on for the rest of my life looking at Peggy Jean, and making new studies of her."

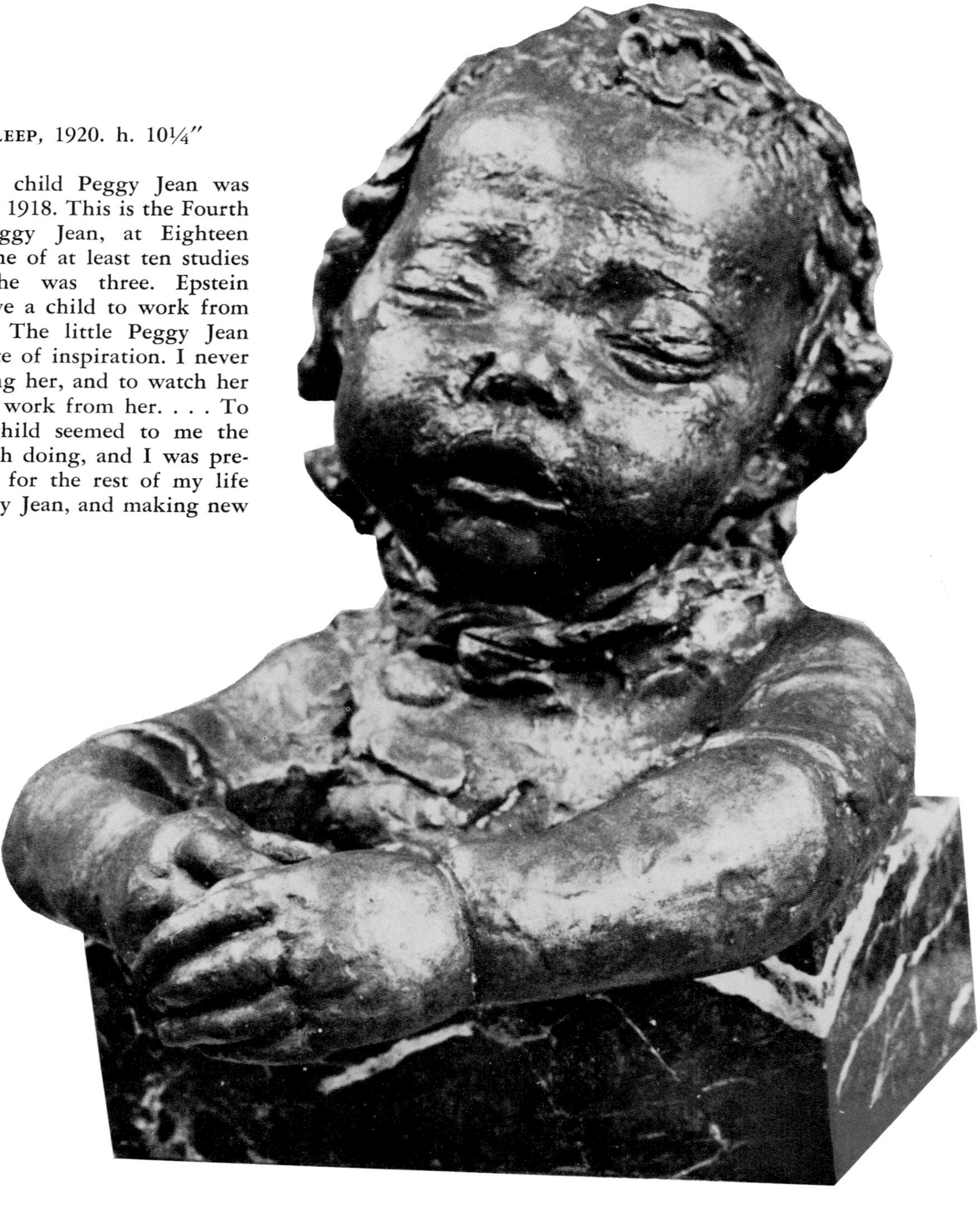

MRS. EPSTEIN, MANTILLA, 1918.
h. 14¾″ w. 16½″

Epstein writes: "This bust, I think, is the most profound—it has that quiet thoughtfulness that I had unconsciously striven for in the other two {second portrait of Mrs. Epstein, 1916 and first portrait of Mrs. Epstein, 1912} or most likely, as I matured in my work, I naturally brought into full play all my powers of observation and expression, and so made this one of my gravest, and I think one of my most beautiful busts. This work was unhurried and brooded over, and the drapery was worked with great care. The lines, all running downward like the rills of a fountain, are essential to the effect of the bust, and help to express its innermost meaning. I think of this bust as a crowning piece, and I place it with any work I have done."

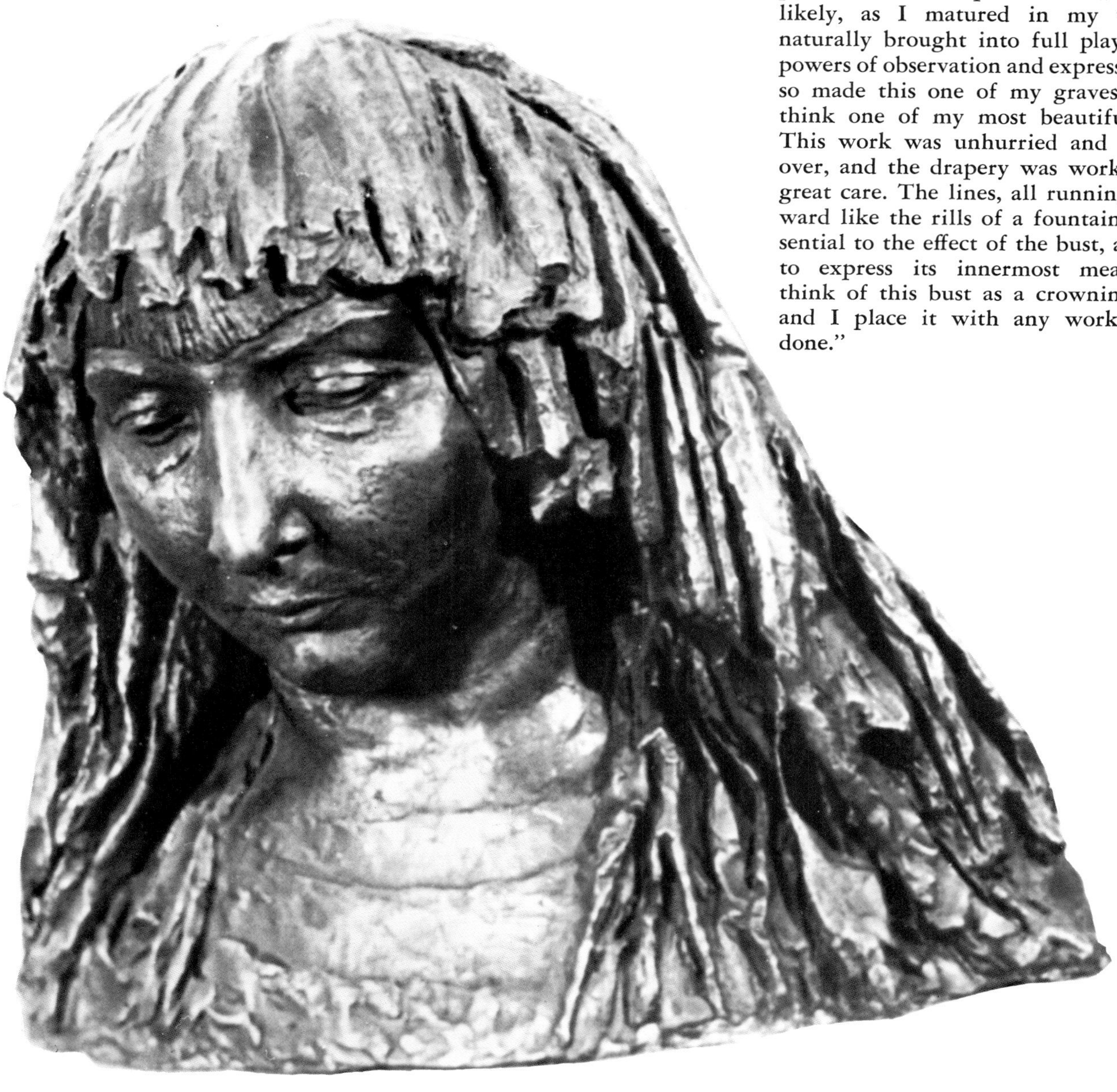

KATHLEEN, 1921. h. 18½″ w. 18¾″ d. 13″

Kathleen Garmen, who was to be Epstein's second wife, met the sculptor in August 1921. Though enamored of her beauty, Epstein chose to exaggerate the irregularities of Kathleen's face. The forehead and cheeks are roughened although the nose and chin are smoothed out. The eyes and brows are not matched either. Epstein told Arnold Haskell, "It is the rough surface that gives both character and likeness to the face. In sculpture it would be an easy mechanical matter to polish and sandpaper until the material was entirely smooth, but to do that would be really to produce a grave distortion."

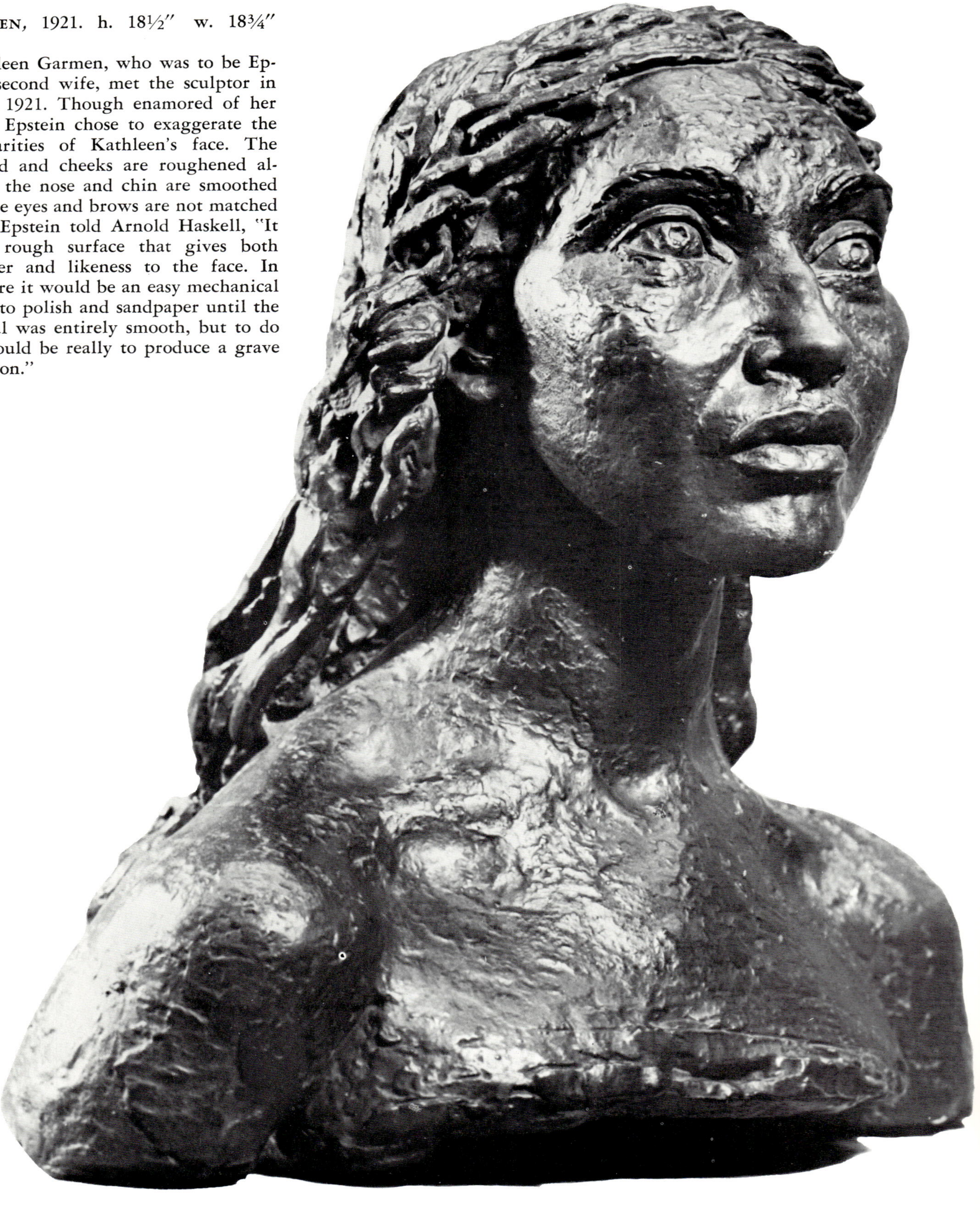

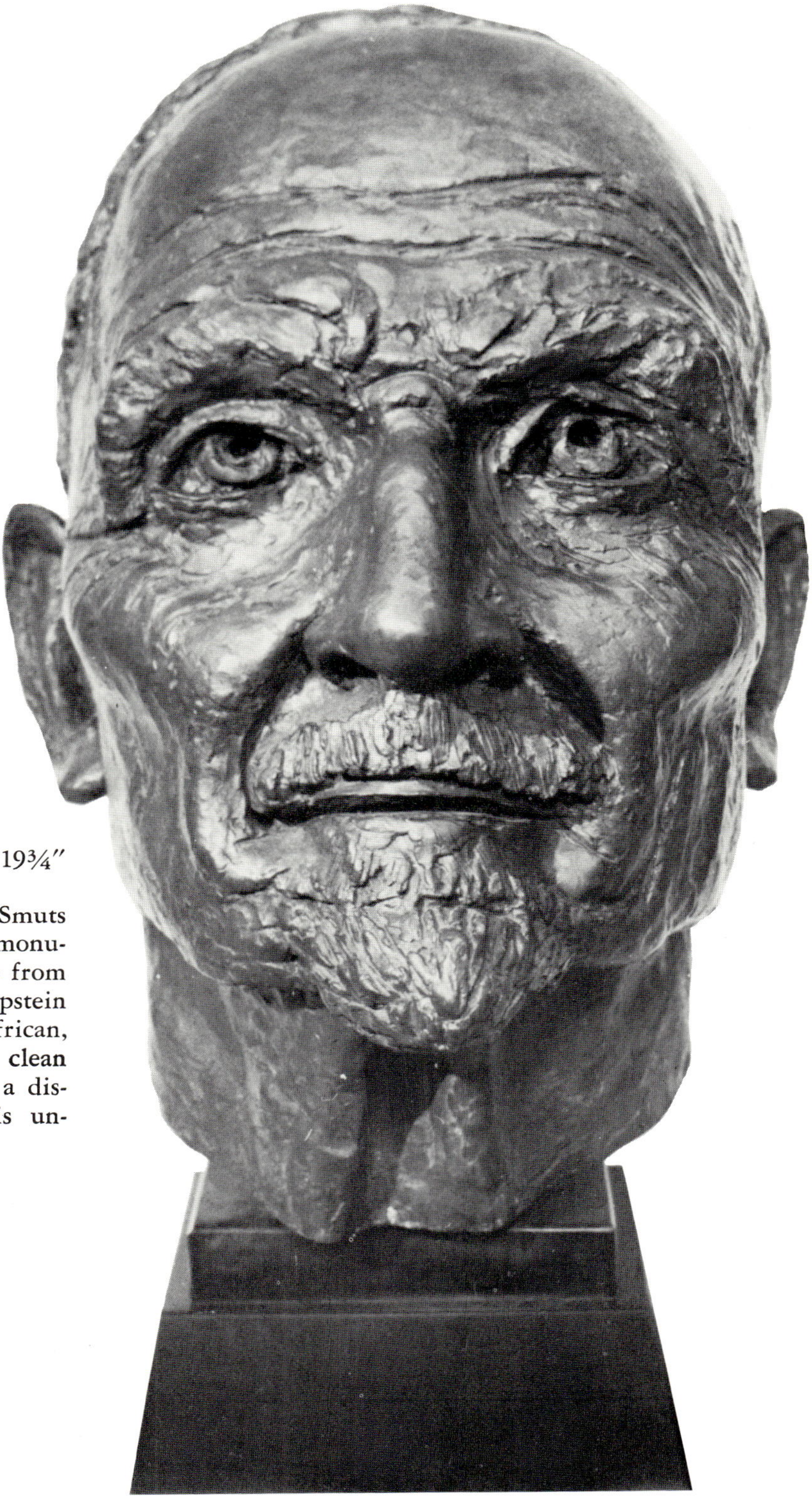

FIELD MARSHAL SMUTS, 1955. h. 19¾″ w. 22″ d. 18″

This head of Field Marshall Smuts was cast separately from a huge monument for Parliament Square. Done from photographs and film because Epstein had never met the heroic South African, the individual features are made clean and separate. When viewed from a distance, the powerful expression is unmistakable.

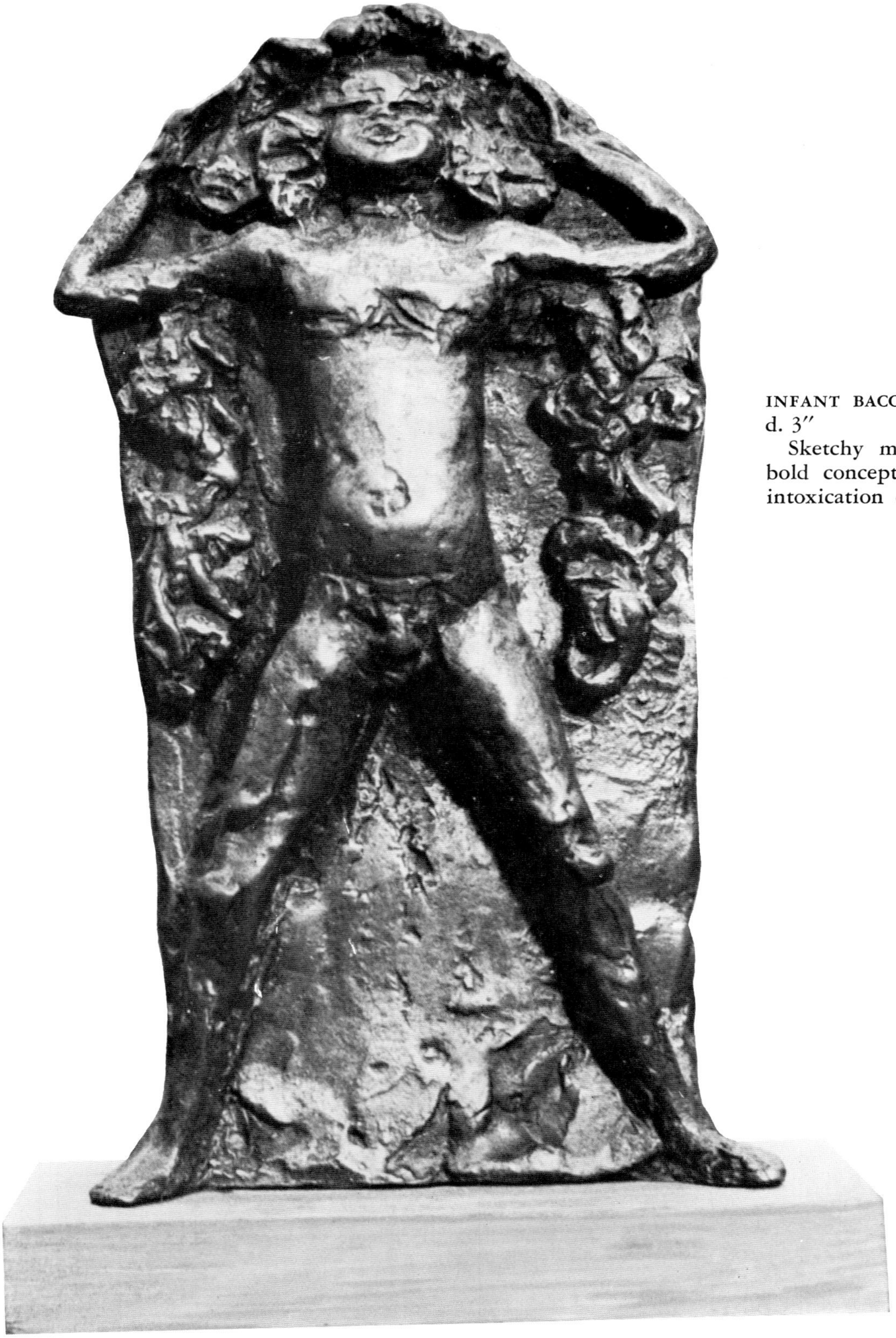

INFANT BACCHUS, 1956. h. 11″ w. 6″ d. 3″

Sketchy modelling characterizes this bold conception in high relief of the intoxication of youth.

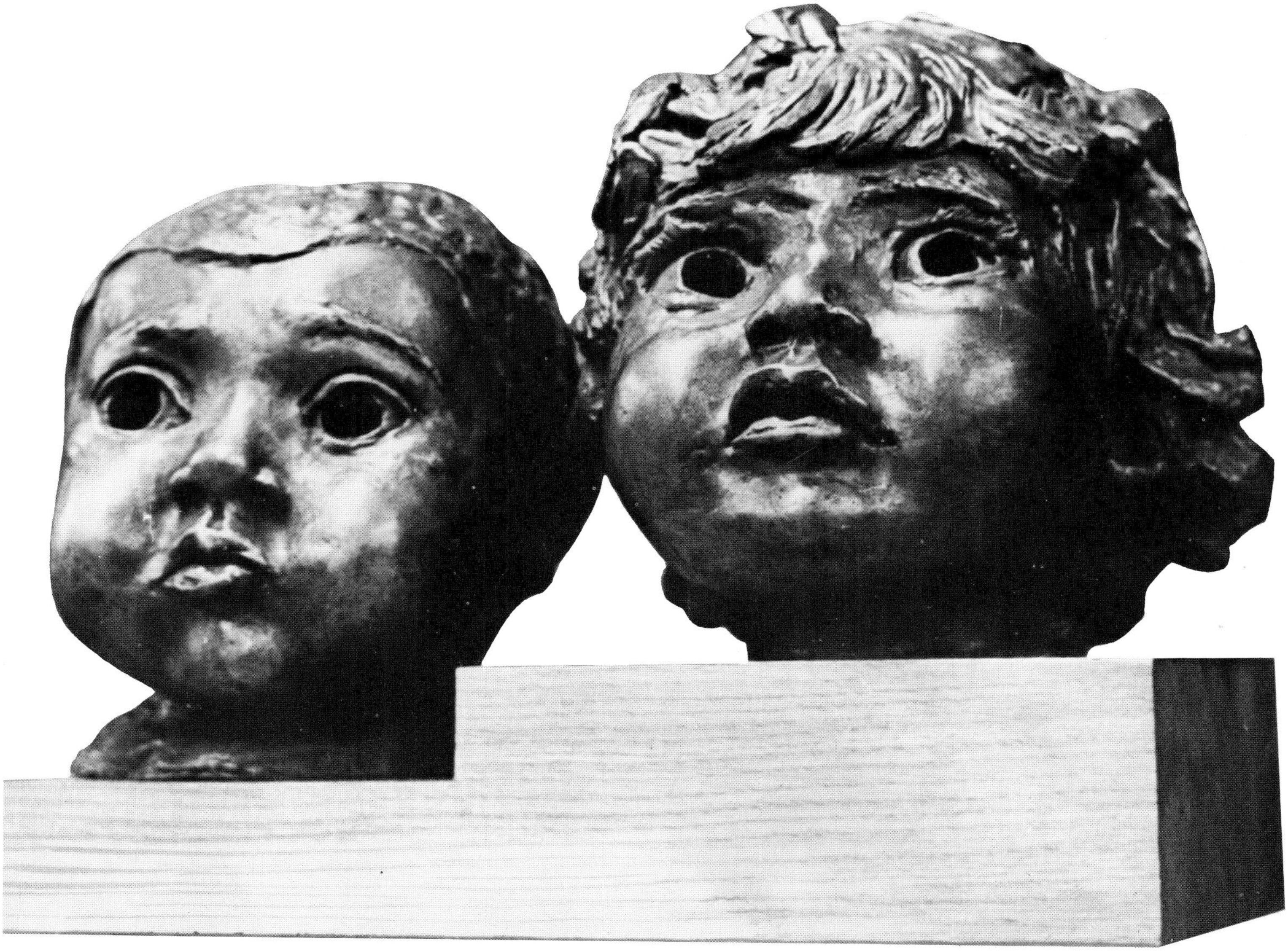

ANN AND ANNABEL (TWO SISTERS), 1950.
h. 7″ w. 7″ d. 5″ (each)

Epstein sculptured members of the family to his delight. His grandchildren, Ann and Annabel, are the children of Kitty and Lucian Freud. Freud was the grandson of renowned Sigmund Freud.

DR. FREDERICK MALLON, 1954. h. 12″ w. 12½″ d. 10¼″

In 1954 Epstein accepted a commission to portray the retiring Irish Governor of Toynbee Hall, Dr. Frederick Mallon. Epstein here portrays the tongue-in-cheek Irish wit of the renowned educator.

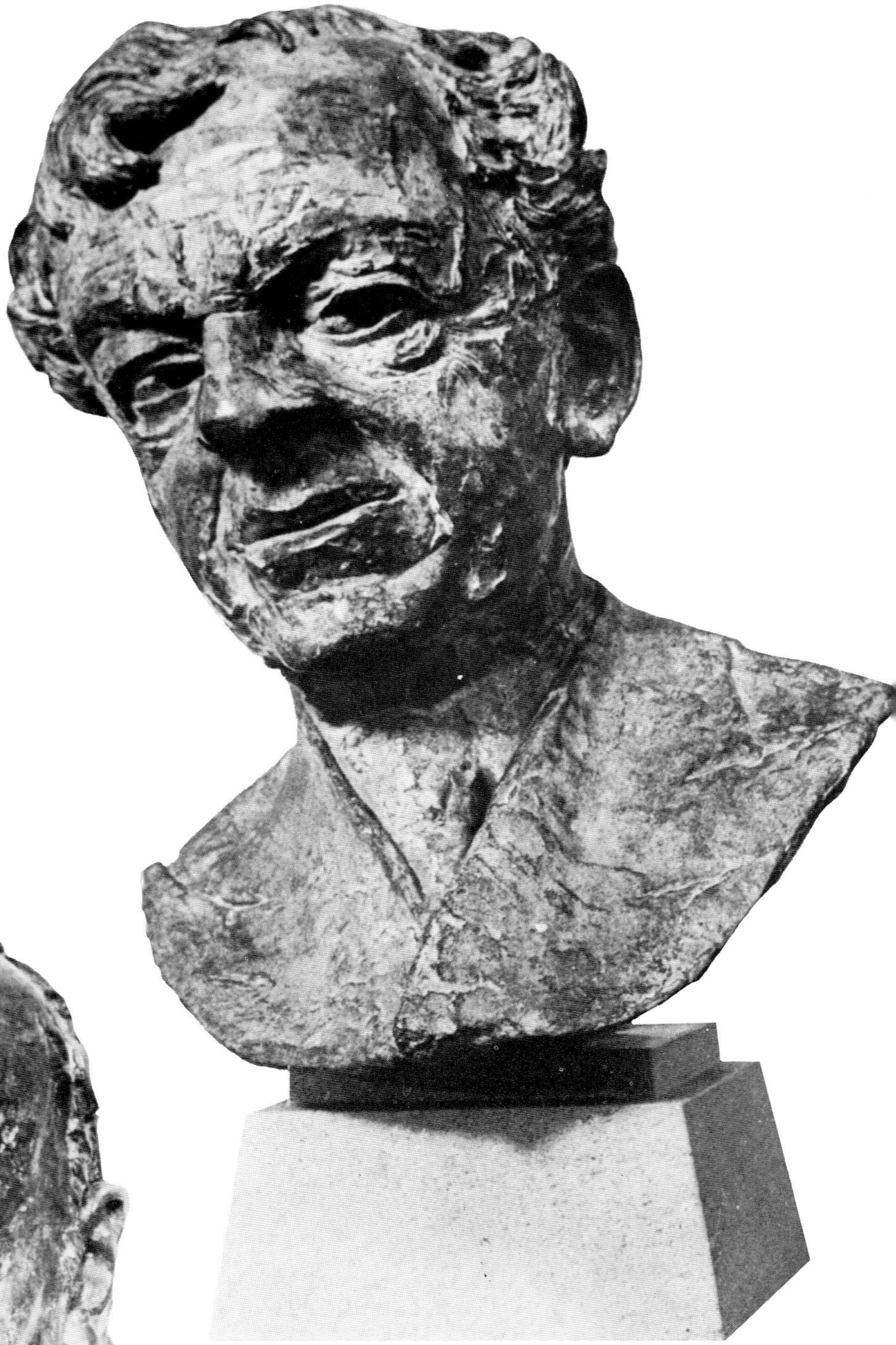

WILLIAM BLAKE, 1956. h. 21¼″ w. 24½″ d. 15½″

This portrait was commissioned by the Blake Society for the Poet's Corner, Westminster Abbey, to commemorate the 200th anniversary of the poet's birth. The penetrating eyes, partially obscured by heavy brows, bespeak a severe tone carried out by the tight-lipped mouth.

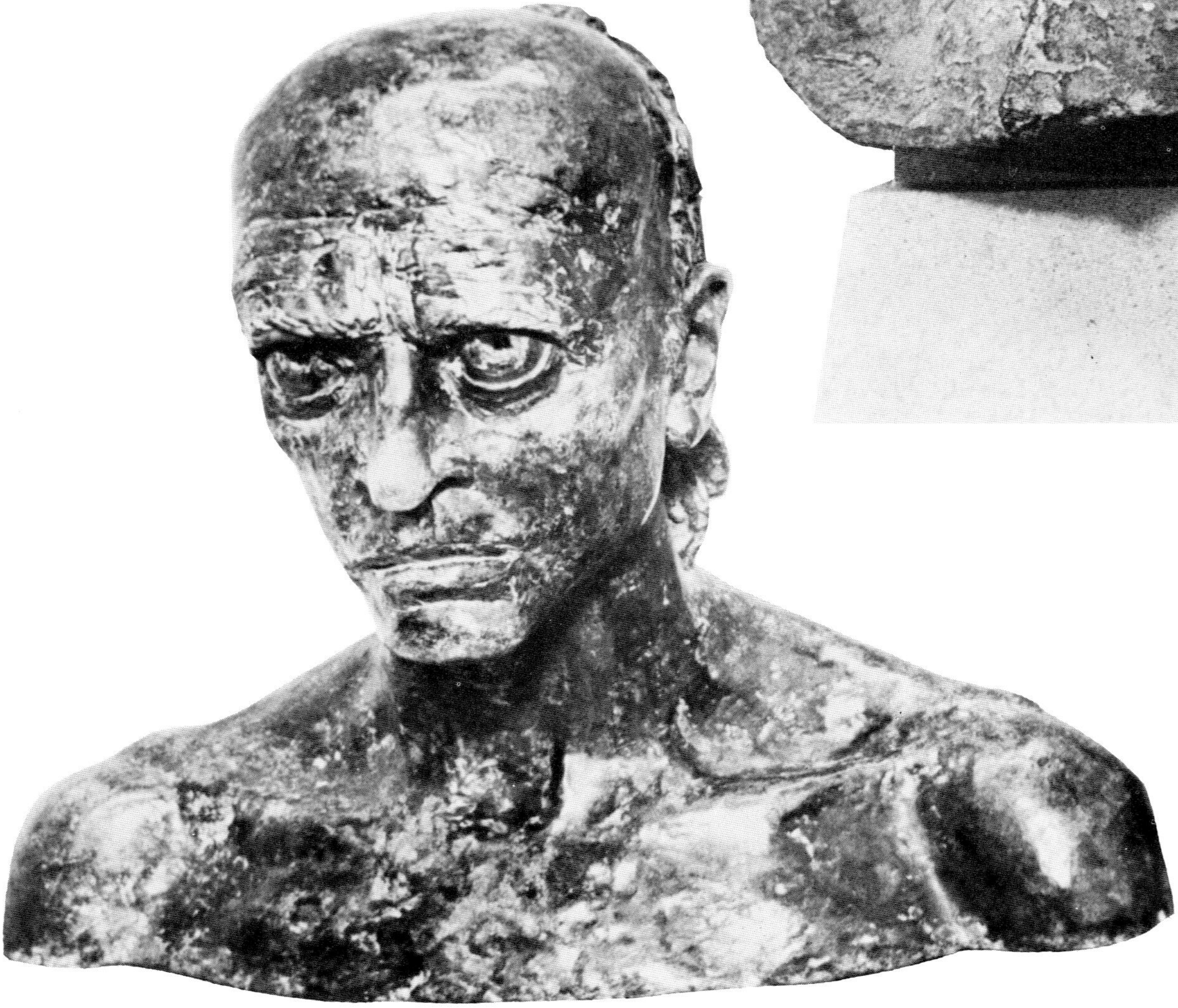

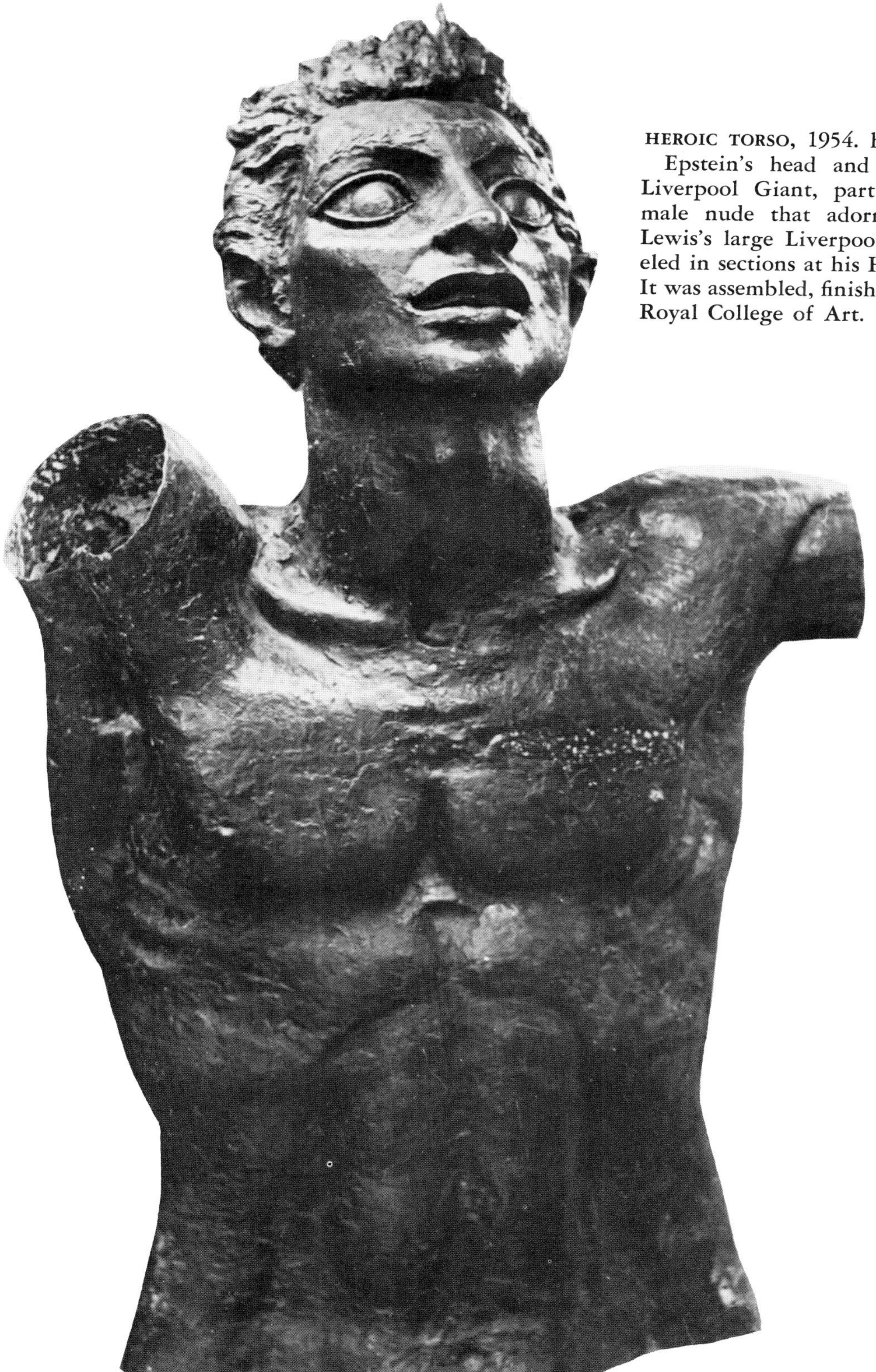

HEROIC TORSO, 1954. h. 84″

Epstein's head and shoulder of the Liverpool Giant, part of the gigantic male nude that adorns the façade of Lewis's large Liverpool store, was modeled in sections at his Hyde Park Studio. It was assembled, finished, and cast at the Royal College of Art.

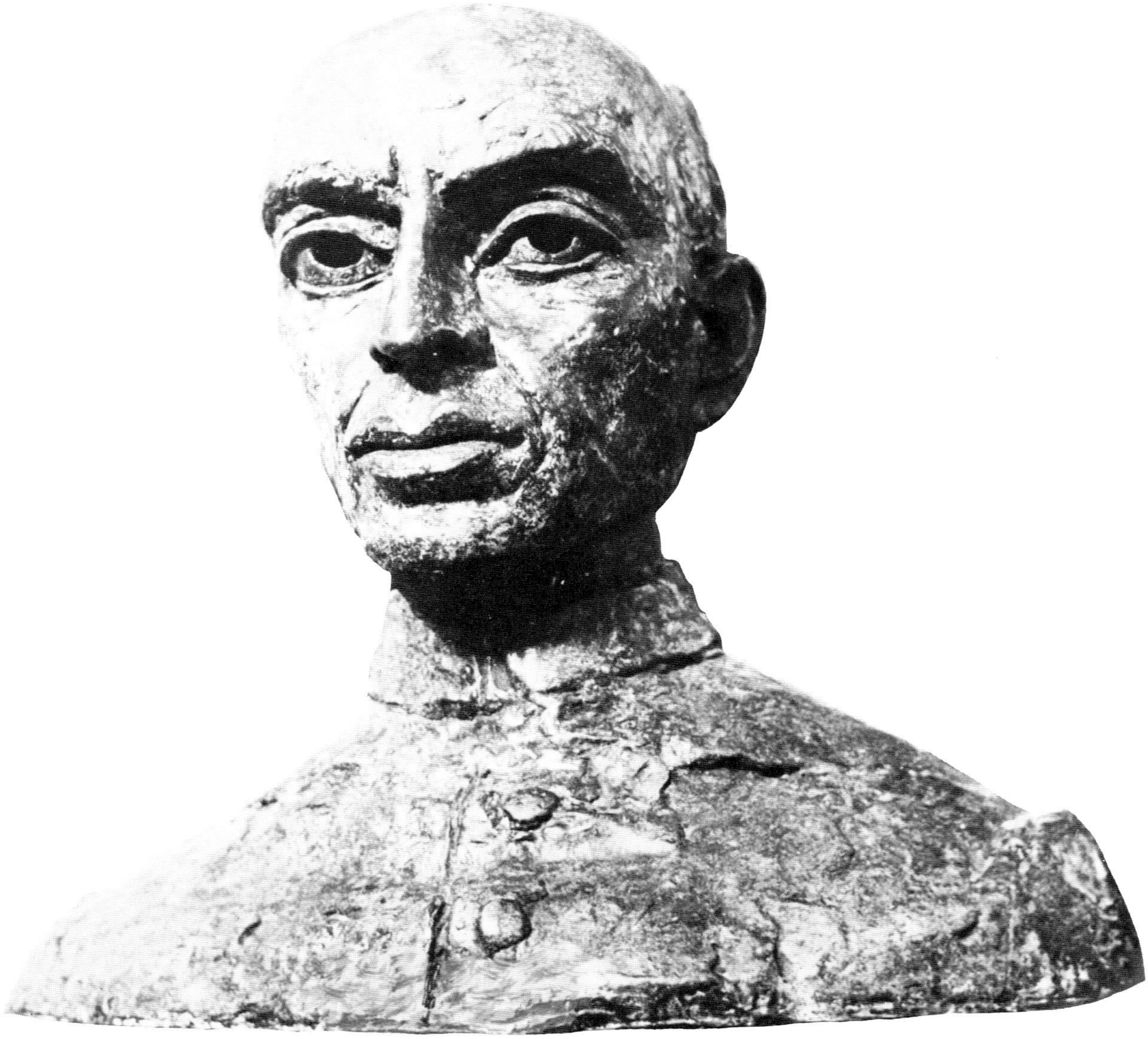

PANDIT NEHRU, 1949. h. 15½″ w. 17″ d. 9½″

Epstein completed this bust of Pandit Nehru when he returned to England a year after he had given the sculptor several brief sittings while attending an Imperial Conference. "At this time," wrote Epstein, "so soon after the assassination of Mahatma Gandhi, Nehru seemed burdened with the cares of office and it was in this mood that I conceived this sombre portrait." One can immediately sense a strange enigmatic quality of the man.

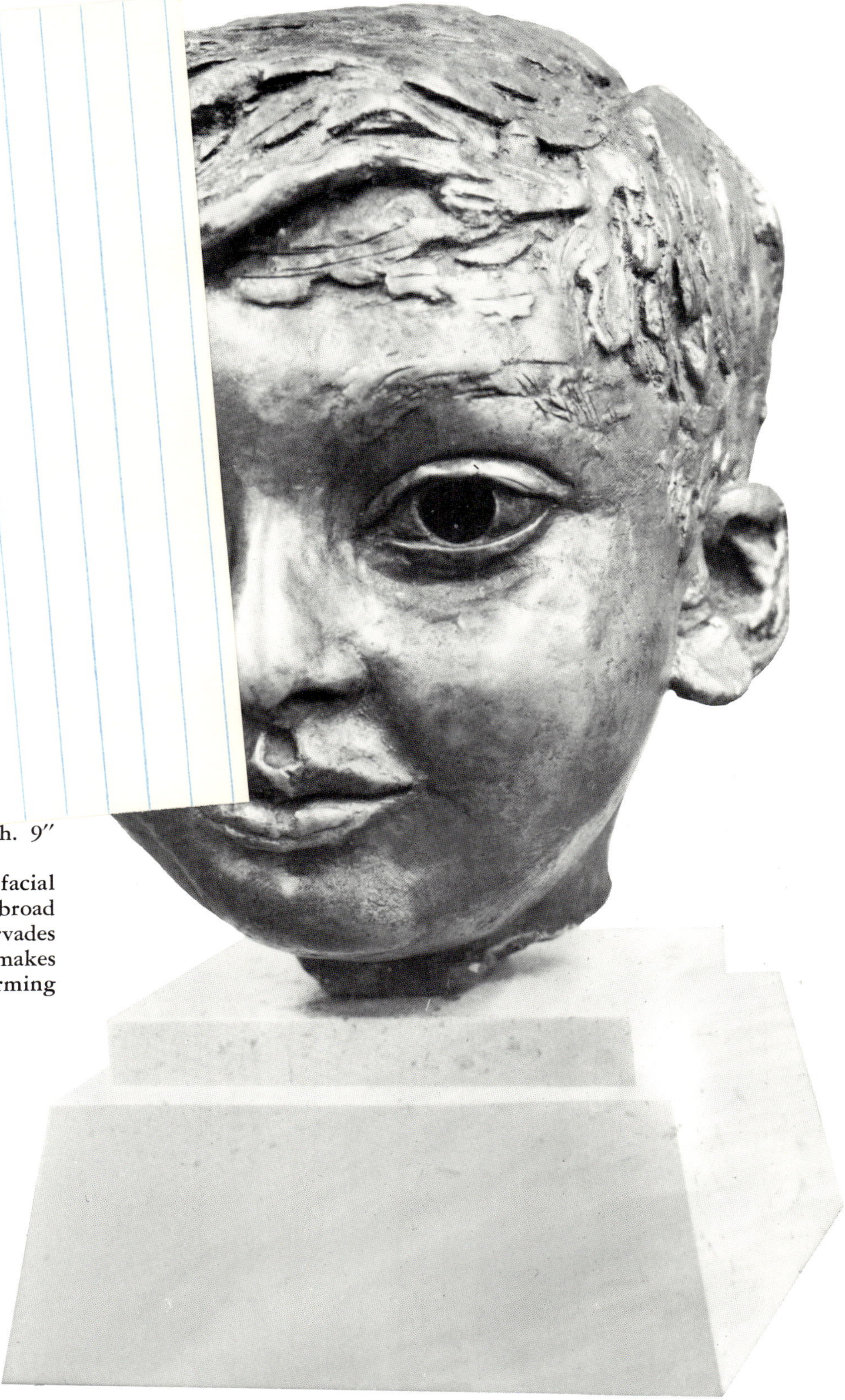

LITTLE PRI[illegible] BARODA, 1951. h. 9″ w. 7″ d. 9″

The soft, subtle curves of the facial features contrast with the thick broad strips of hair. The calm that pervades the wondering eyes and sweet lips makes this one of Epstein's most charming child portraits.

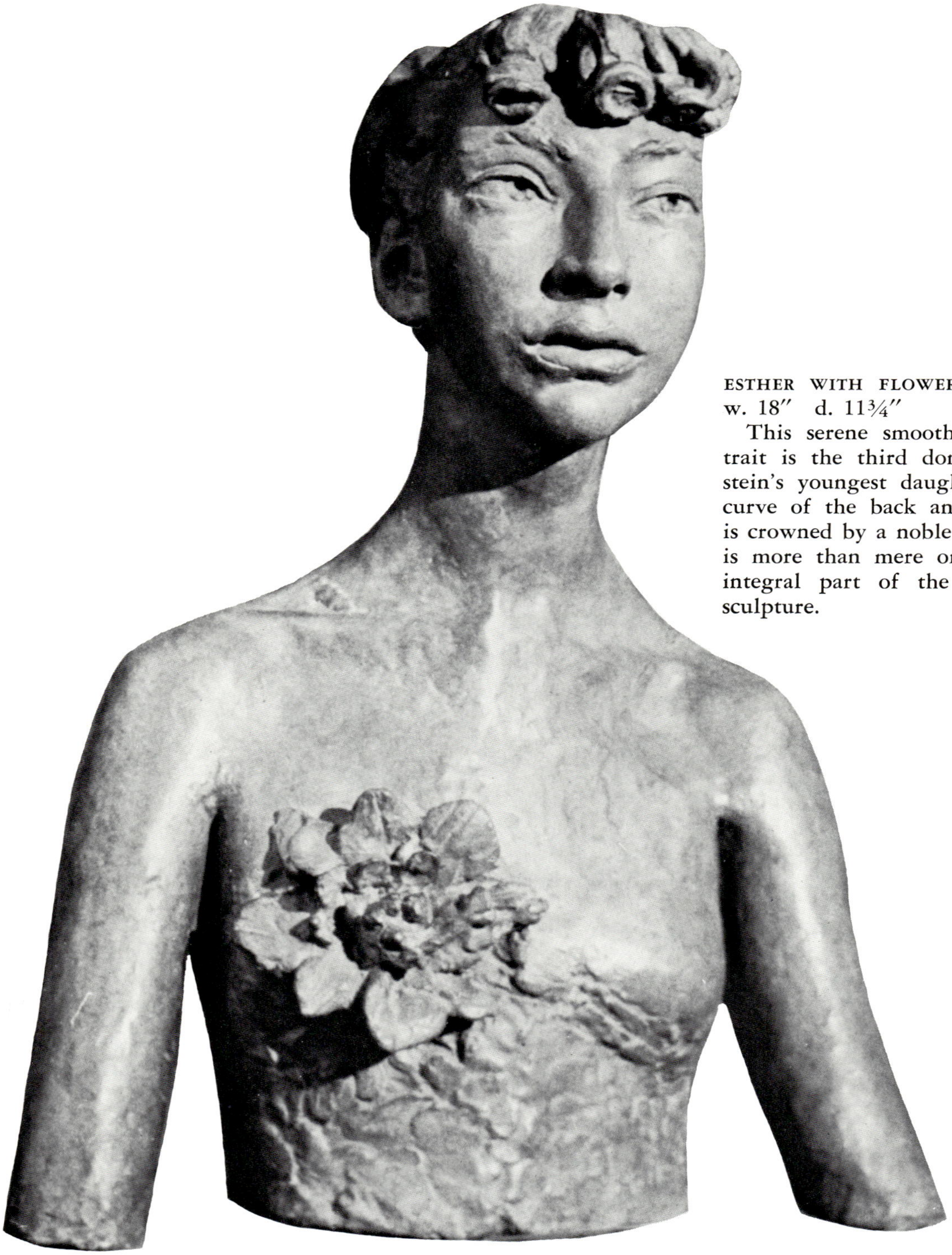

ESTHER WITH FLOWER, 1949. h. 23¾″ w. 18″ d. 11¾″

This serene smoothly modelled portrait is the third done of Esther, Epstein's youngest daughter. The elegant curve of the back and elongated neck is crowned by a noble head. The flower is more than mere ornament; it is an integral part of the balance in this sculpture.

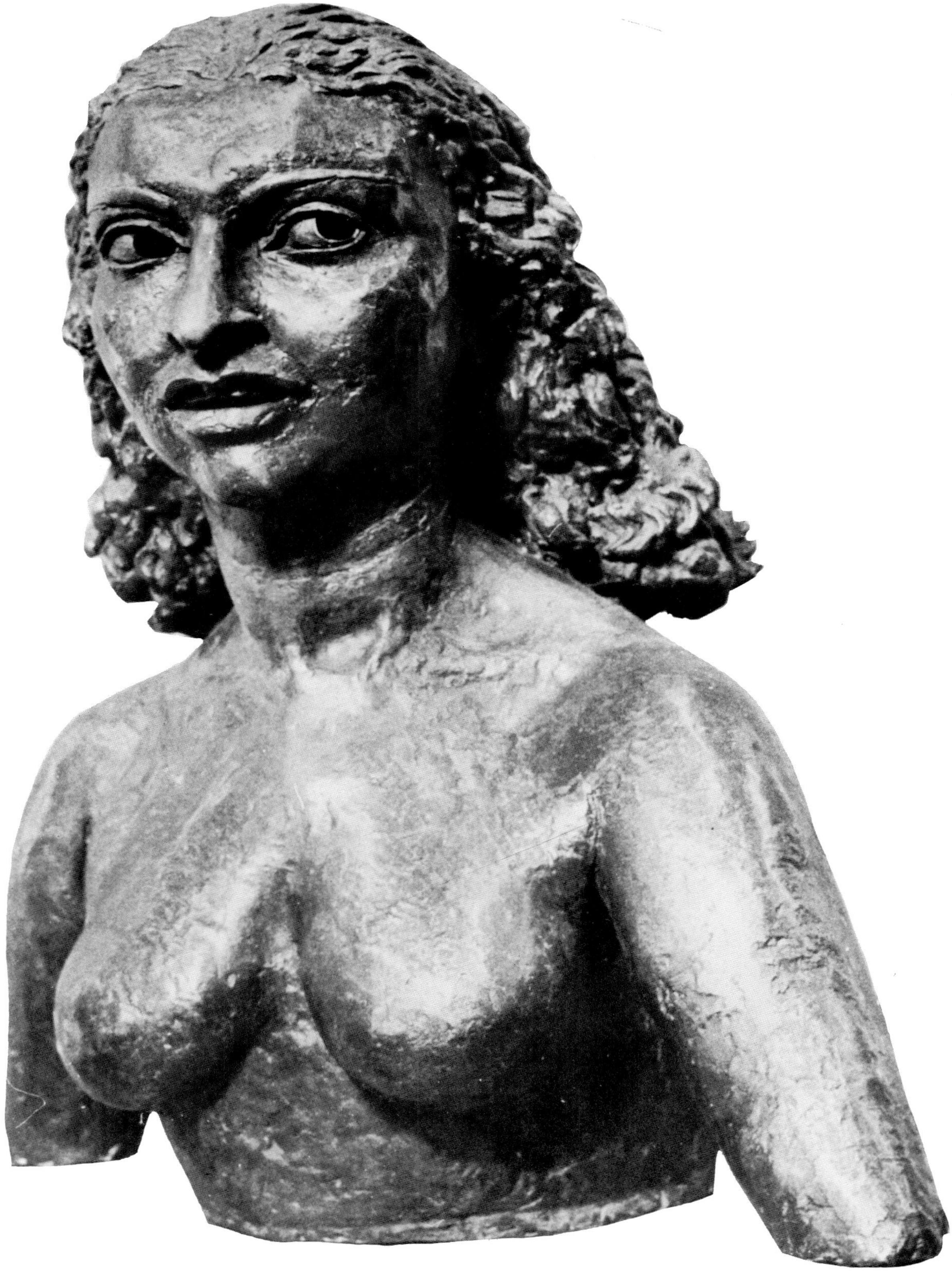

PRINCESS DESTA, 1949. h. 21″ w. 21″ d. 15″

The half Belgian niece of the Empress of Abyssinia, Princess Desta, generates a feeling of tremendous force created by the mass of hair which seems electrified with an energy of its own. The intense eyes and brows, open mouth, and extended arm evoke impending action.

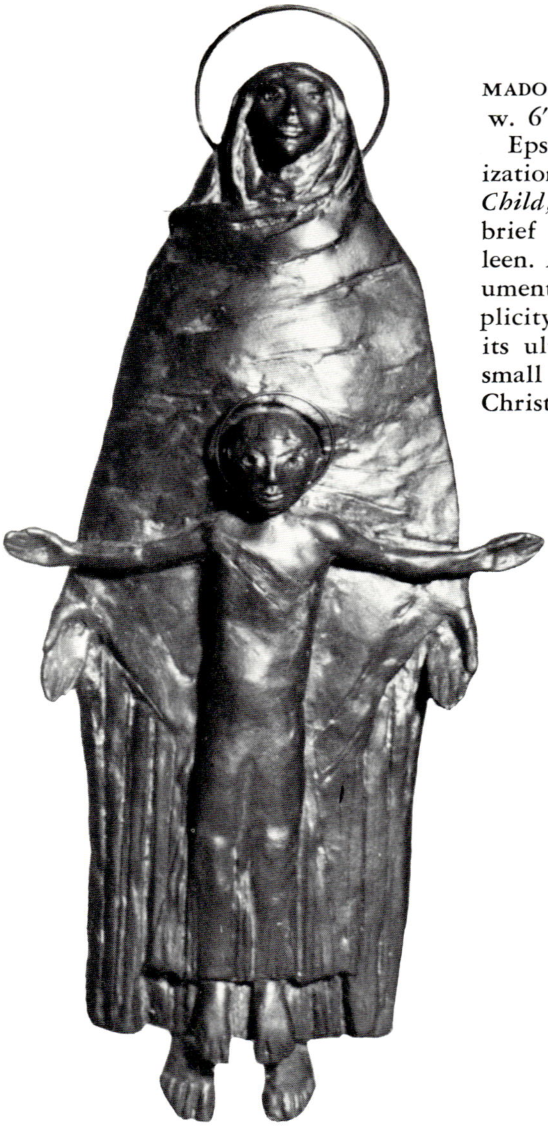

MADONNA AND CHILD, 1950. h. 14″ w. 6″

Epstein's uncanny ability at characterization is revealed in *Madonna and Child,* where we recognize, even in this brief sketch, essential features of Kathleen. A study for the thirteen-foot monument for Cavendish Square, the simplicity and smoothness of form hint at its ultimate state as a monument. The small outstretched arms of the young Christ form the cross.

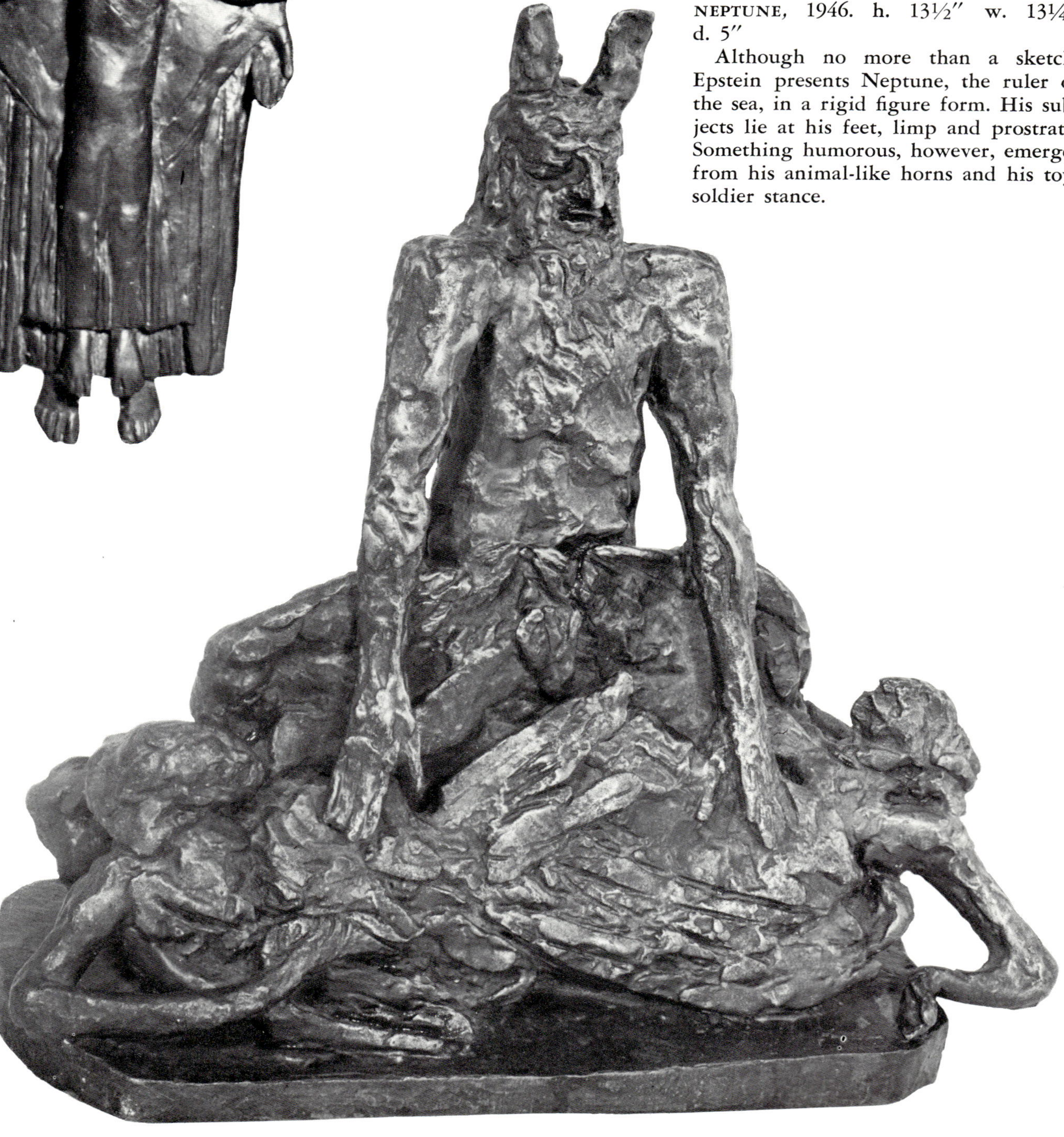

NEPTUNE, 1946. h. 13½″ w. 13¼″ d. 5″

Although no more than a sketch, Epstein presents Neptune, the ruler of the sea, in a rigid figure form. His subjects lie at his feet, limp and prostrate. Something humorous, however, emerges from his animal-like horns and his toy-soldier stance.

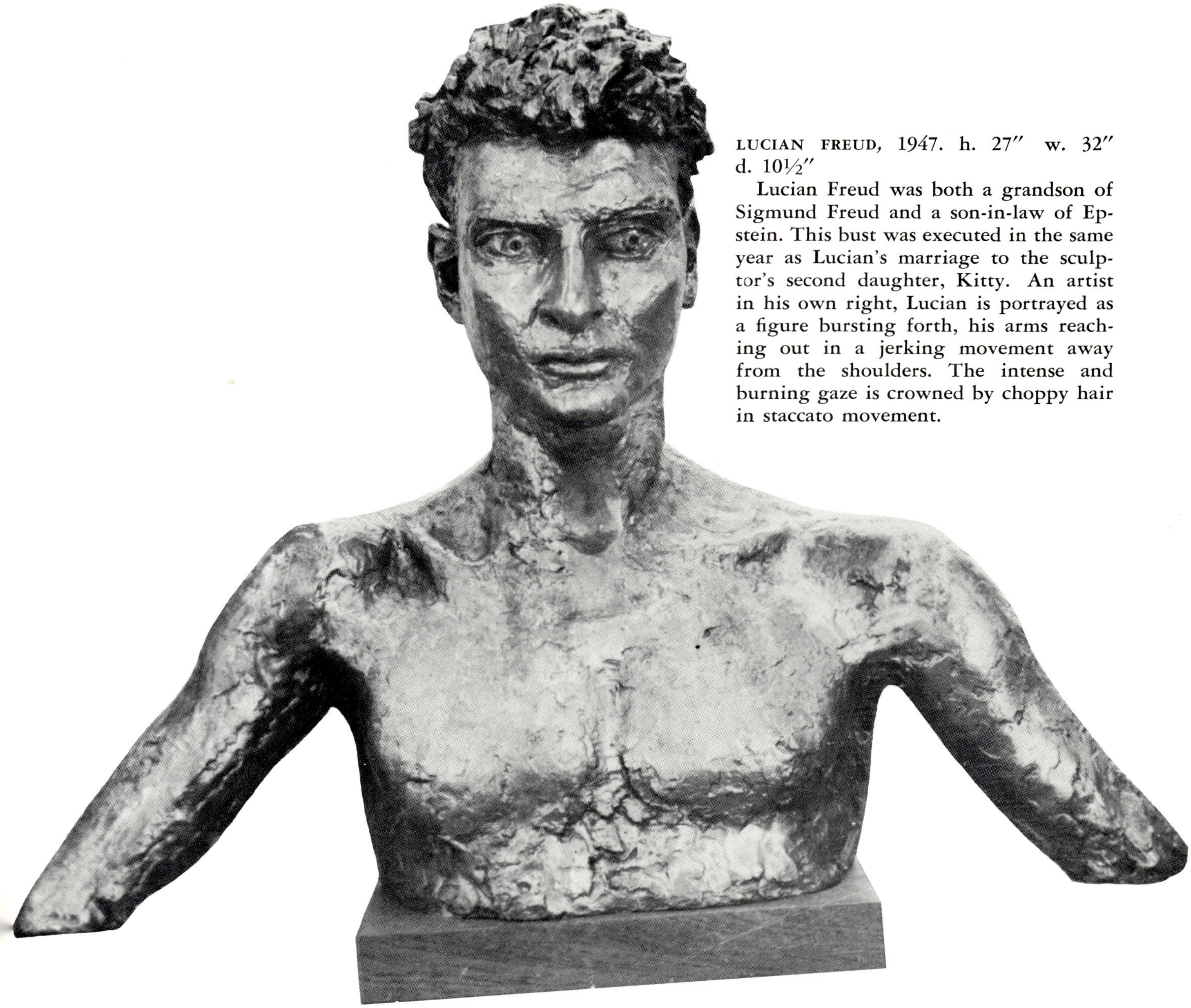

LUCIAN FREUD, 1947. h. 27″ w. 32″ d. 10½″

Lucian Freud was both a grandson of Sigmund Freud and a son-in-law of Epstein. This bust was executed in the same year as Lucian's marriage to the sculptor's second daughter, Kitty. An artist in his own right, Lucian is portrayed as a figure bursting forth, his arms reaching out in a jerking movement away from the shoulders. The intense and burning gaze is crowned by choppy hair in staccato movement.

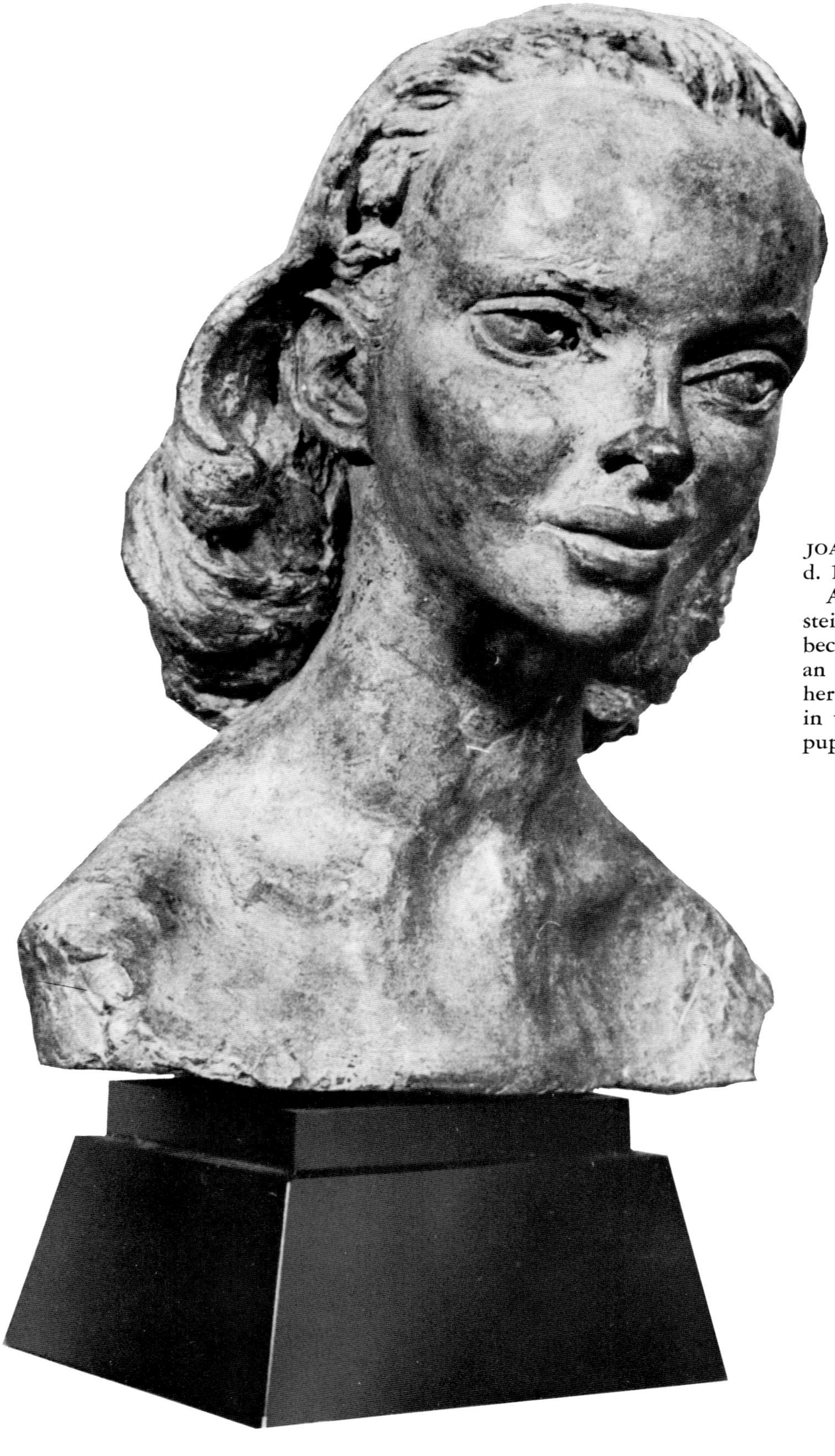

JOAN GREENWOOD, 1948. h. 15″ w. 12″ d. 10″

A childhood friend of Peggy Jean, Epstein's oldest daughter, Joan Greenwood became an actress. The sculpture achieves an elfin quality in her fluid features, her half smile and strange smiling eyes in which he has hollowed out only the pupils.

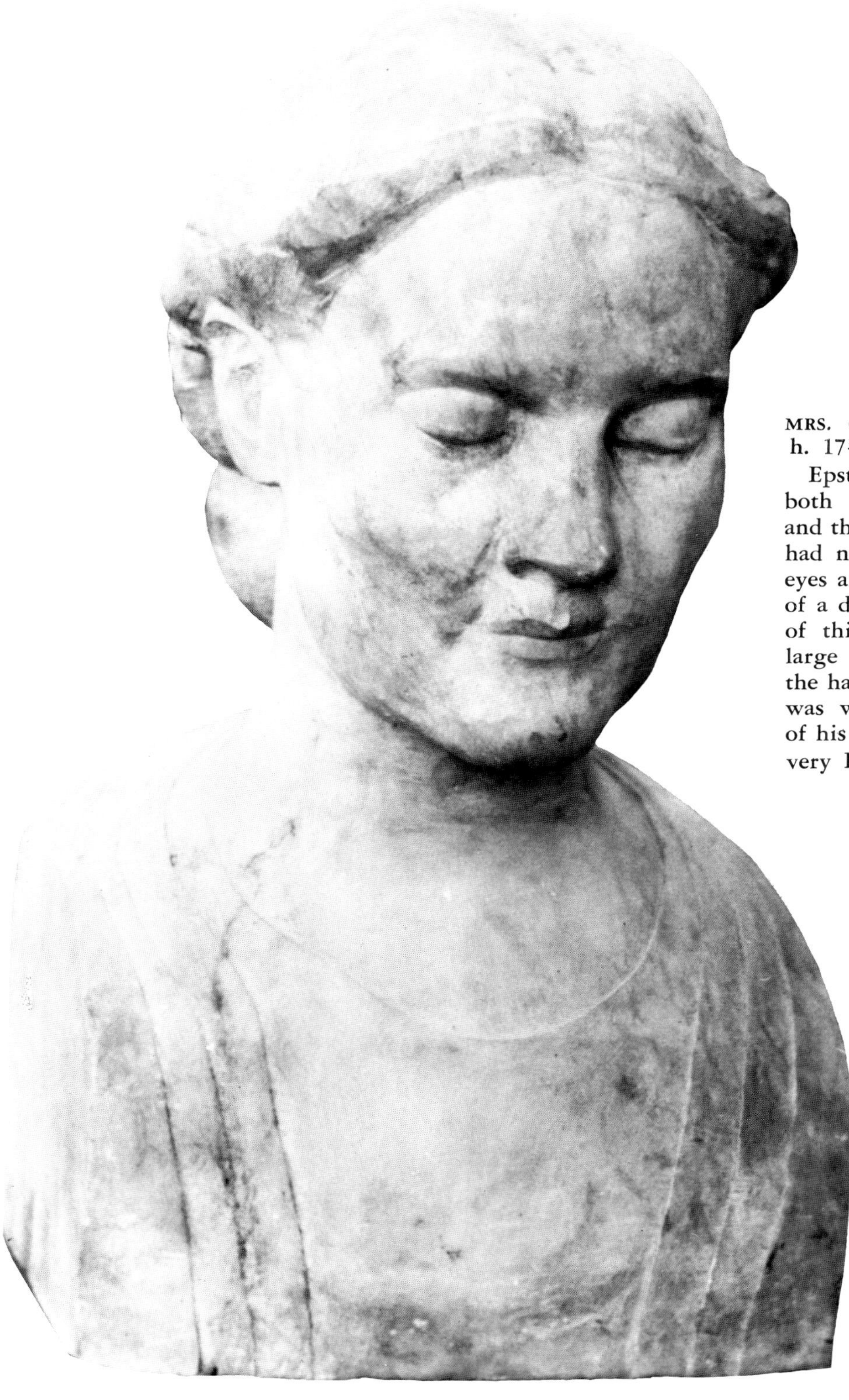

MRS. CHADBURN—*Stone Carving,* 1910. h. 17¾″

Epstein did only two carved portraits, both in 1910, one of Mrs. Chadburn and the other of Mrs. McEvoy. As yet, he had not mastered the art of modelling eyes and avoided the problem by means of a downward gaze. The face and hair of this alabaster bust are chiselled in large smooth planes partly because of the hardness of the medium in which he was working. Unlike the exotic types of his later portraits, Mrs. Chadburn has very British features.

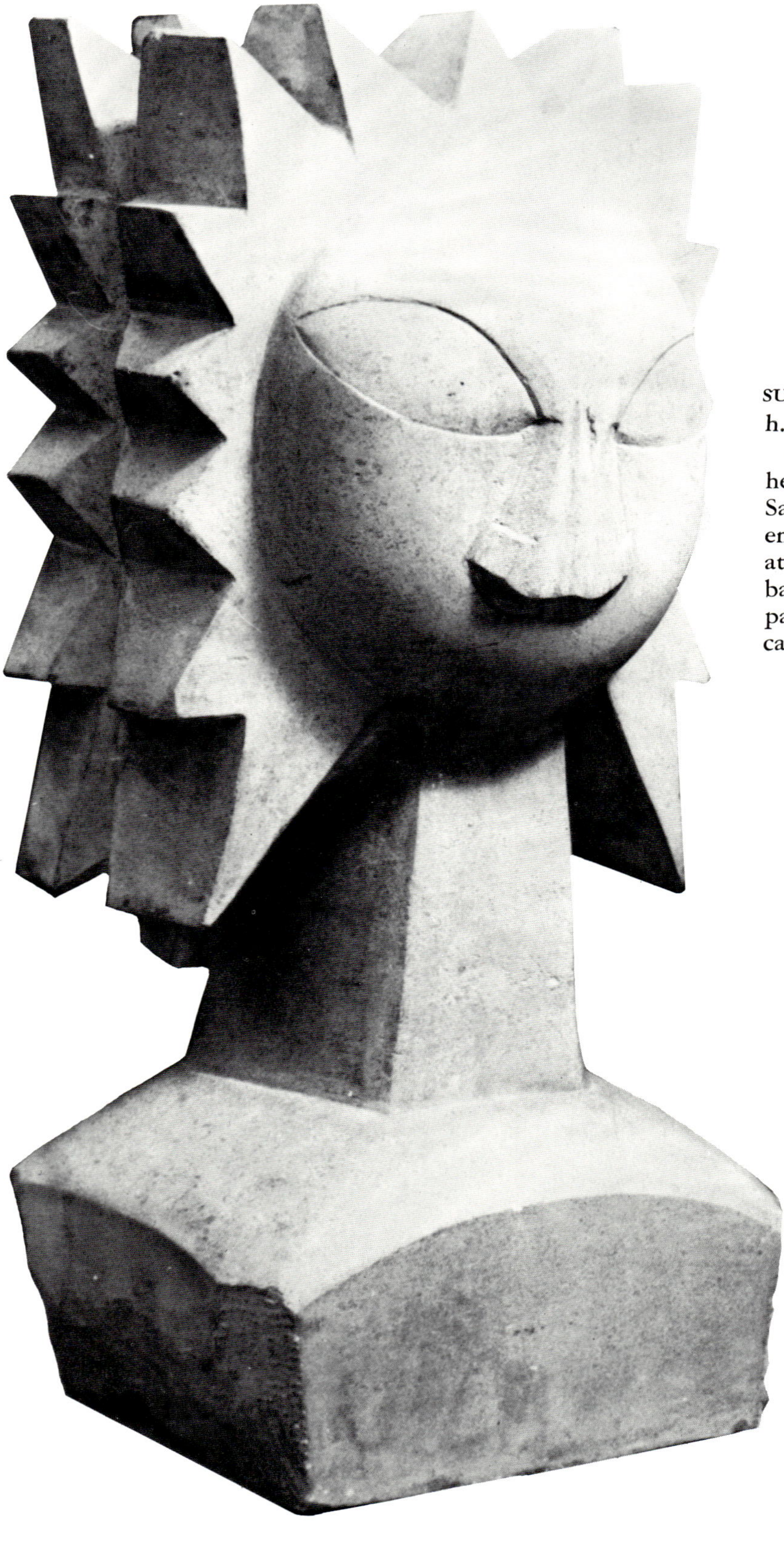

SUNFLOWER—*Stone Carving,* 1910. 24″ h. 24″

Concerned with abstract form, Epstein here carves sun, flower and face out of San Stefano stone. Saw-toothed flames encircle a spherical face on either side atop a truncated pyramid and rounded base. An experimental work, it anticipates his encounter in Paris with Picasso, Brancusi, and Modigliani in 1912.

ELEMENTAL MAN—*Stone Carving,* 1932.
h. 31¼″ w. 24″ d. 20¾″

Like his other carvings, Epstein retains the form of the block of alabaster. Conceived in Epping Forest, the sculpture was inspired by the primeval forces of nature. Here he creates the pent-up energy of a primitive man by huddling him into a ball with the hands gripping his ankles and the head raised in surrender to the unknown powers over him. The unfinished state is in keeping with the content of the sculpture.

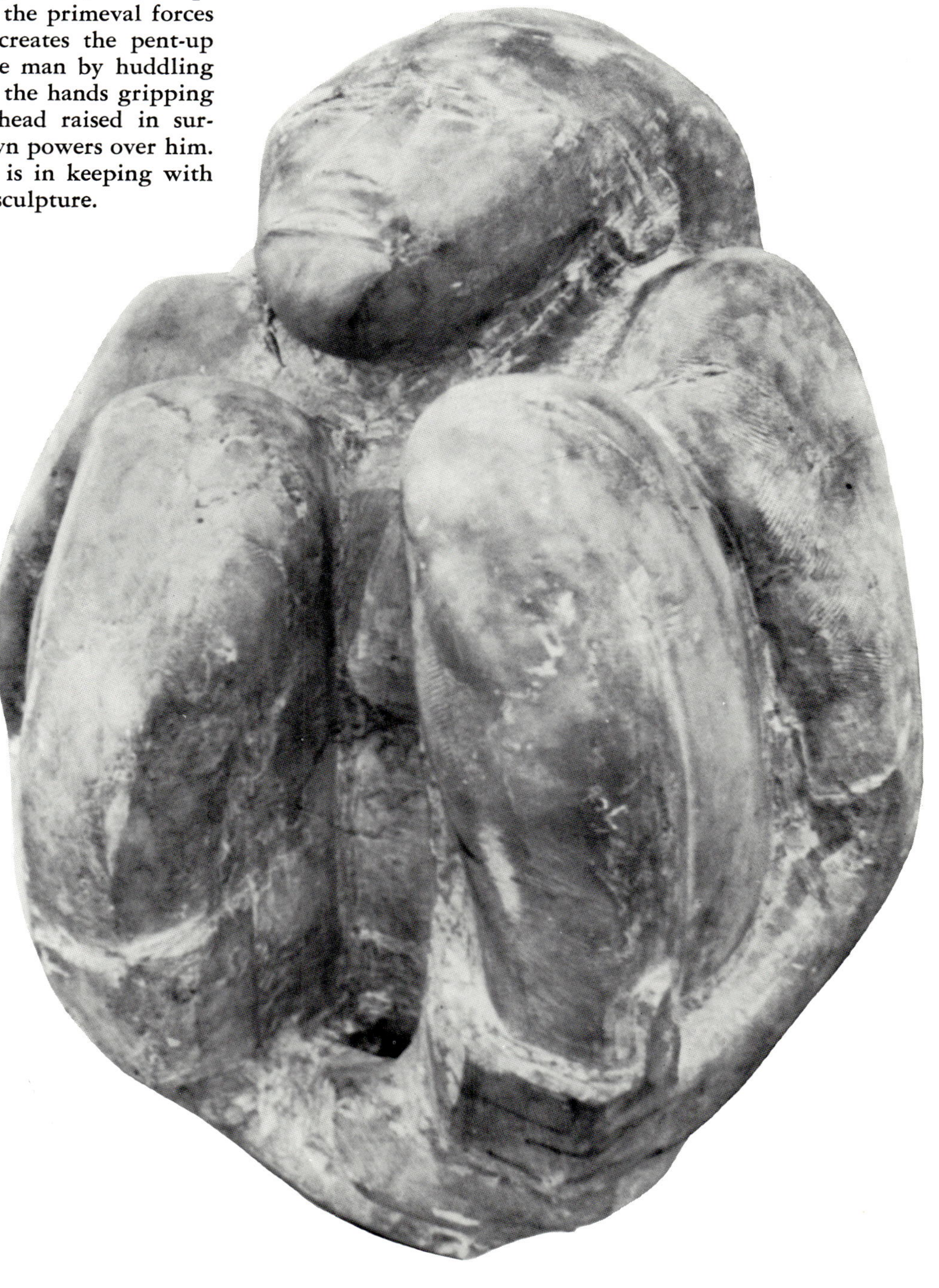

FEMALE FIGURE—*Stone Carving,* 1913.
h. 18″

This curious question-mark shaped figure in green flenite is at once an abstract form and a pregnant woman.

The smooth surface color and form combine to suggest an African amulet.

Every part is directed to the enclosed fetus: the drooping head, sloped back and arms, and arching legs.

FLENITE RELIEF—*Stone Carving,* 1913.
h. 12″ x w. 11″

Another experimental piece is this two-sided bas-relief in the hard material flenite. The least articulated side shows crossed arms and breasts, but the other side has a symmetric frontal figure in a crouching position.

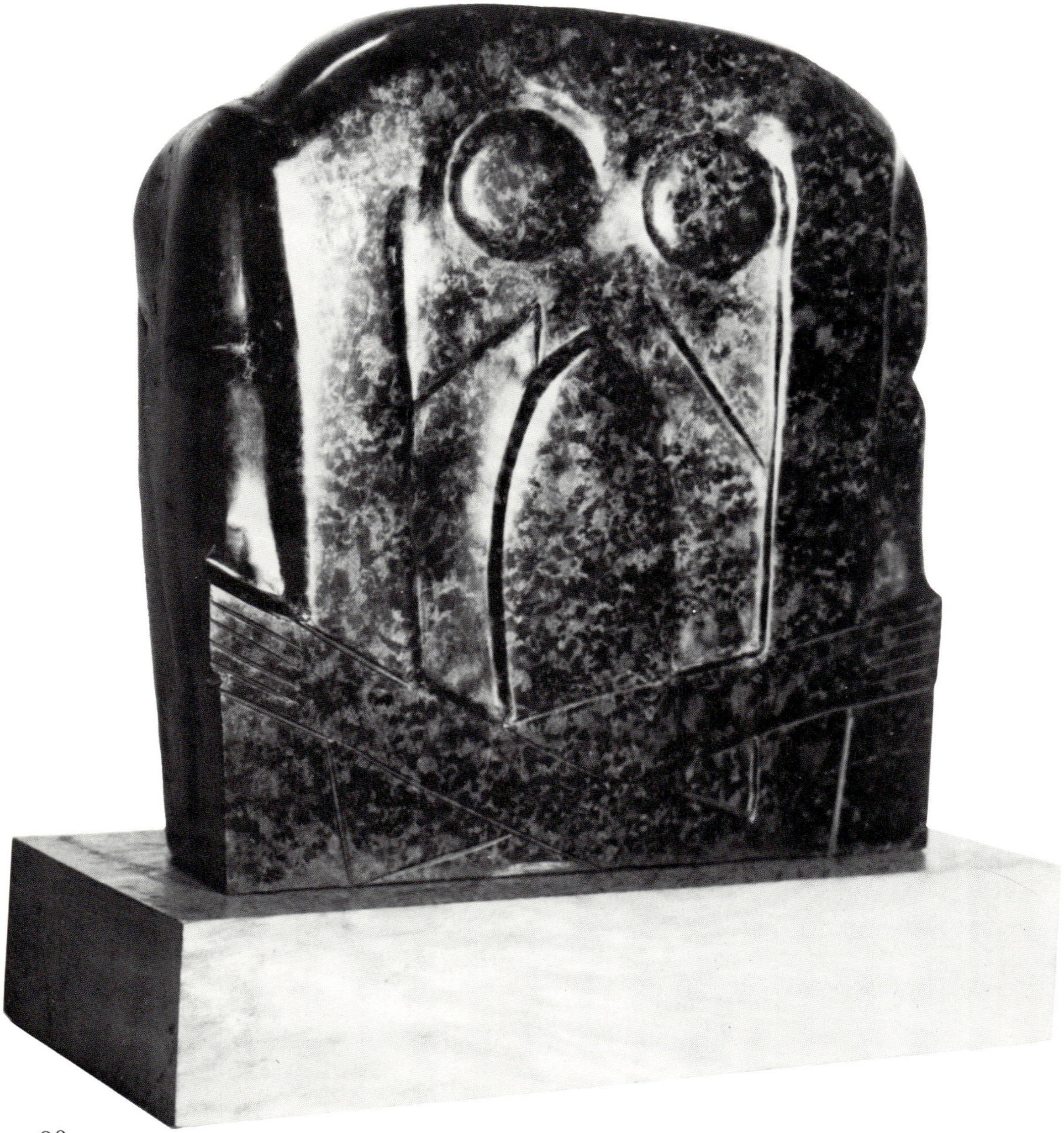

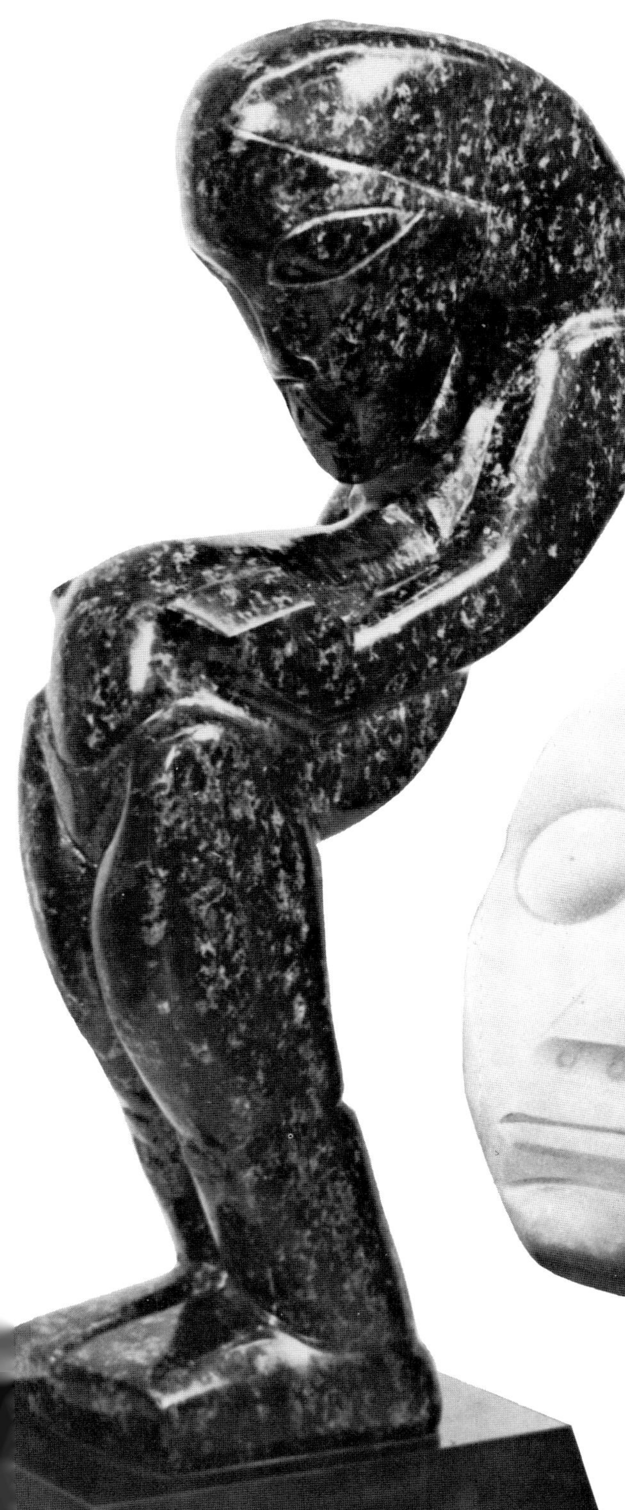

CHIMERA—*Stone Carving,* 1932. h. 10″ x d. 26″

This strange creature strains forward like a monster. The unit of head and neck could perhaps have been planned as an appendage to another object or more likely could have been simply an experiment in alabaster.

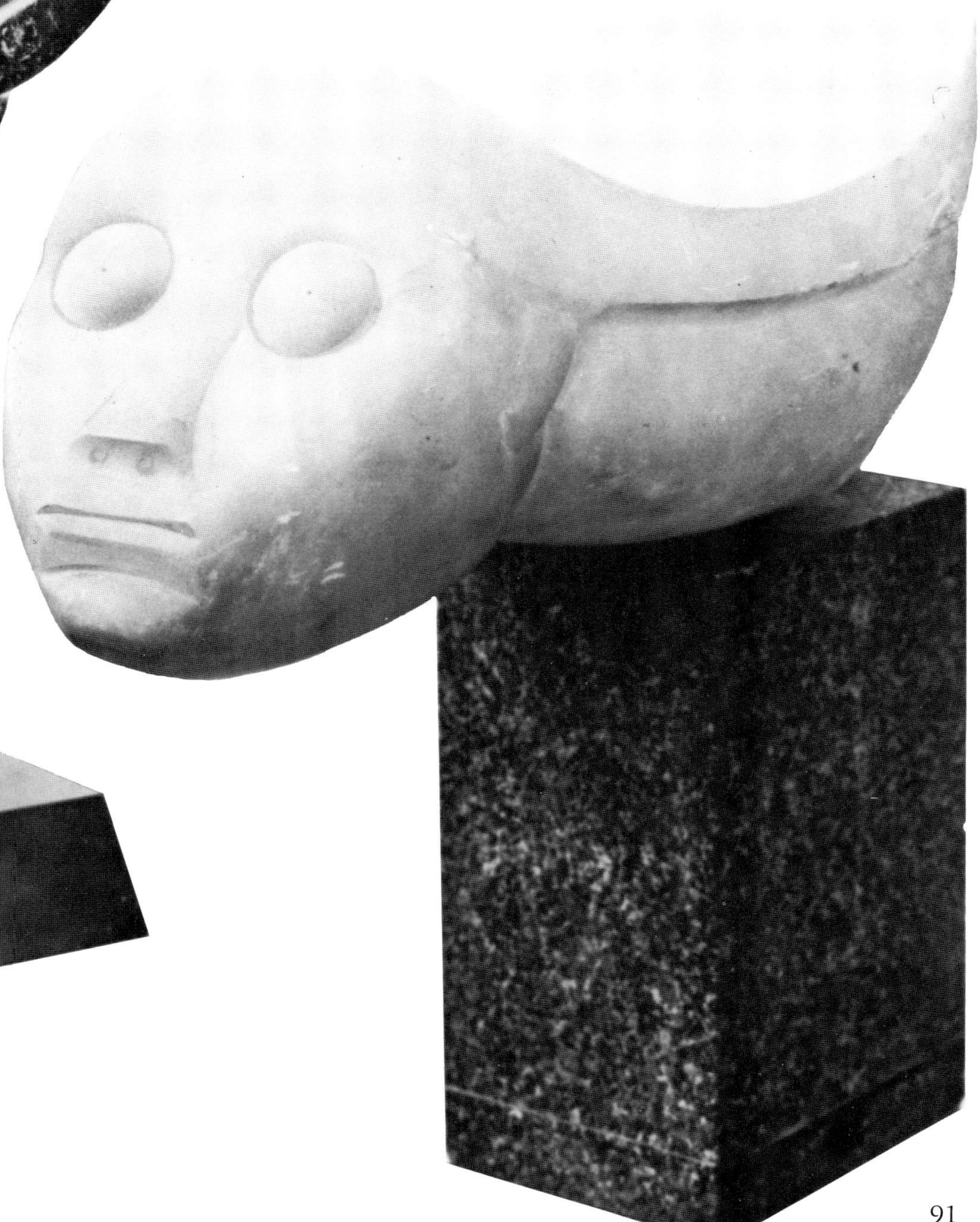

CONSUMMATUM EST—*Stone Carving,* 1936. h. 24″ x l. 88″ x w. 32″

The stylized body is monumental in stature. The position of the arms and head seems to indicate the figure's struggle to rise. Epstein wrote: "The unworked alabaster block lies in my studio for a year. While I work at other things I look at it from time to time. The block lies prone in its length, and I consider whether I should raise it, but decide to leave it where it is. I can conceive any number of works in it. I can conceive a single figure or a group of figures. I have been listening to Bach's *B minor Mass*. In the section, Crucifixus, I have a feeling of tremendous quiet, of awe. The music comes from a great distance and in this mood I conceive my 'Consummatum Est.' I see the figure complete as a whole. I see immediately the upturned hands, with the wounds in the feet, stark, crude, with the stigmata. I even imagine the setting for the finished figure, a dim crypt with a subdued light on the semi-transparent alabaster."

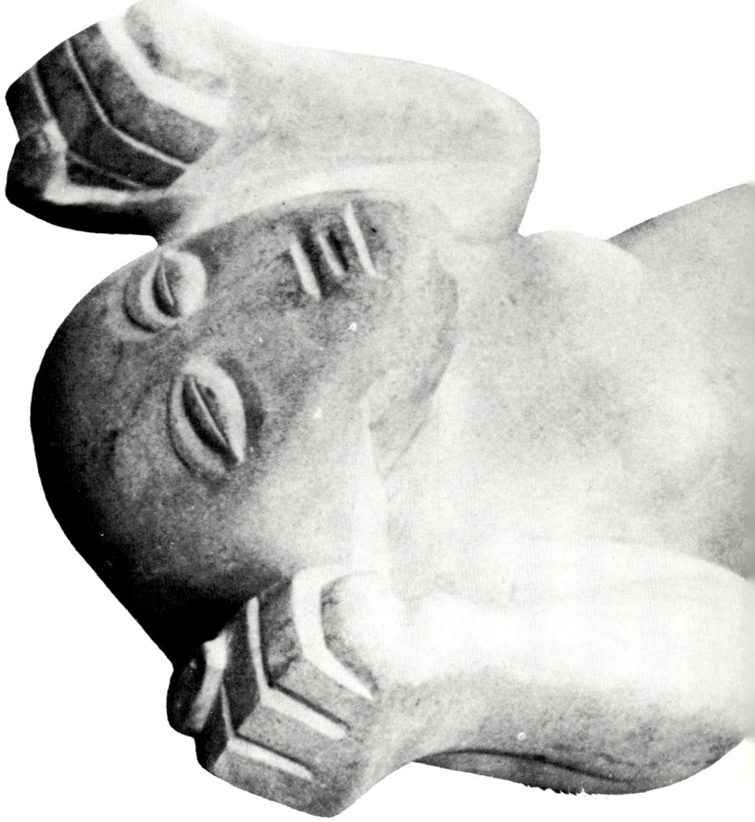

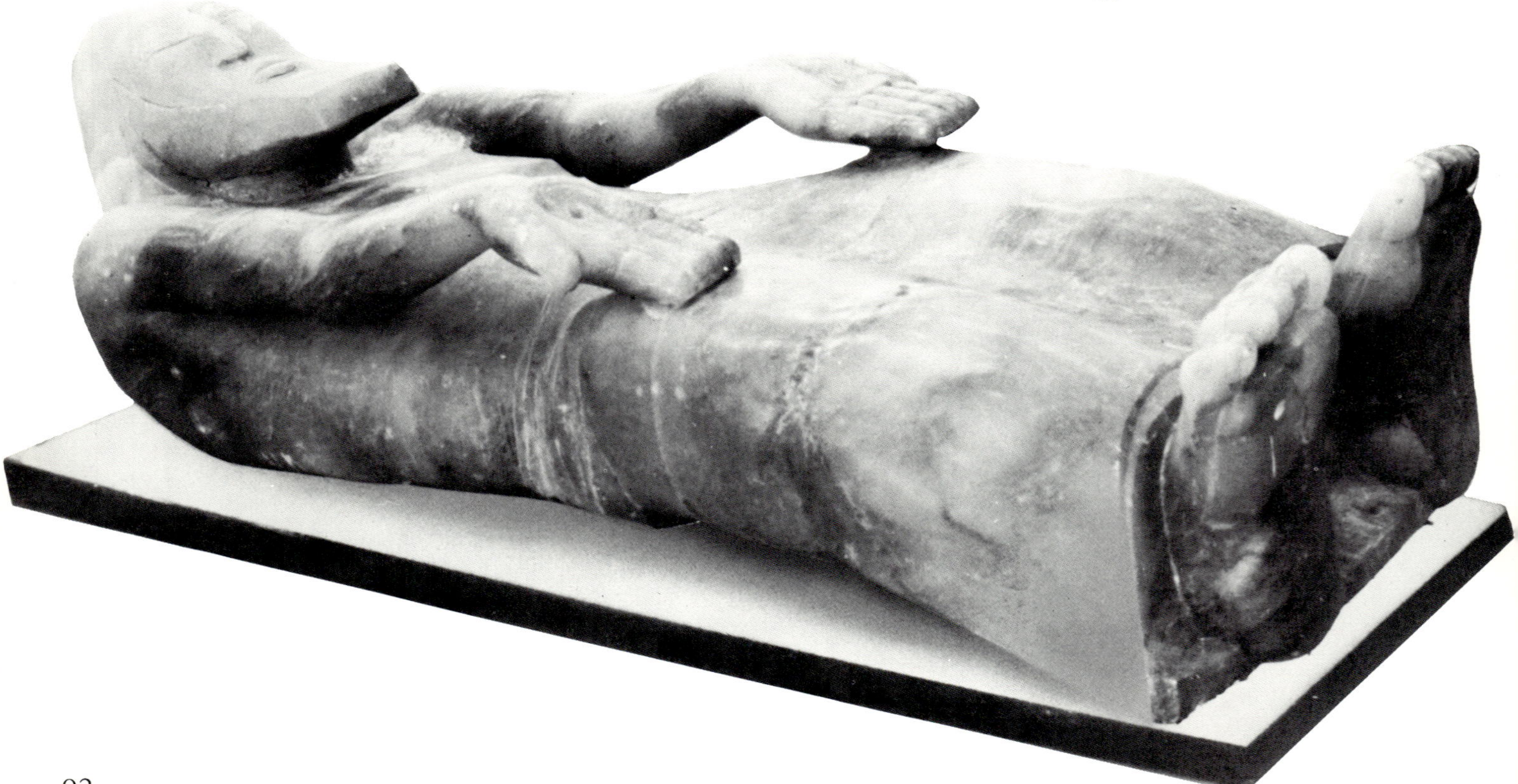

WOMAN POSSESSED—*Stone Carving,* 1932. 17″ x 40″

Made of Hopton Wood stone, this figure seems possessed by a spirit so strong that the back is arched, the fists are clenched and the eyes are closed. The influence of primitive sculpture is evident in the stylized face, hands, and feet. Even the lips are mysteriously open.

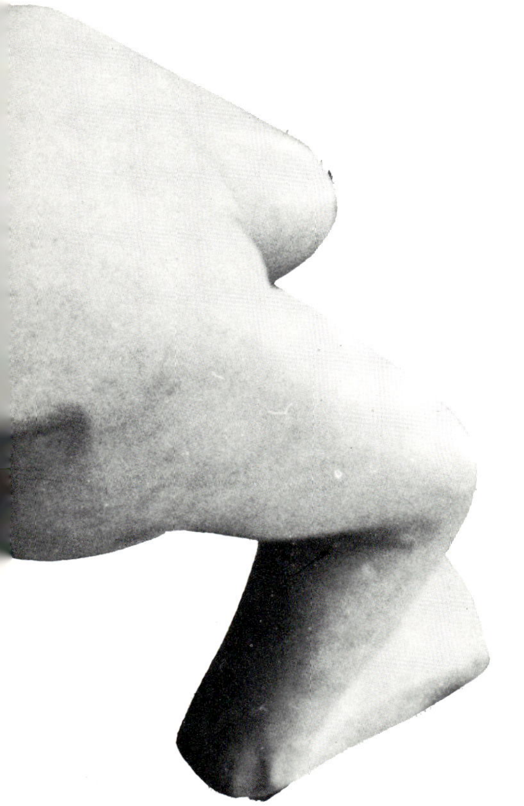

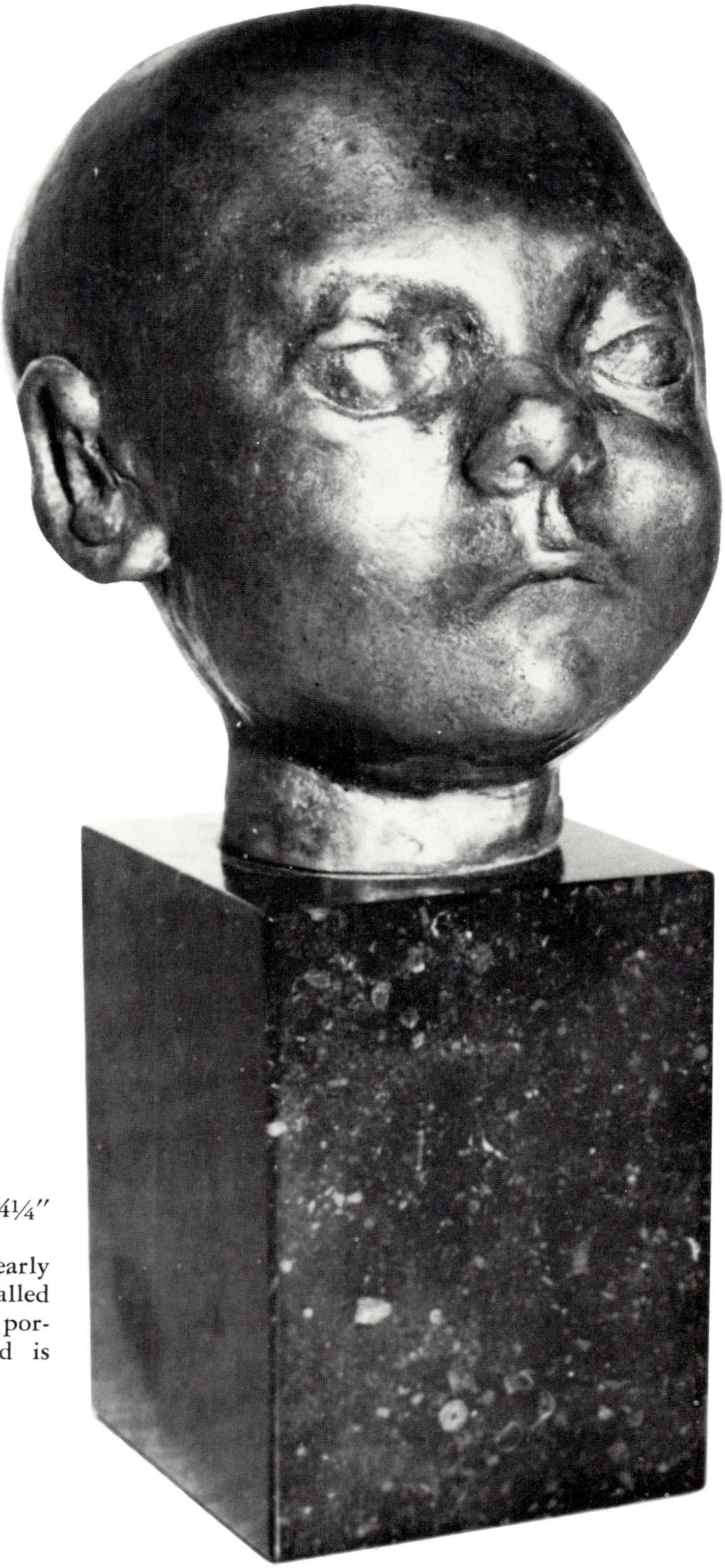

BABY AWAKE, 1902–04. h. 5″ w. 4¼″ d. 6″

Epstein destroyed much of his early work, but this statue and another called *Sleeping Baby* survive. Unlike the portraits to come, this life size head is smoothly and simply modelled.

ROMILLY JOHN, 1907–08. h. 8″ w. 6¼″ d. 8″

Romilly John was the son of the renowned British painter Augustus John, a long-time friend of Epstein.

Compared to *Annabel Freud with Bonnet,* done forty-five years later, *Romilly John* is a stylized portrait. The heavy smooth bonnet is like a helmet; it frames two deep-set eyes sunk in shadow, fat cheeks, and broad nose and lips. Epstein has not lost the character of the piece in his efforts to simplify the portrait. The precise edge of metal is merged with the soft surface contours.

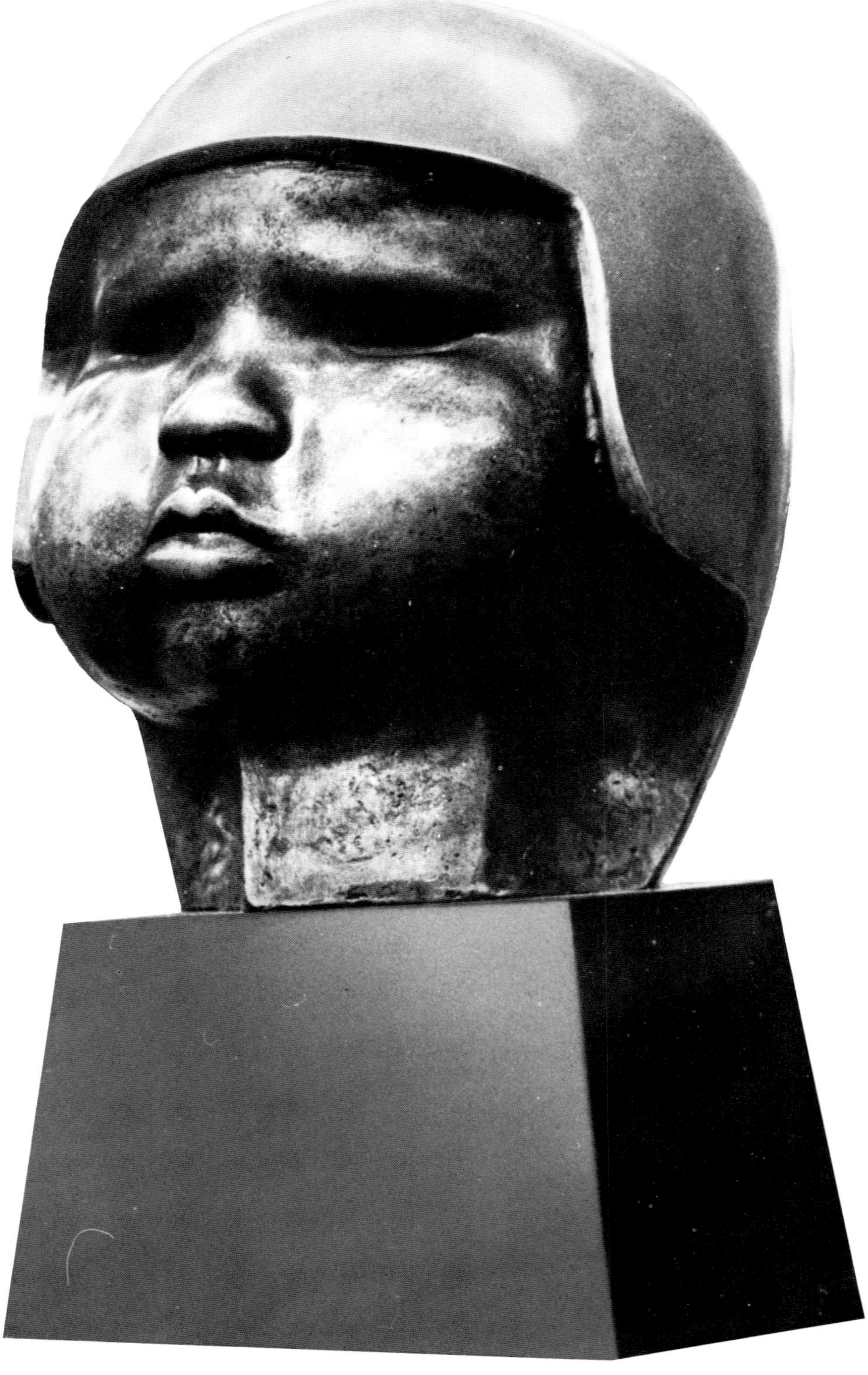

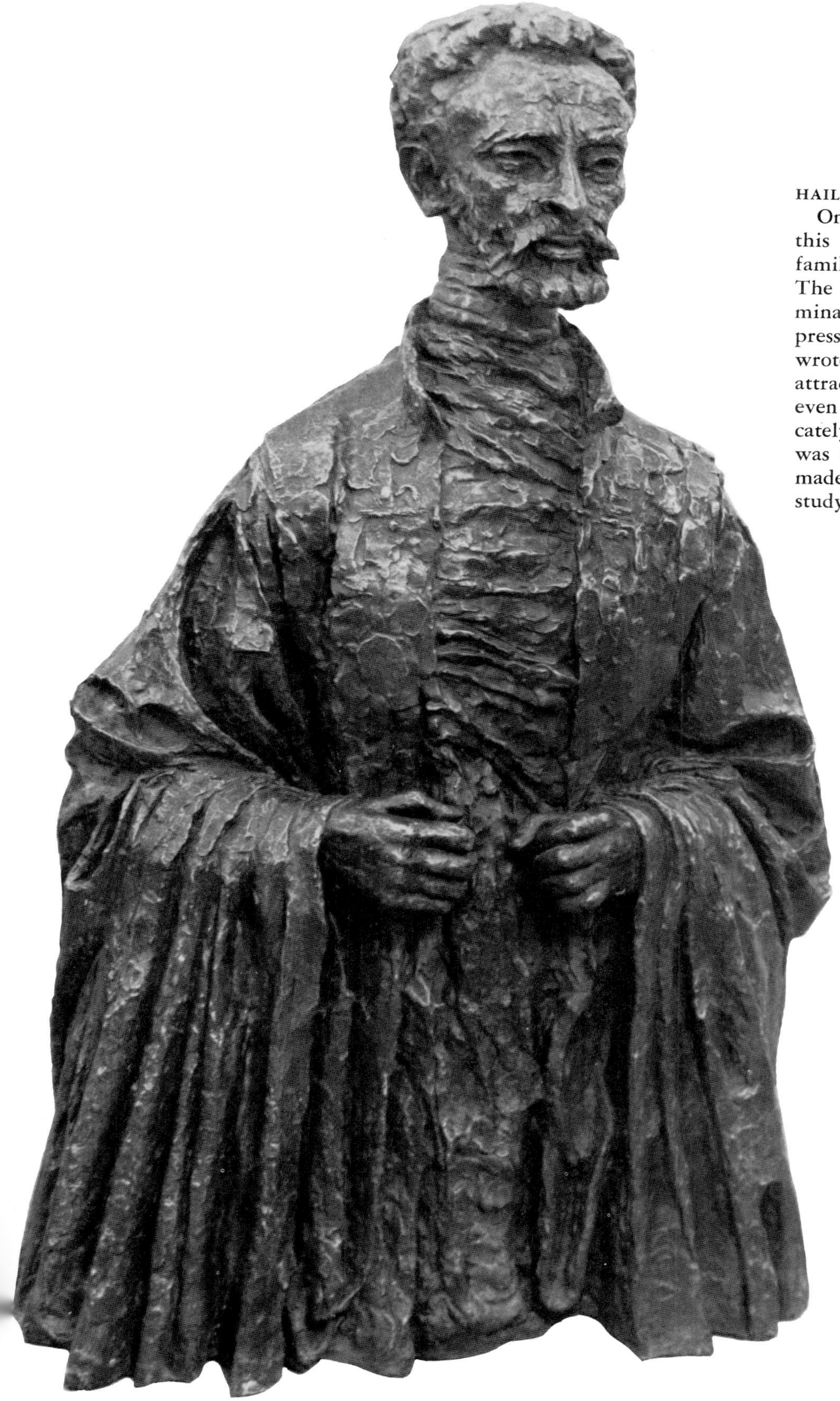

HAILE SELASSIE, 1936. h. 48″ w. 27″

One of Epstein's most tender works, this portrait shows an emperor whose family has ruled for a thousand years. The sadness of his exile and the determination to return are forcefully expressed in the hands and face. Epstein wrote: "The Emperor's hands especially attracted my attention. They were fine, even feminine. He was altogether delicately fashioned, although this delicacy was tempered with a Semitic virility. I made what I considered an interesting study, although an unfinished one."

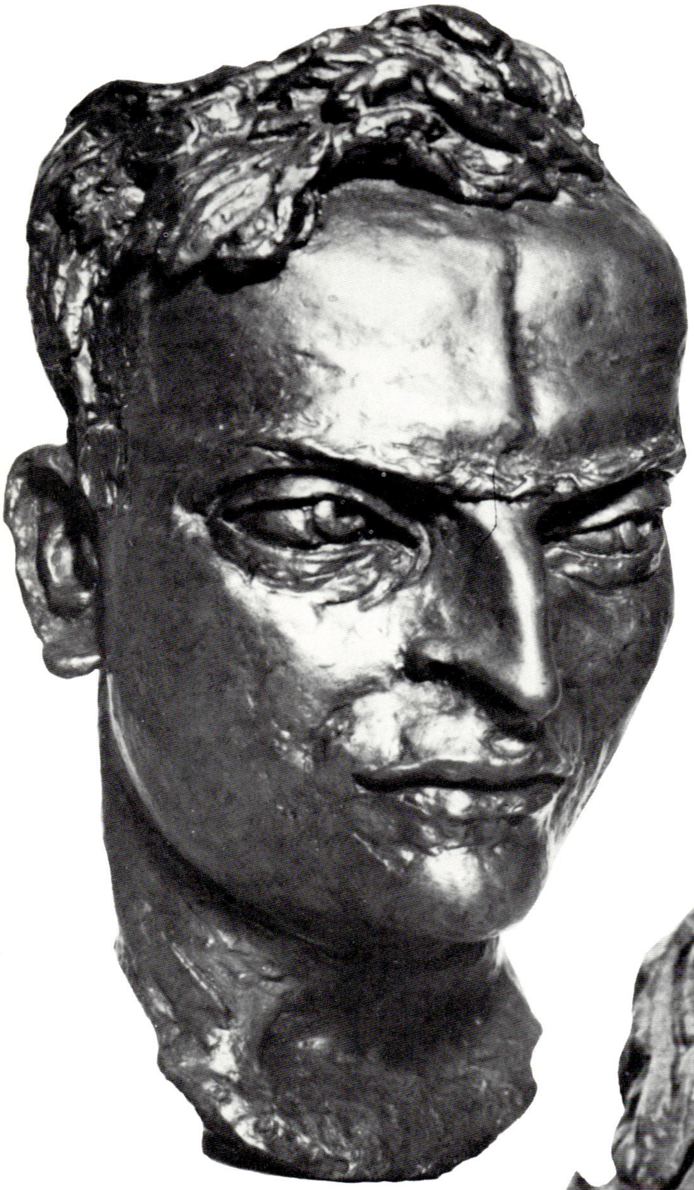

YEHUDI MENUHIN, 1943. h. 14″ w. 8½″ d. 9¾″

Epstein created a powerful bust of Yehudi Menuhin. The eyes look askance, the nose is flared, the brows are tightly knit, and the mouth is drawn to create a kinetic intensity.

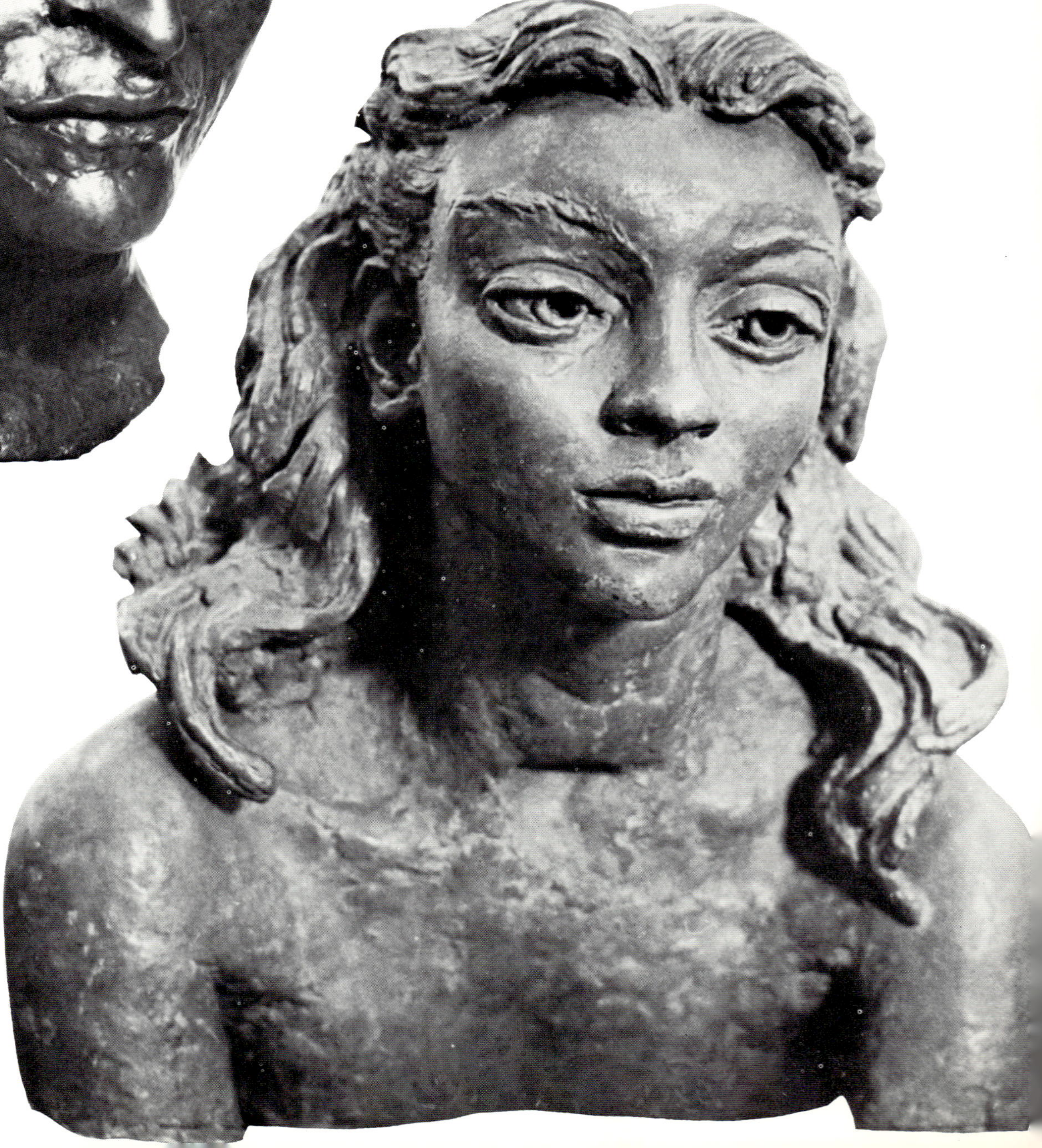

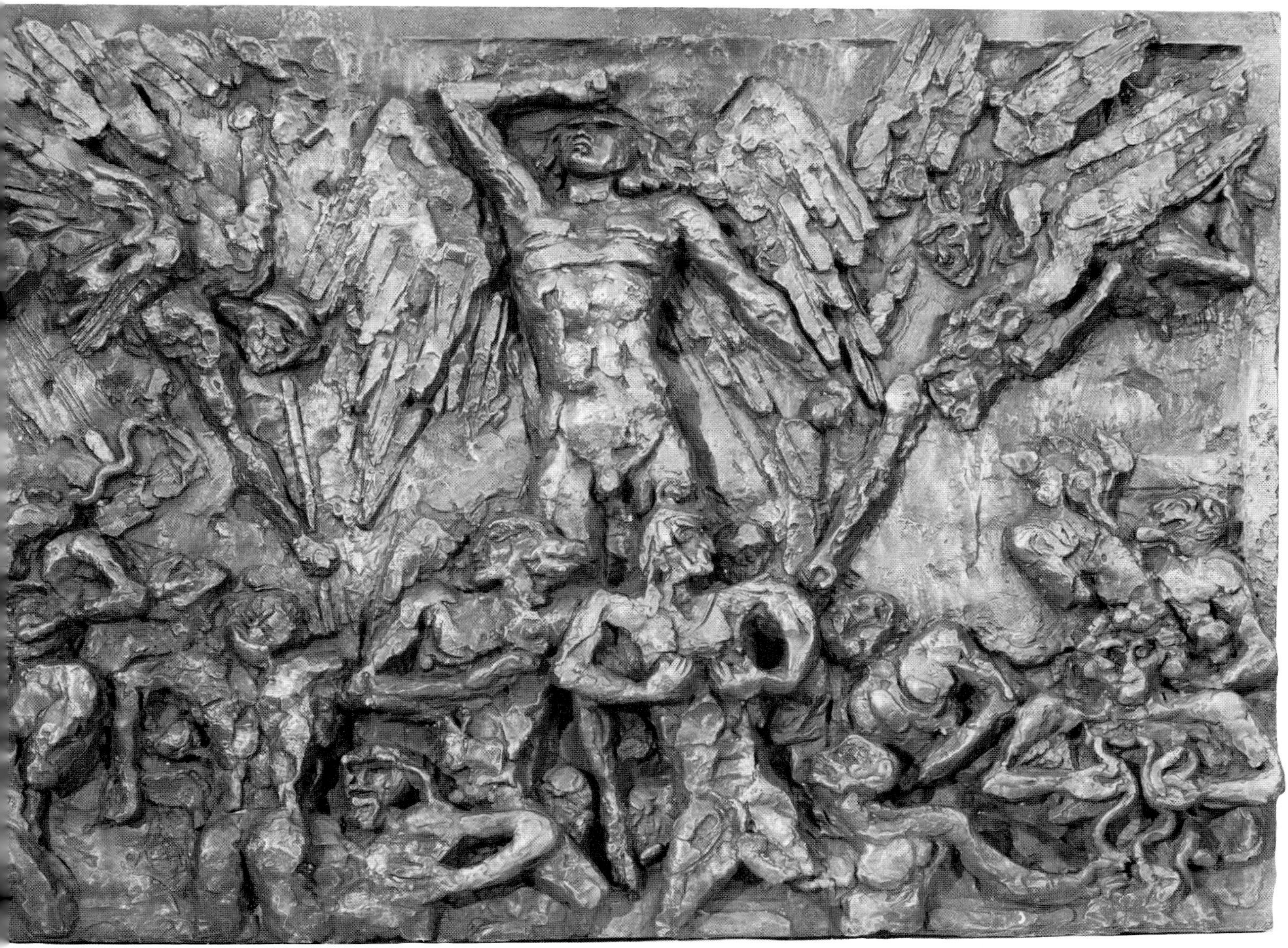

FALL OF LUCIFER, 1944. 24″ x 35″

An unfinished panel in relief, *Fall of Lucifer* is a complex of slashing diagonal strokes unleashing the fury of Lucifer's downfall. He shields his face in despair and sheer terror at God's wrath. The crowded damned below are in marked contrast to the good Angels who are isolated to the left and right of Lucifer.

EIRDRE—*Third Portrait,* 1942. h. 16¾″
v. 15½″ d. 16½″

This final portrait of Deirdre has her eaning forward with her hair flowing lown her back and shoulders. The lreamy expression is matched by the low-moving strands of hair. Deirdre vent to work for the War Office and ventually married an officer bound for ustralia.

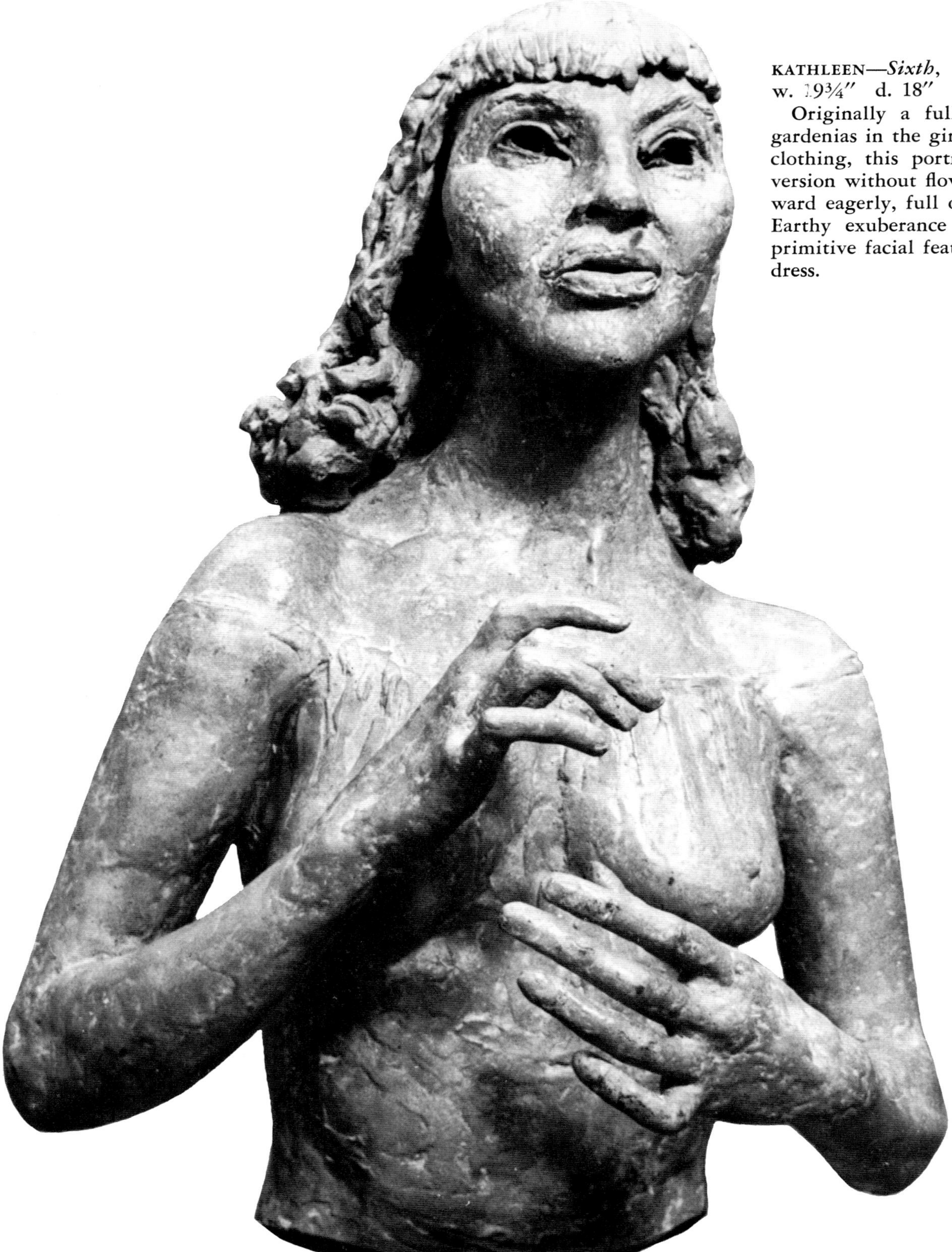

KATHLEEN—*Sixth*, 1941. h. 26½″ w. 19¾″ d. 18″

Originally a full-length figure with gardenias in the girl's hands and on her clothing, this portrait is a half-length version without flowers. She presses forward eagerly, full of youth and energy. Earthy exuberance is captured by the primitive facial features and transparent dress.

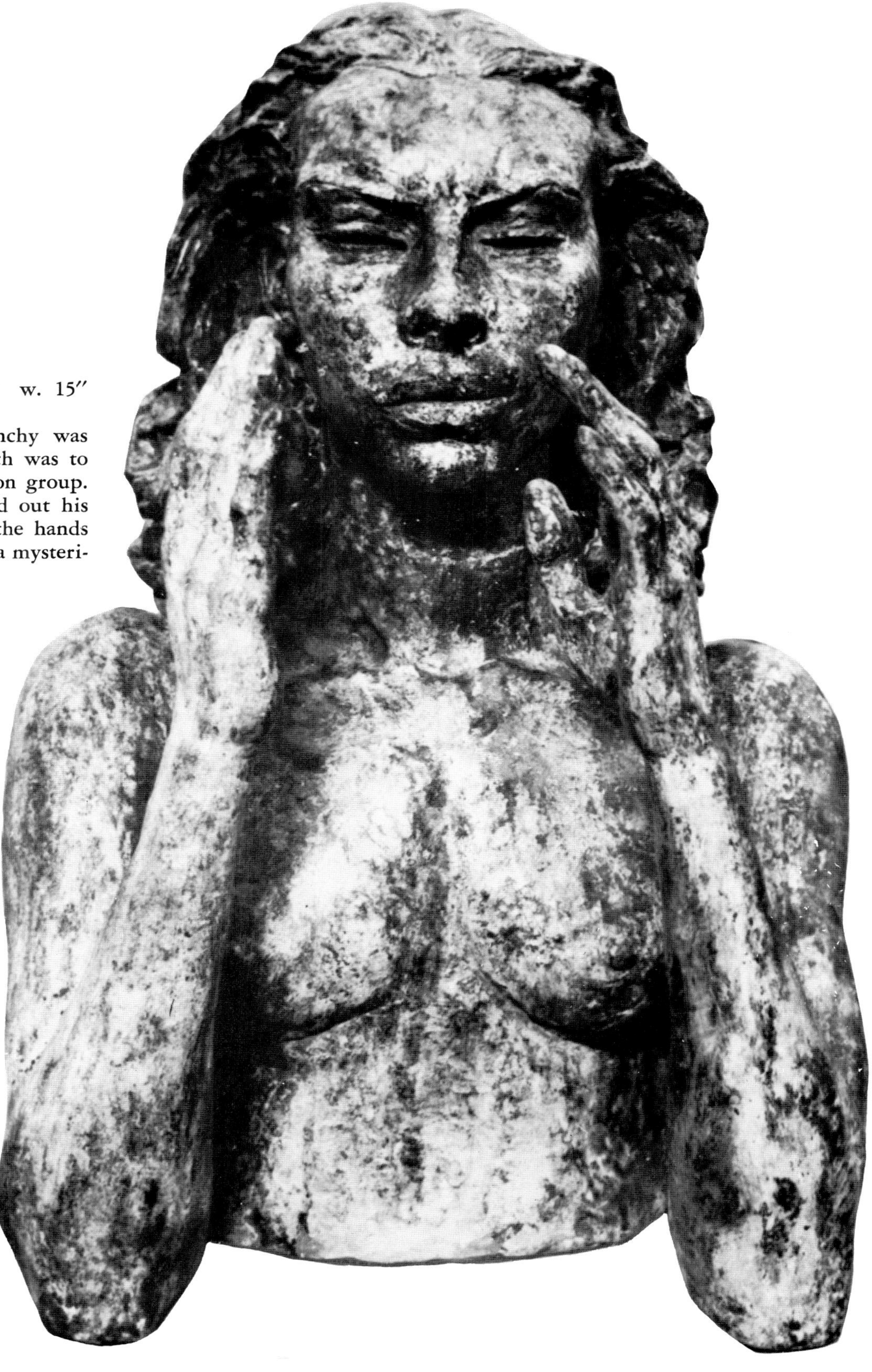

RESURRECTION, 1941. h. 22½″ w. 15″ d. 13″

The Polish girl Pola Givenchy was the model for this study, which was to have been part of a Resurrection group. However, Epstein never carried out his plan. The unusual gesture of the hands and the half-closed eyes render a mysterious mood.

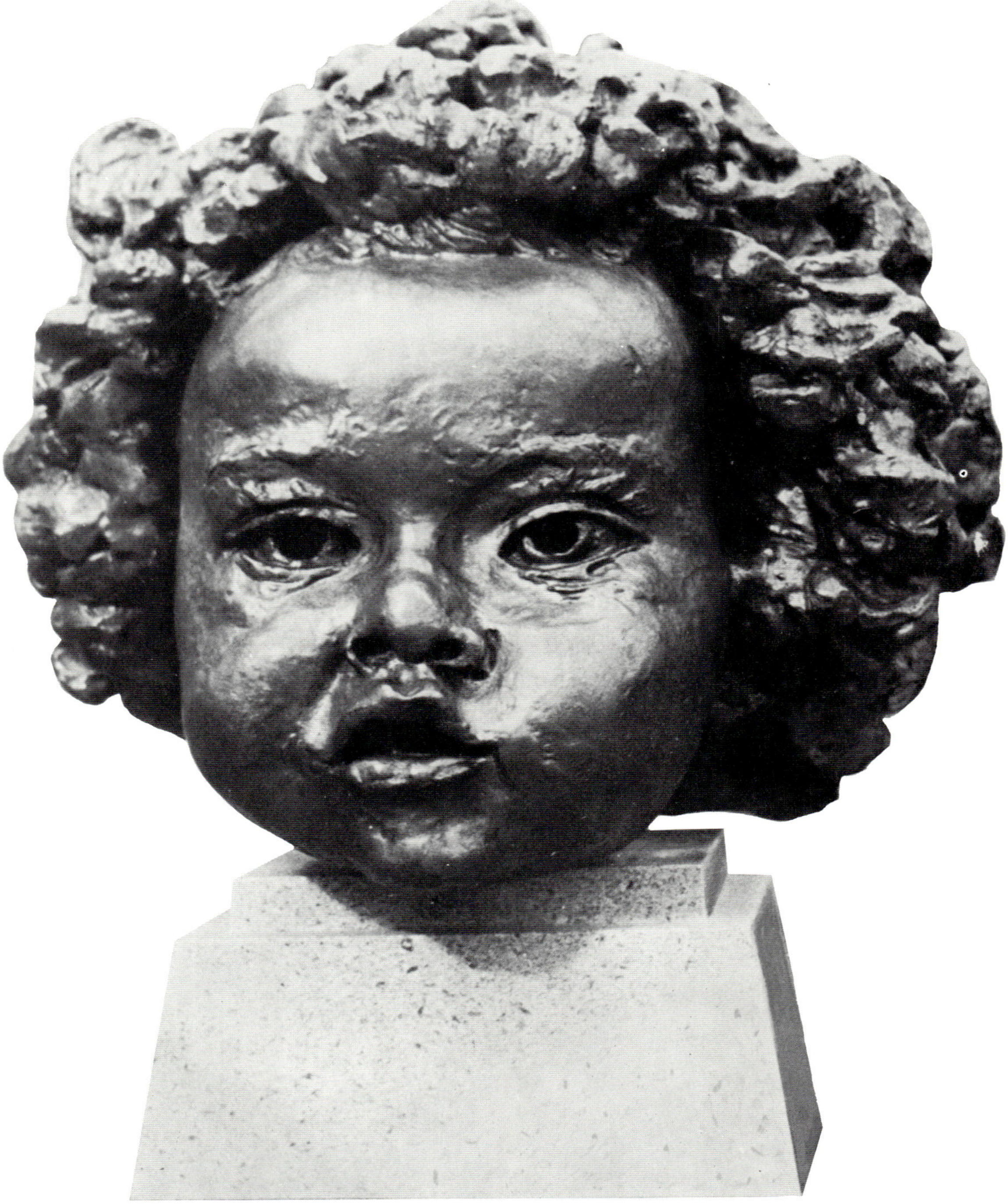

IAN, 1942. h. w. 10″ d. 9½″

Ian was Epstein's grandson and the son of Peggy Jean. Here, precocious and serious as only a child can be, Ian juts out his lower lip. The huge mass of flaming hair heightens the intensity of the eyes which reveal a certain maturity. One feels that Ian is quite capable of understanding in his own way.

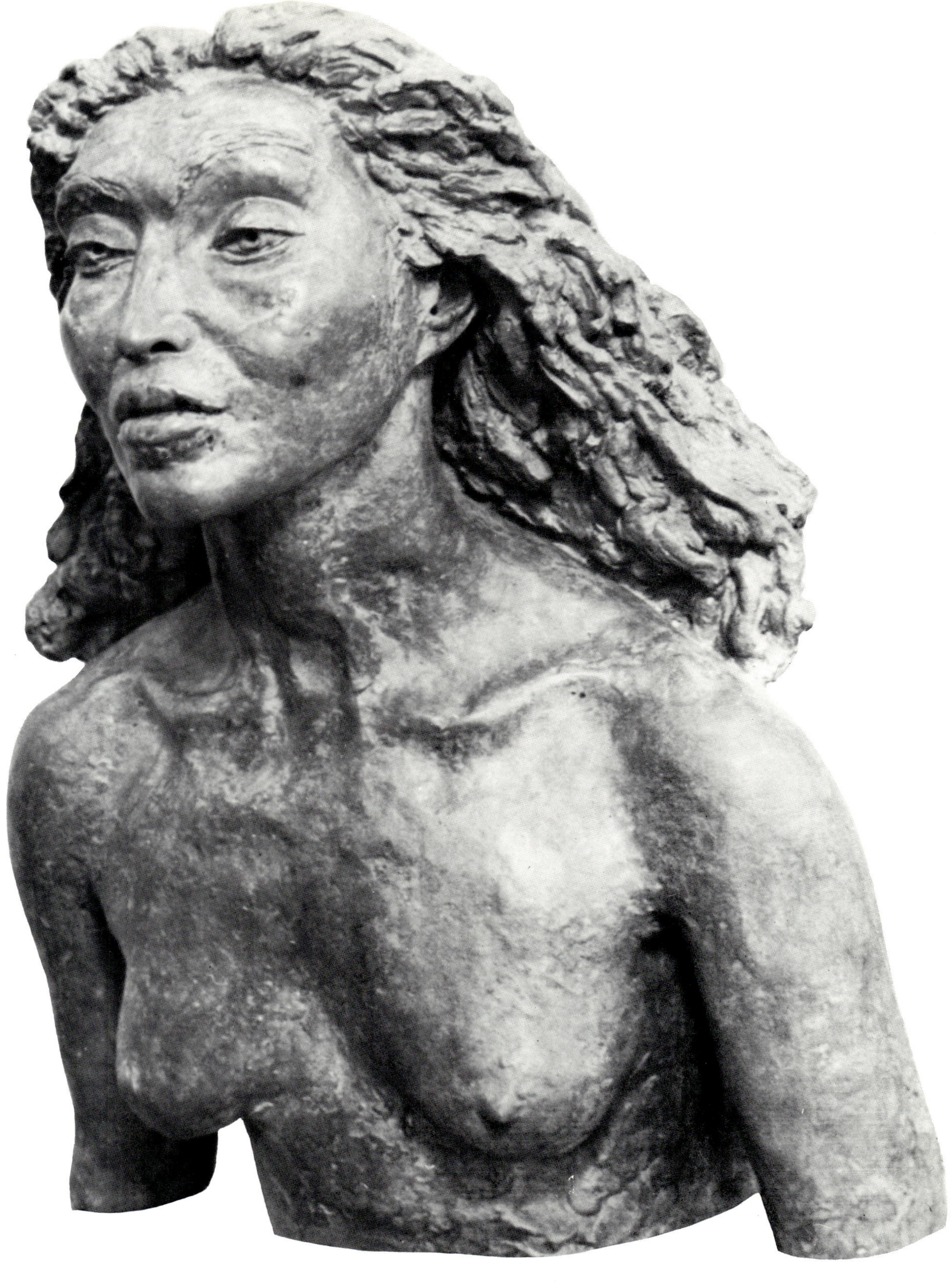

GIRL FROM BAKU, 1944. h. 21½″ w. 17″ d. 13″

Most of Epstein's female models possess similar facial features: long narrow noses, high prominent cheekbones, and thick lips. Chosen for her primitive quality, the *Girl from Baku* bursts with the primal forces of her Slavic ancestry. Hair rushing down behind her, she leans forward in an expectant mood.

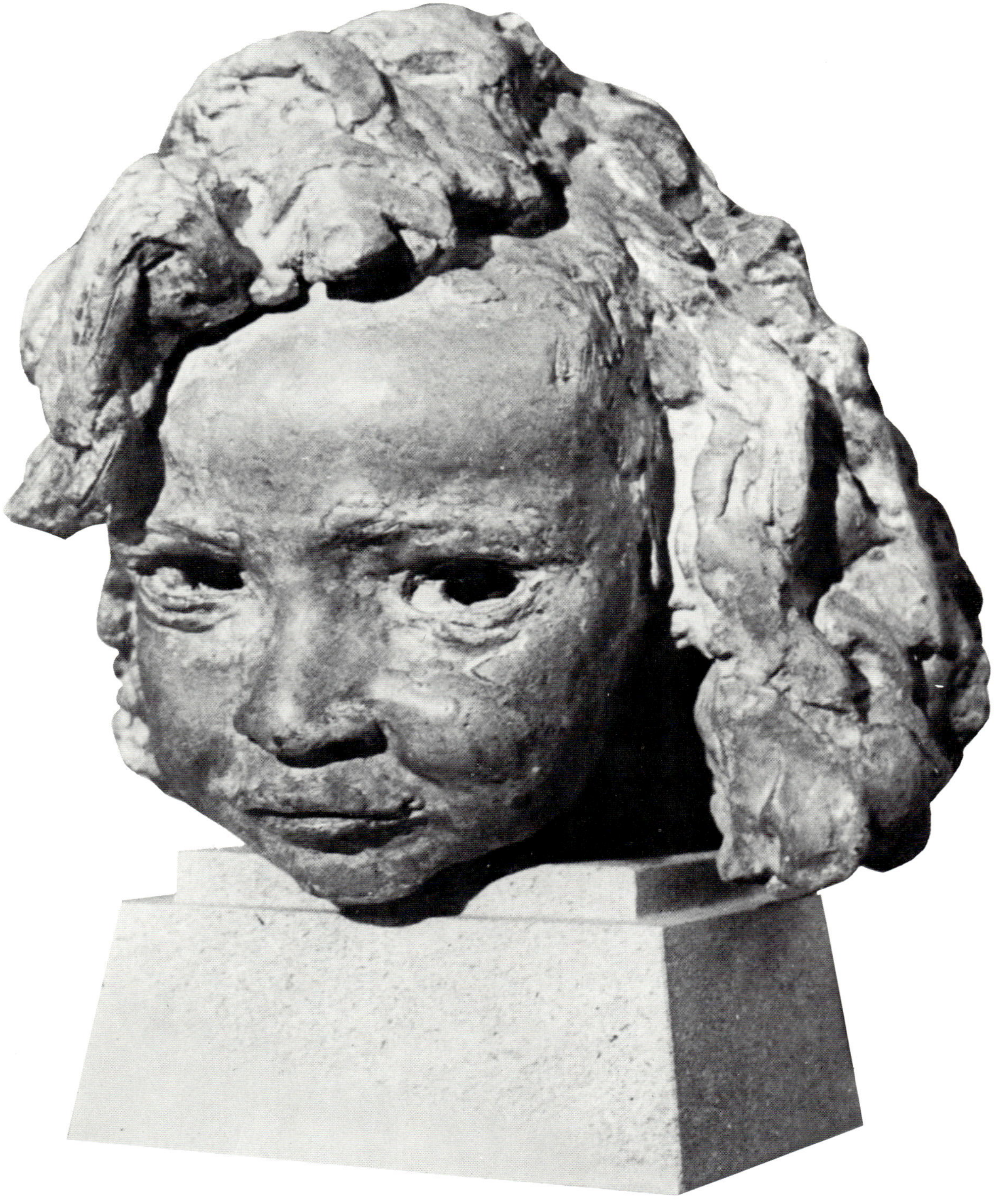

LEDA—*Fifth Portrait,* 1944. h. 8½″ w. 9½″ d. 11½″

Leda was Epstein's granddaughter and the sister of Ian. Here, the sculptor portrays her as a pouting four-year-old. Massive curly hair and an inward expression guard the private world of the child.

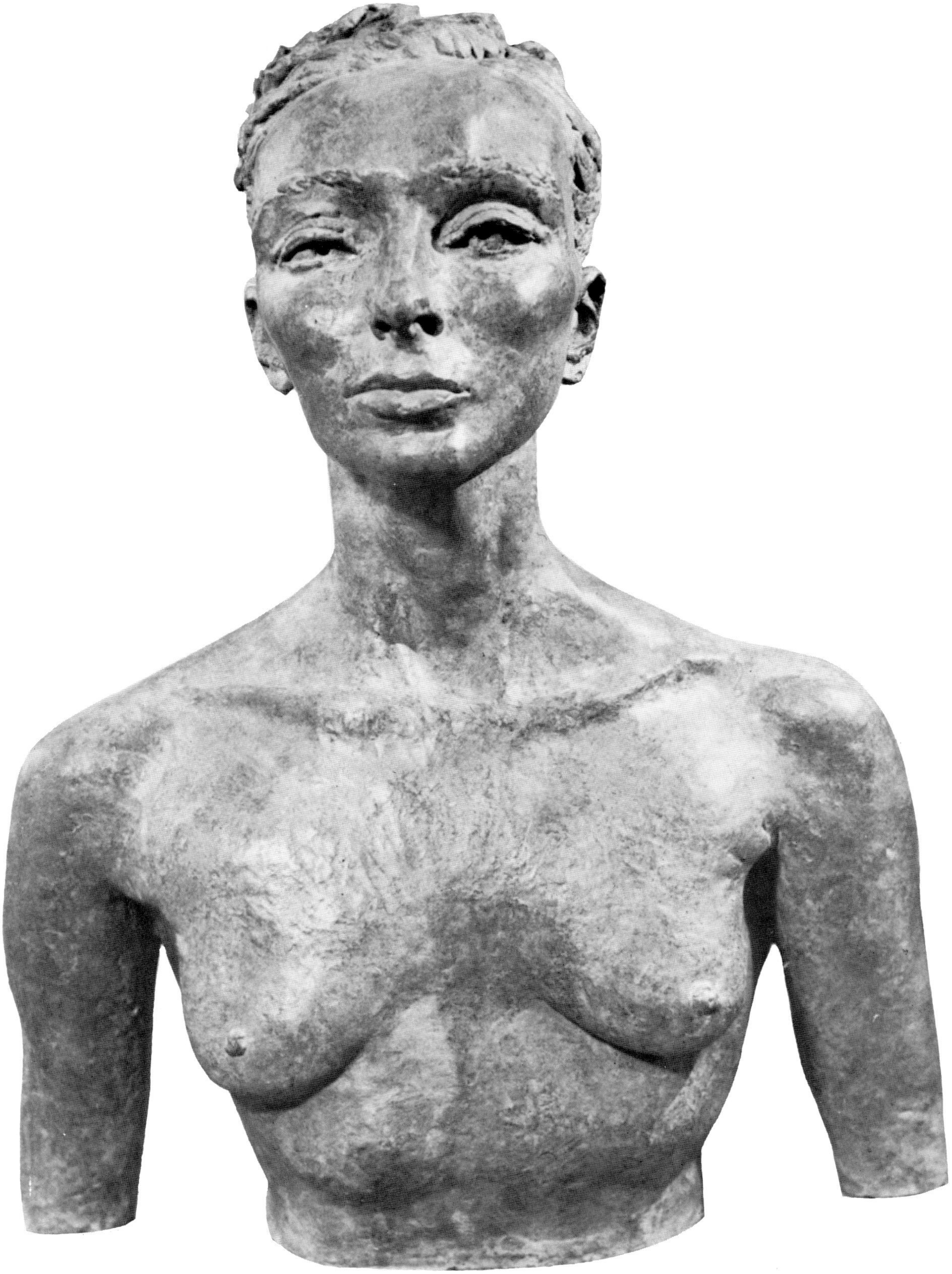

PRINCESSE DE BRAGANZA, 1944. h. 24¼″ w. 18¼″ d. 10″

Married to a Portuguese, this American woman is the epitome of sincere dignity. The sculpture, with its straight, vertical, and clear forms, reminds one, perhaps, of the noble stone carvings of Egyptian Emperors.

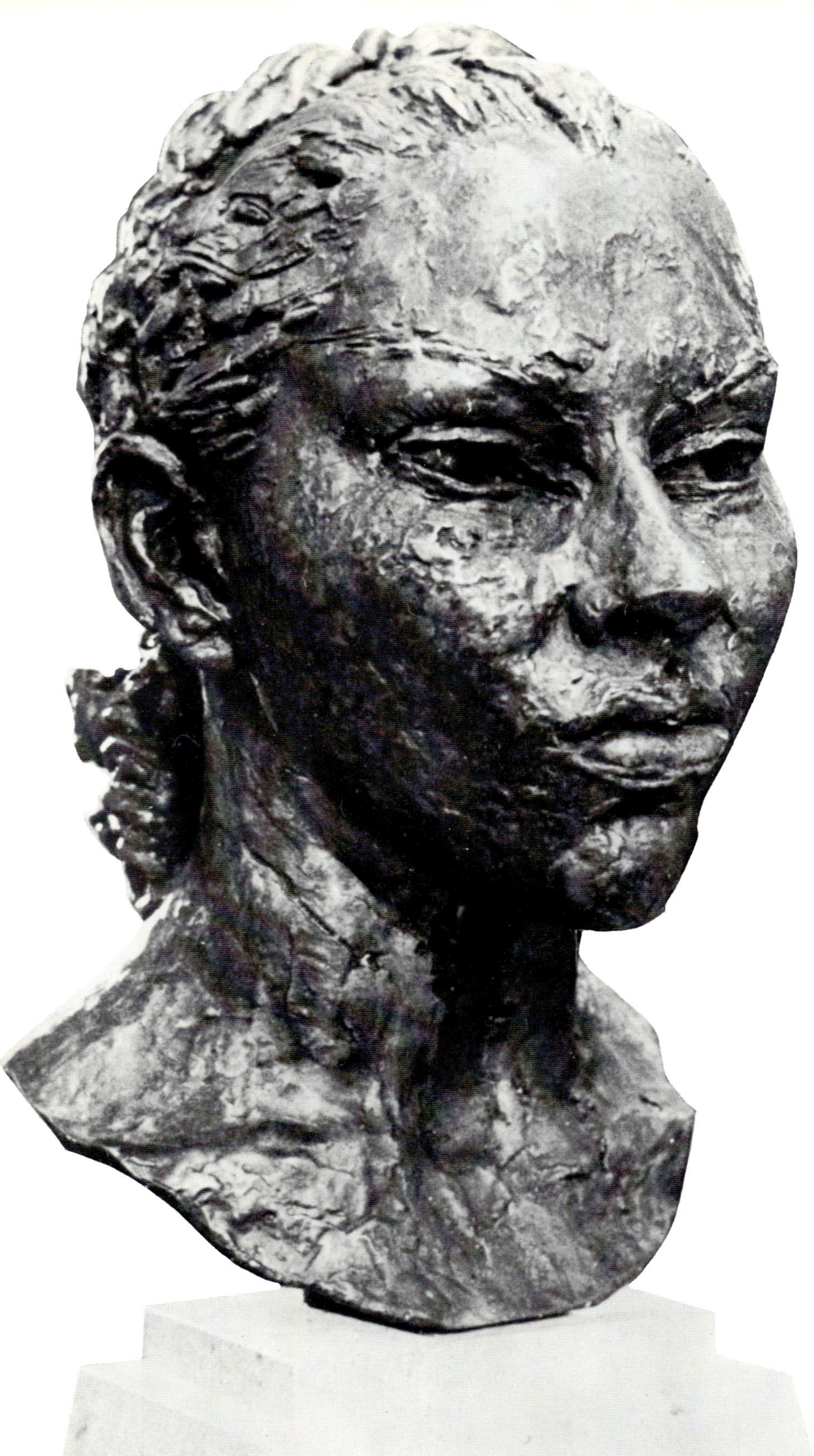

TI-YI, 1938. h. 15″ w. 8″ d. 11″

Epstein was commissioned to do the head of the aspiring young opera singer, TI-YI. By accentuating the asymmetric qualities of face and hair, Epstein has enabled the viewer to see more of the head at a glance than would normally be possible. This is the sculptor's method of projecting movement into bronze.

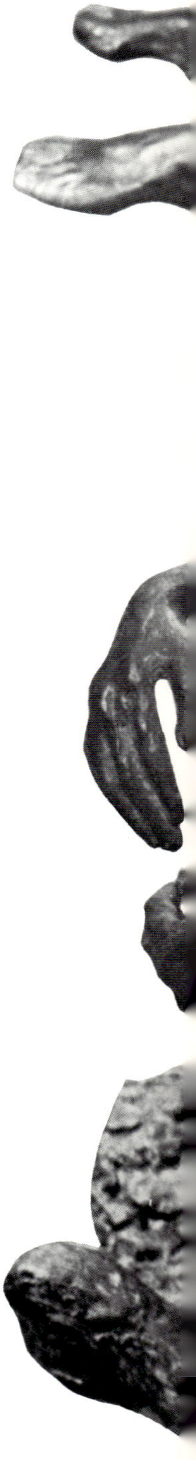

BETTY PETERS RECLINING, 1939. h. 28½′ w. 12½″ d. 7½″

The short arms and legs relate thi nude to Epstein's figure of Sunita as Re clining Goddess. While the upper half o Betty Peters's body is relaxed, a violen energy possesses her legs which floa and pull away from her body.

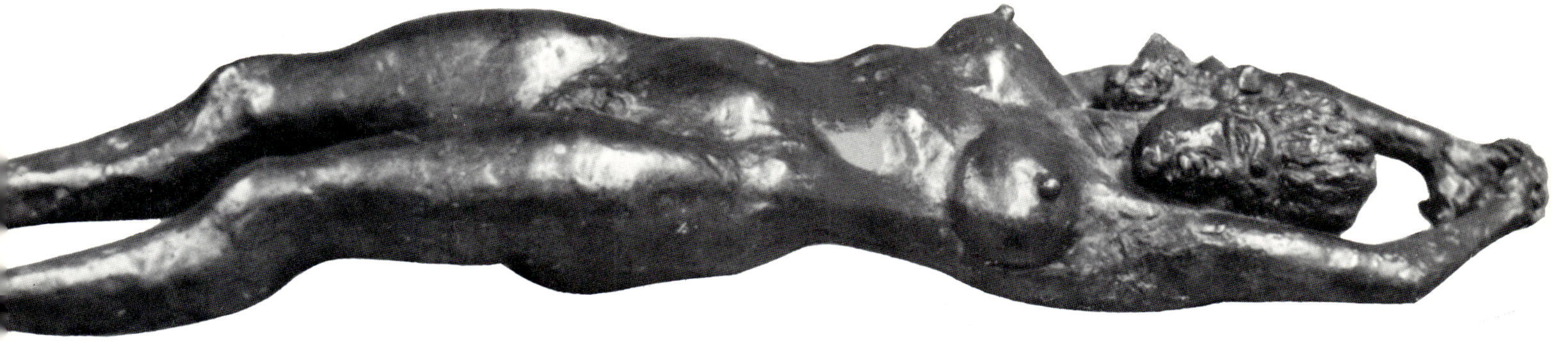

BETTY PETERS, 1939. h. 4″ w. 6″ d. 28½″

In *Betty Peters,* because of the extended arms, seeming repose becomes extreme tension as the body arches with almost the full weight off the ground. This piece is one of a series of studies from the nude begun at the outbreak of World War II.

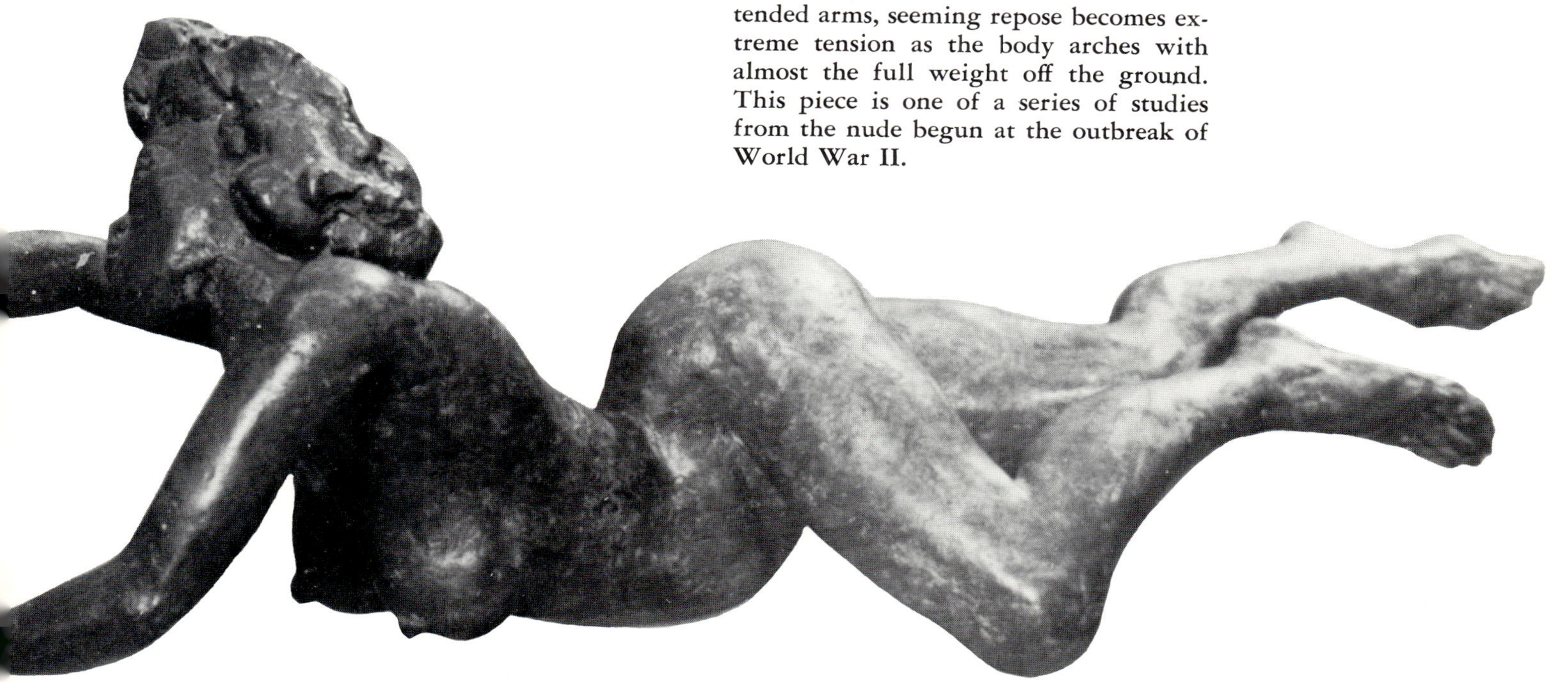

THE SWIMMER, 1939. h. 18¼″ w. 8″ d. 6¼″

Using the model Betty Peters, Epstein alters the horizontal with the use of curves. Here the curves rise and fall as waves which carry *The Swimmer* along. The flow of energy is made tense by the sudden breaking of the motion in the small of the back.

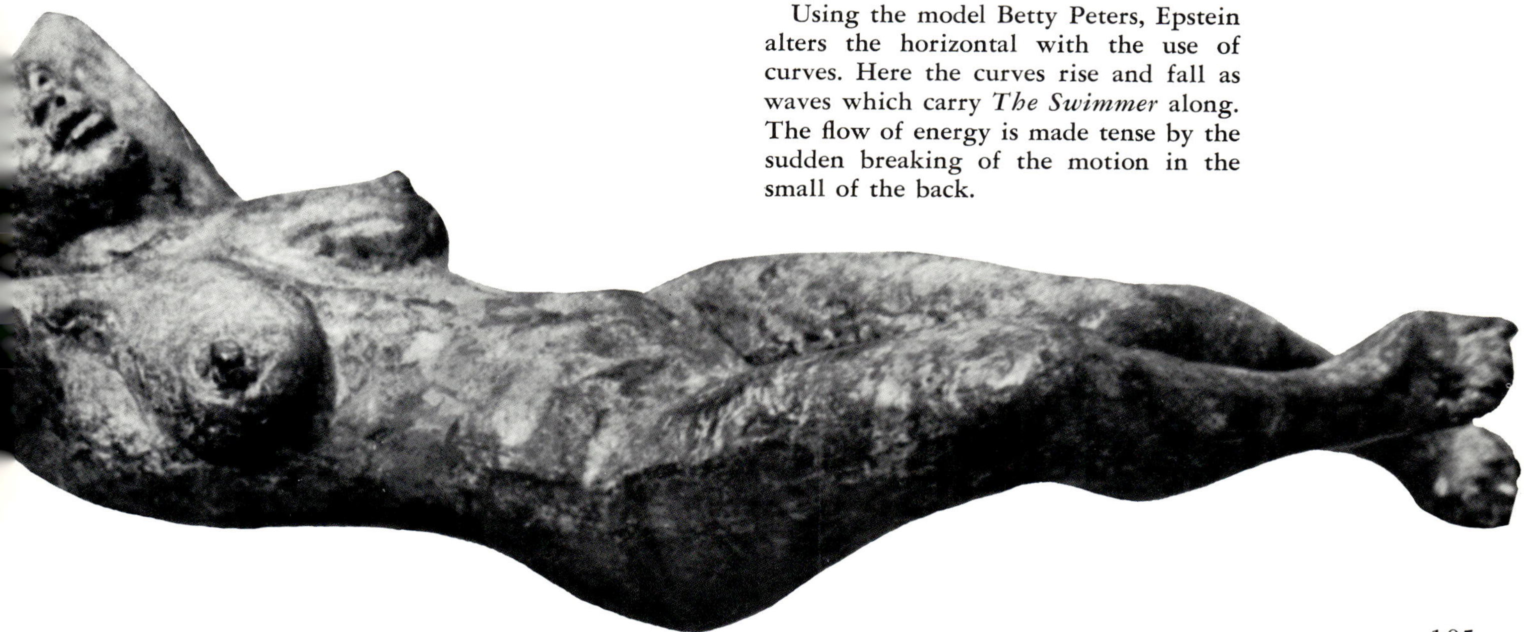

DEIRDRE—*First Portrait*, 1941. h. 25″

Deirdre was first hired as a cook-housekeeper but was found more suitable for modelling.

Asymmetric qualities, the feeling of motion of the arms, and the airy way in which the figure rests upon the base create a lithe, snakelike movement. The graceful gesture of the slender arms gives a mood of uncertainty.

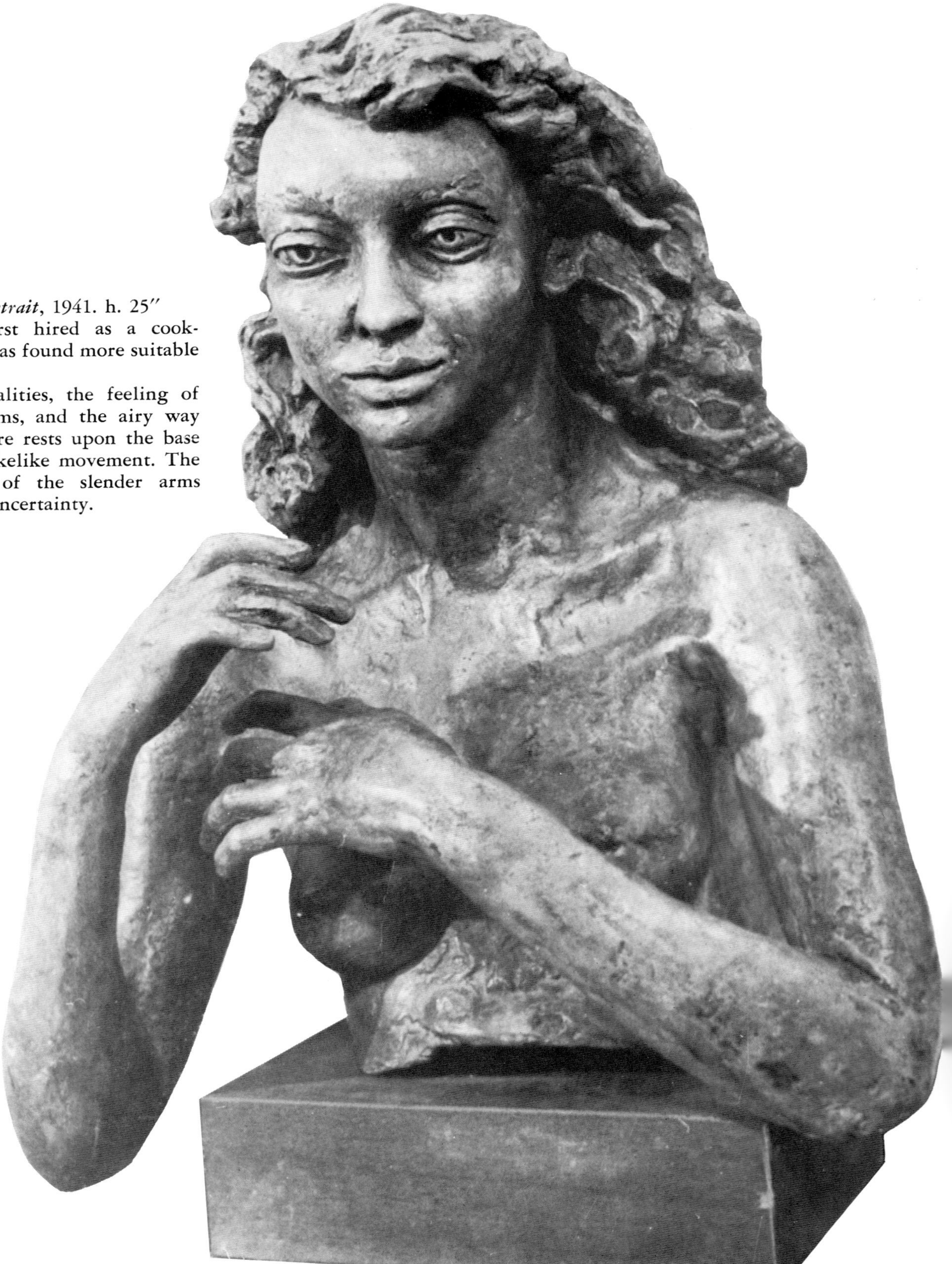

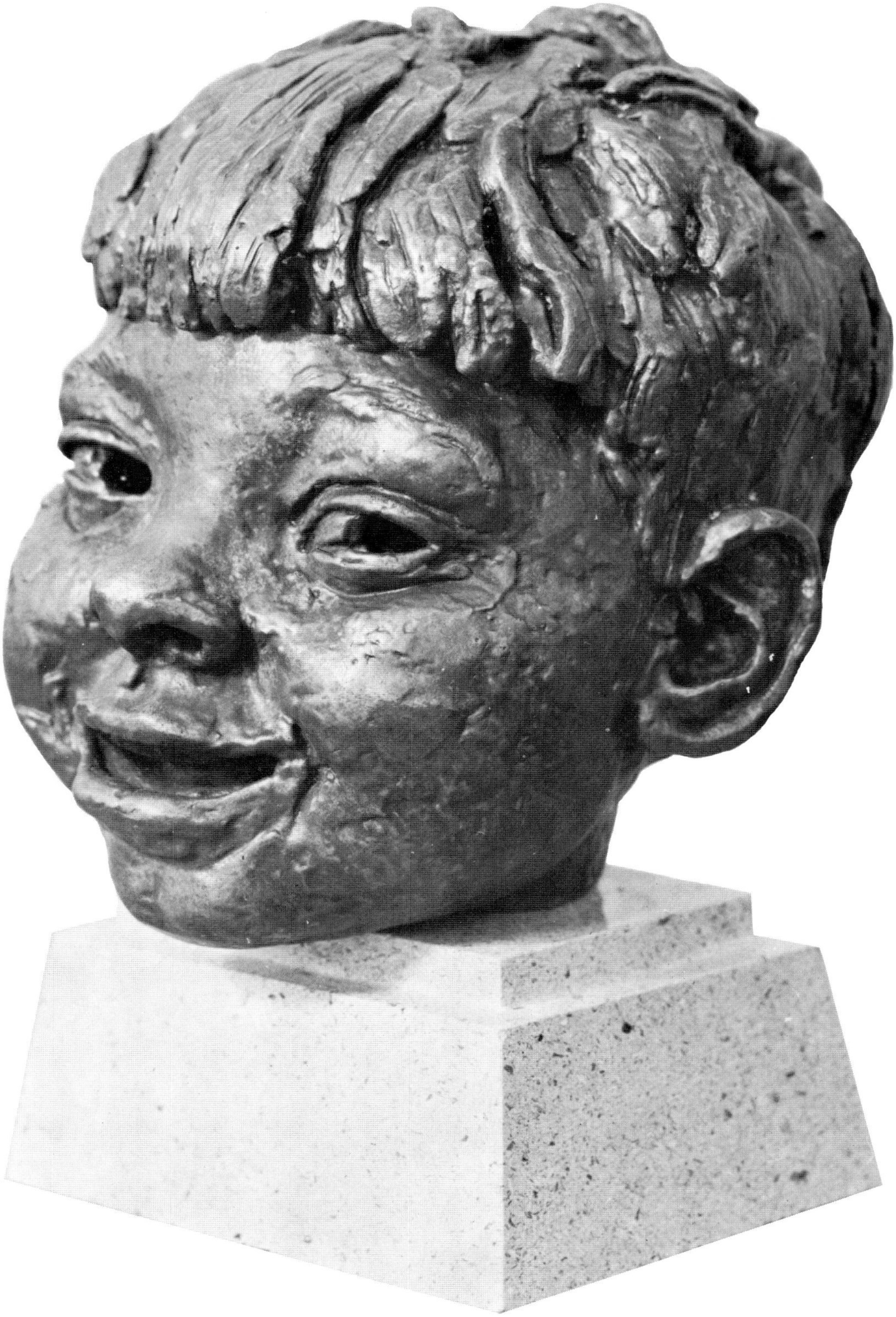

RAGAMUFFIN, 1940. h. 9″ w. 8″ d. 9″

Ragamuffin is the third portrait of Jackie, Epstein's second son. Lines of force, as in a magnetic field, radiate from the eyes and mouth while they project the sparkling warmth which is youth.

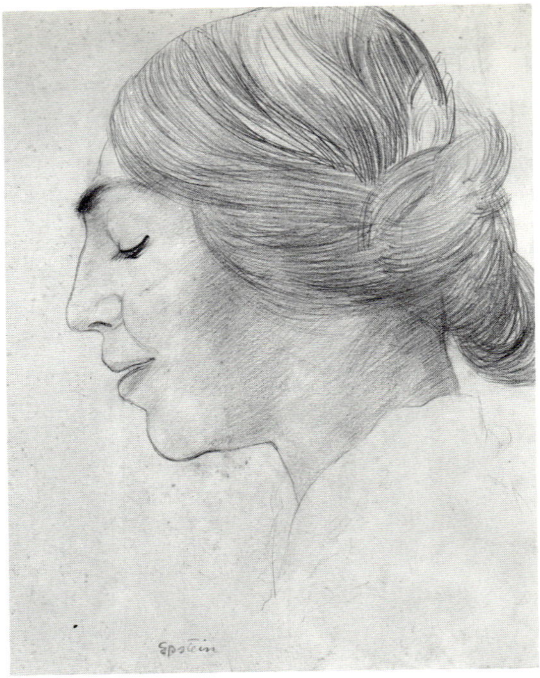

PROFILE OF WOMAN, 1906—*Drawing.*
h. 11⅝″ x w. 8¾″

Pencil drawing of unknown sitter—a more disciplined line which he was to drop in the 1920s.

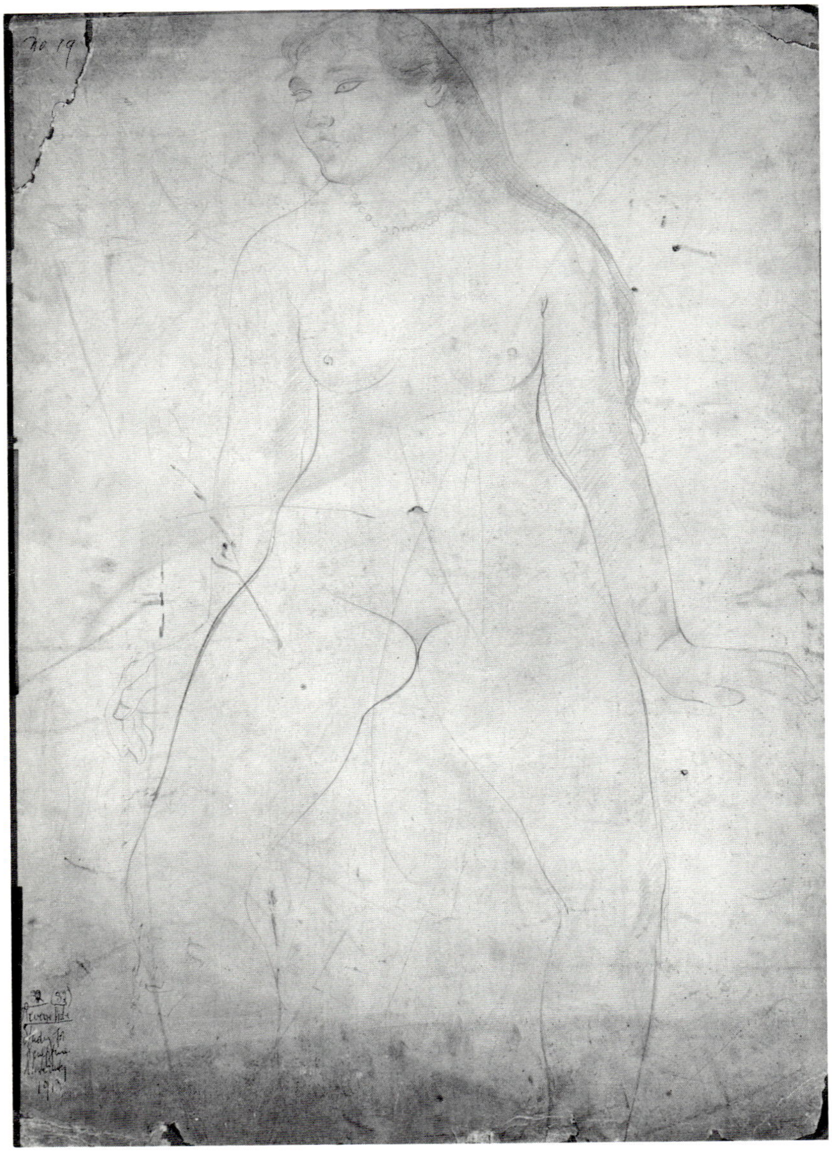

STUDY FOR "MATERNITY", 1910 (Backside of Maternity)—*Drawing*

One of the original sketches for Epstein's highly stylized marble carving, which he started in 1909 and worked on intermittently during the next forty years.

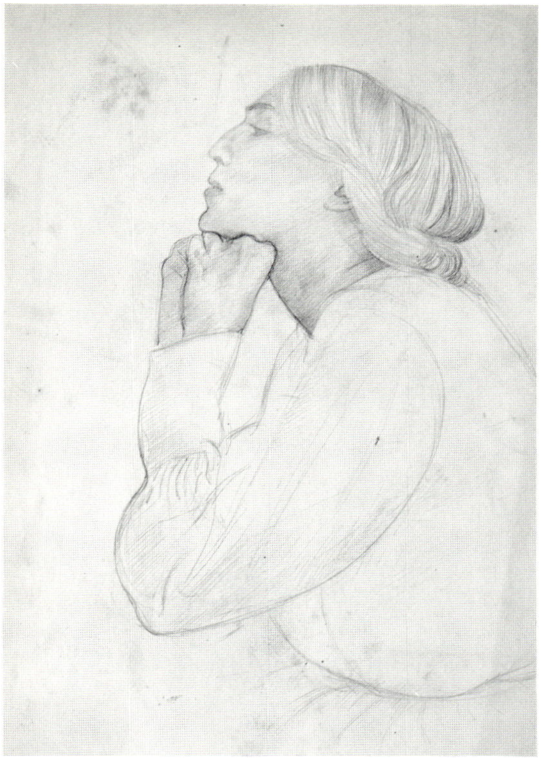

WOMAN RESTING ON ARMS, 1906—*Drawings.* h. 15½″ x w. 11″

This pencil drawing emphasizes face and hands by shading these areas and by showing only the contours of the blouse.

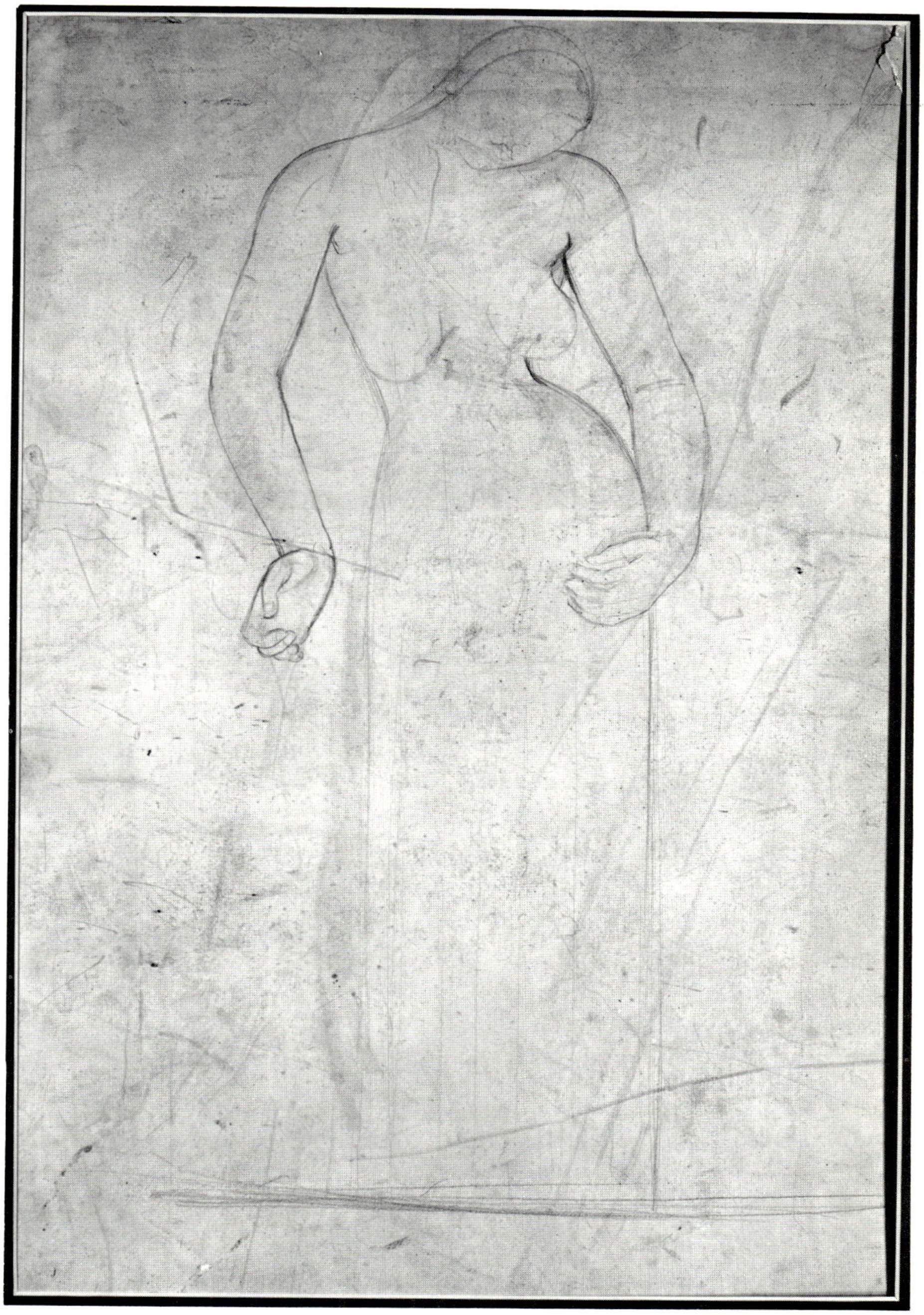

MATERNITY, 1910—*Drawing.* h. 32″ x w. 22½″

Pencil study for an unfinished statute begun in 1910. Note the slow moving curves, the delicate gestures of the hands, and the sleep-like pose of the head which lend serenity to the sketch.

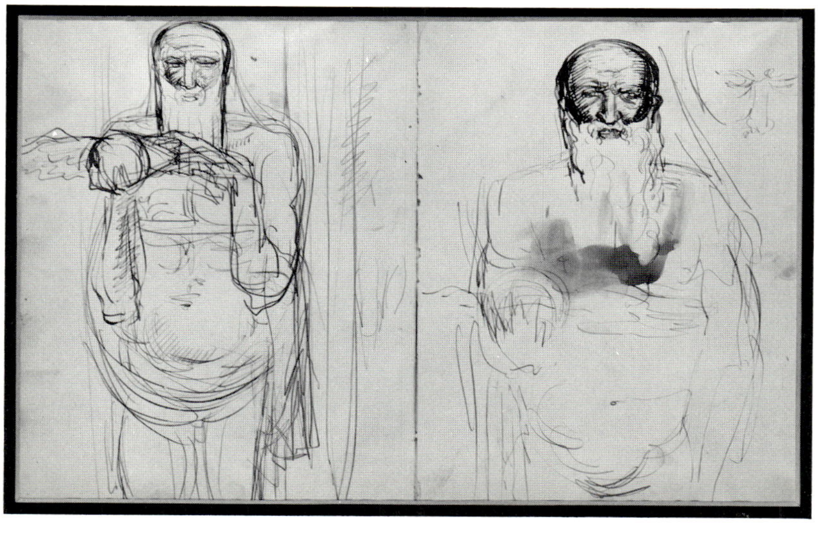

PHILOSOPHER (STRAND STATUE), 1907—*Drawing.* h. 15¼″ x w. 21″

These pencil studies show an old man, later carved as a young man, holding a winged skull symbolic of human thought. The two heads show the dramatic difference between flat and modelled drawing.

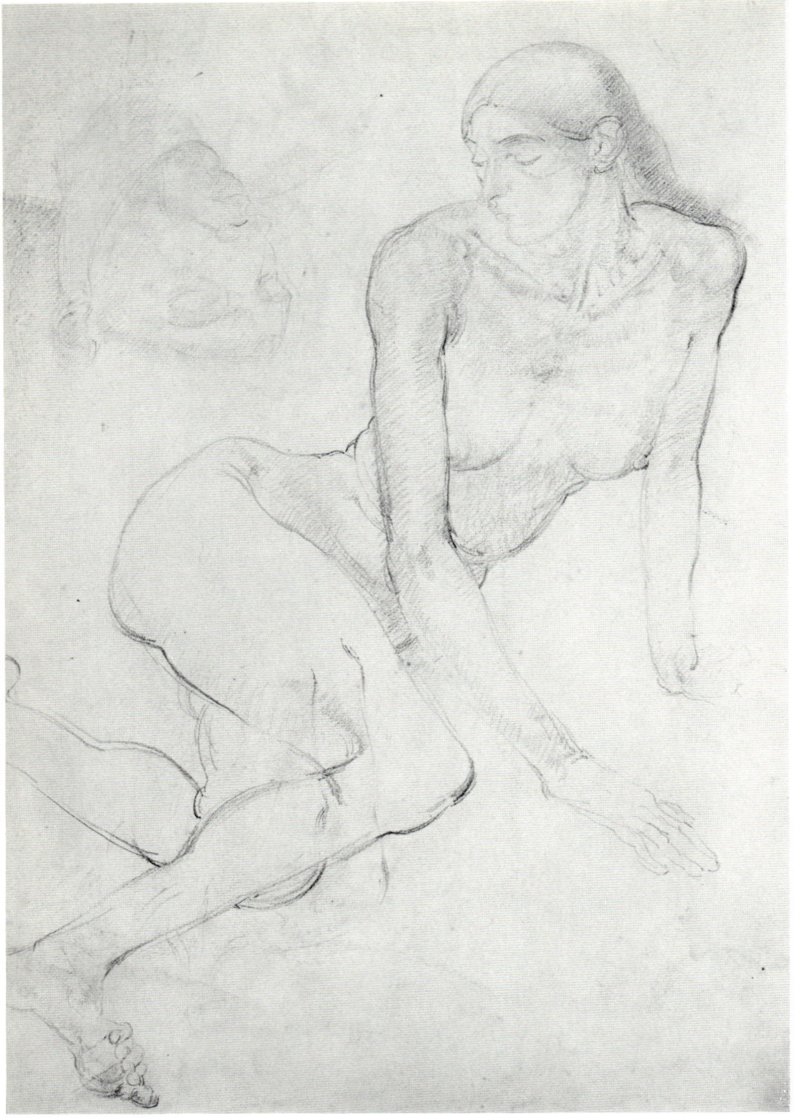

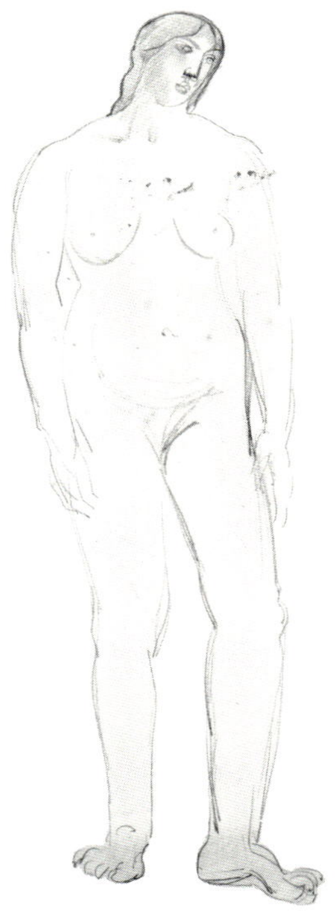

STANDING NUDE, 1911—*Drawing*
A figure study of a model who interested Epstein.

NAN THE DREAMER, 1911—*Pencil Drawing.* h. 20″ x w. 14″
A professional model and gypsy, Nan Condron was the subject of many studies in these early years.

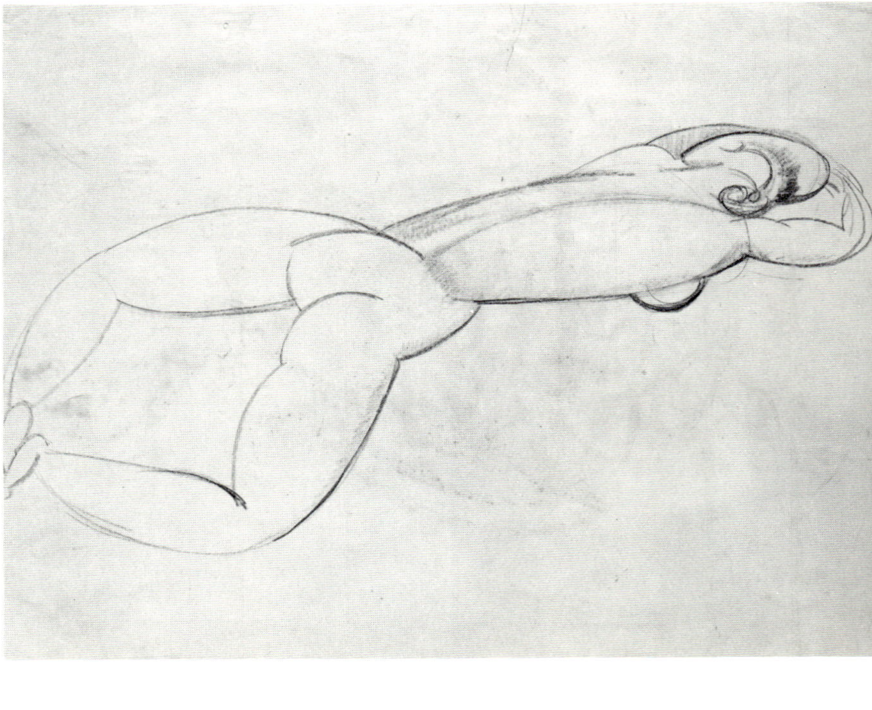

VORTICIST FIGURE, 1913—*Drawing.* h. 25¼″ x w. 20¾″
This blue chalk drawing is an example of his short-lived abstract period. It shows an interest in form alone. The pattern created by the legs is echoed on a smaller scale by the arms.

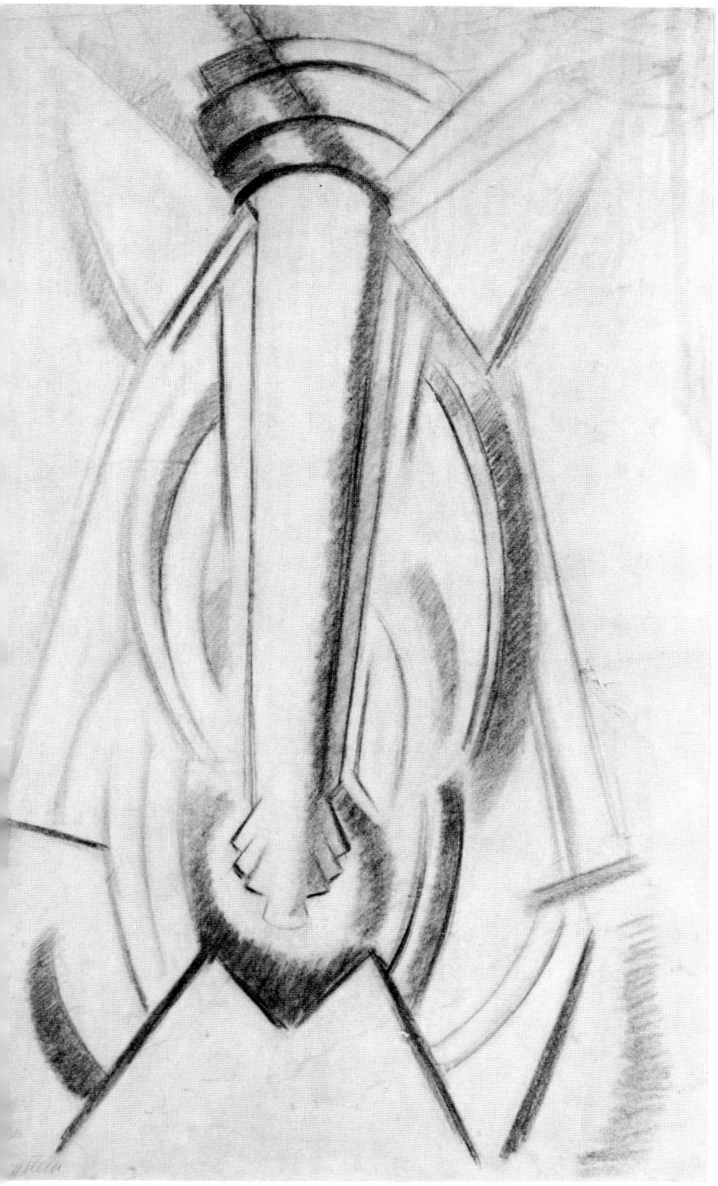

ROCK DRILL REFLECTIONS, 1915—*Drawing.* h. 27″ x w. 17″

Charcoal sketch of rock drill in motion entering the ground. Movement is created by the repetition of shapes.

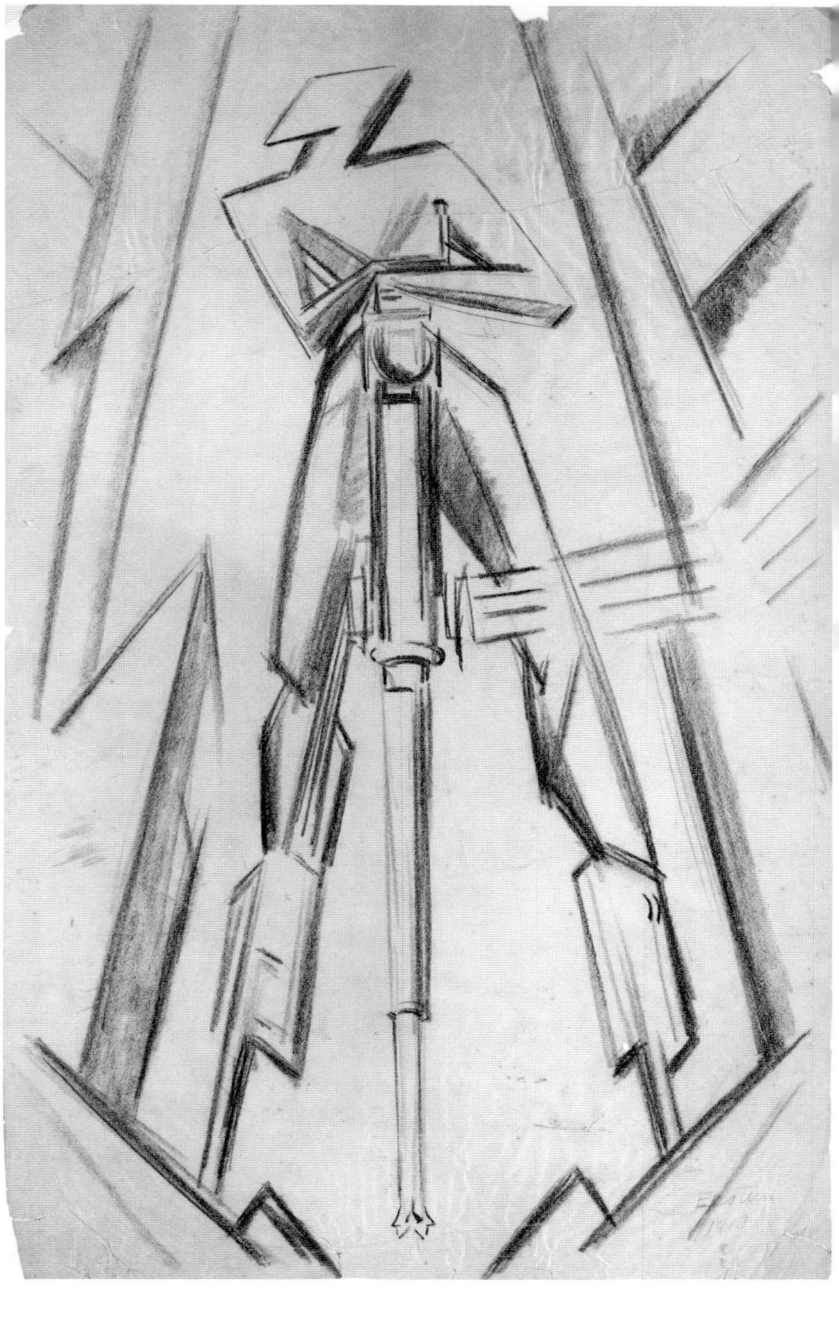

ROCK DRILL STUDY, 1915—*Drawing.* h. 27″ x w. 16⅞″

This is a charcoal study for the bronze Rock Drill. The Vorticists were interested in machinery and functional equipment. The dehumanization of man's body is achieved by angular abstraction and the extension of legs into parts of the tripod.

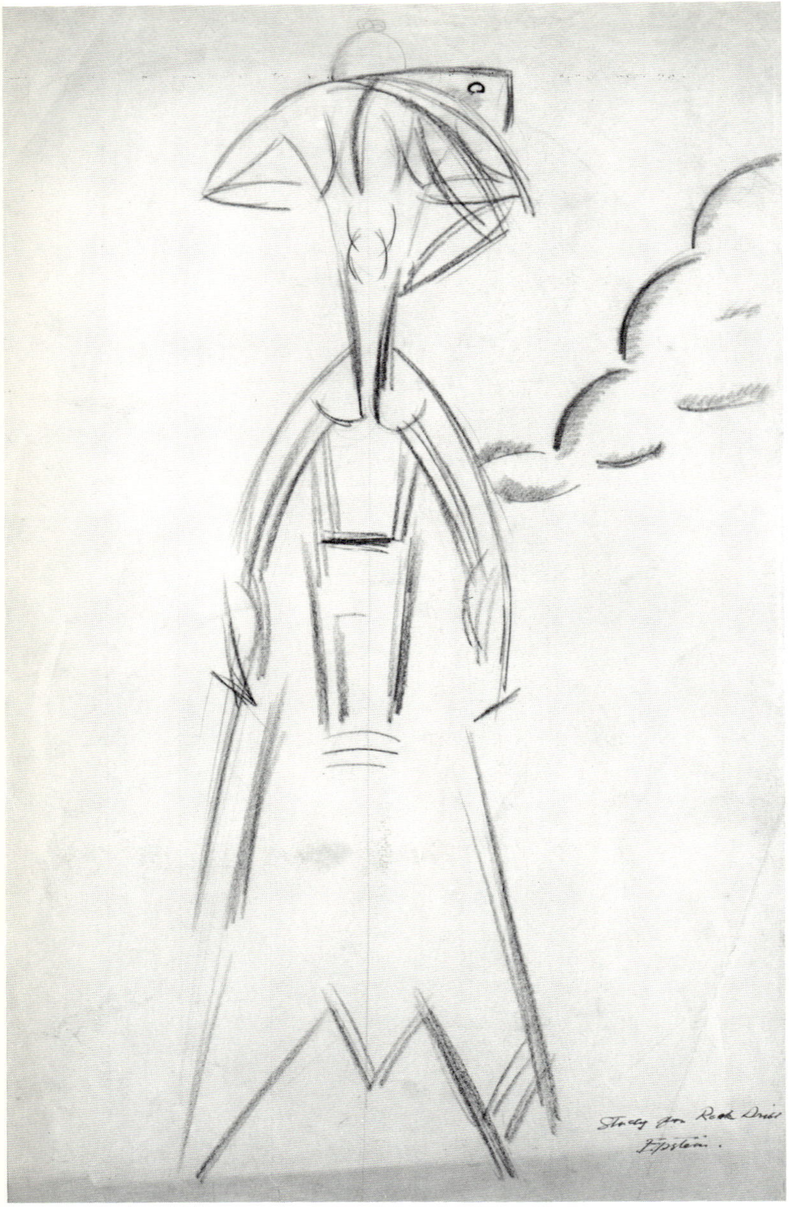

STUDY FOR "ROCK DRILL," 1915—*Drawing.* h. 27″ x w. 17″
Back View, Charcoal.

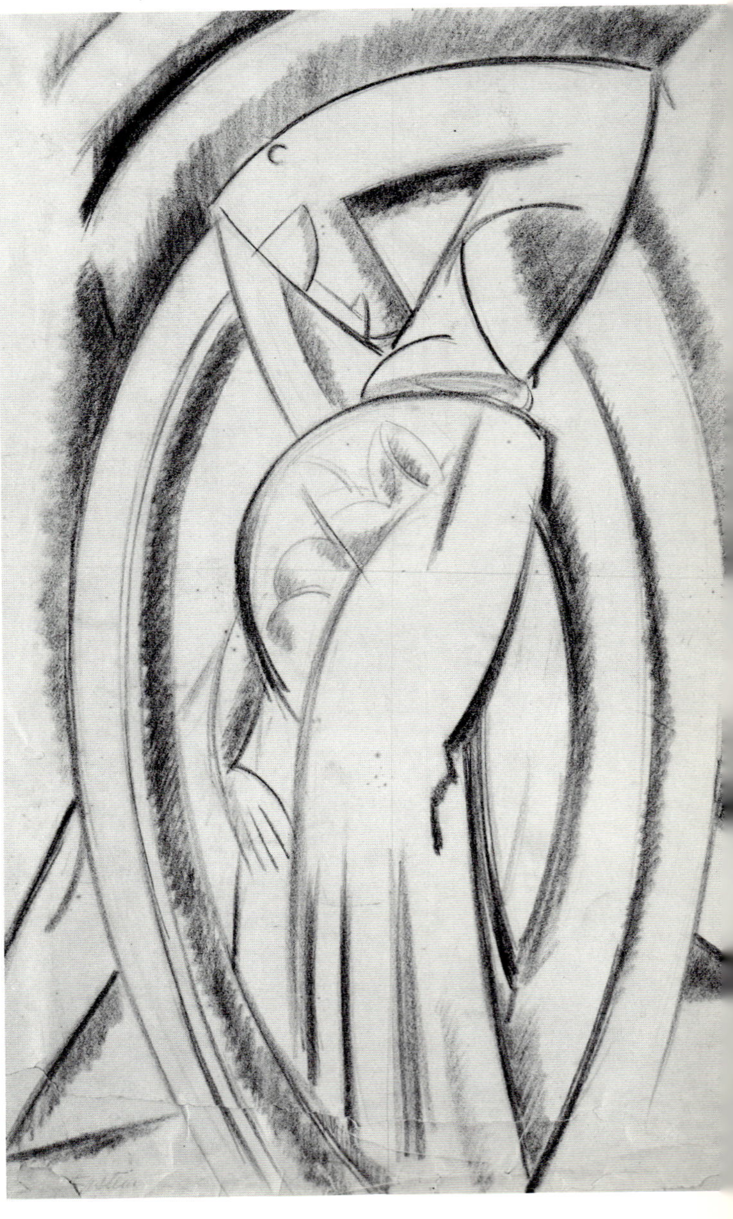

VORTICIST COMPOSITION, 1915—*Drawing.* h. 27⅛″ x w. 17″

The energized convex shells enclose a female figure who in turn contains a fetus.

Charcoal study possibly of flenite figures for a pregnant woman which he later carved in stone as an architectural building decoration.

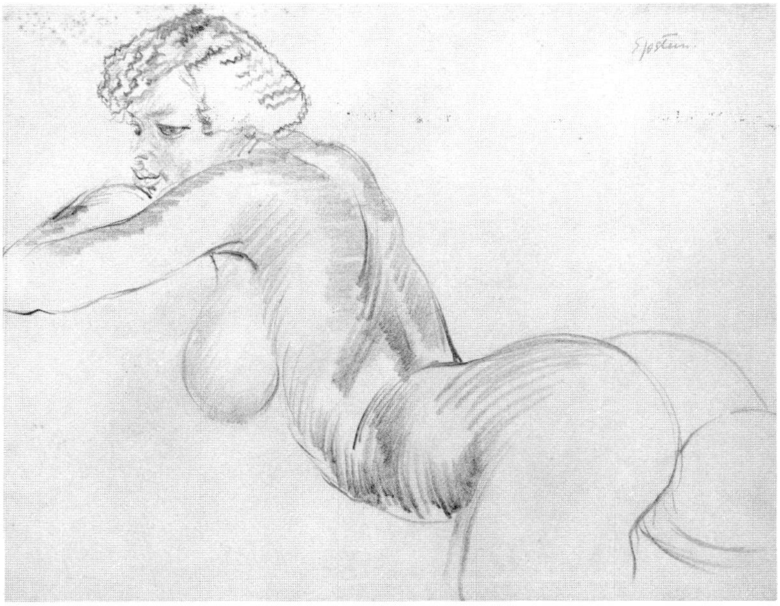

RECUMBENT NEGRESS, 1925—*Drawing.* h. 20″ x w. 16⅜″

This sketch stresses the roundness of forms in contrast to the *Reclining Nude,* which concentrates on the angularity of the body.

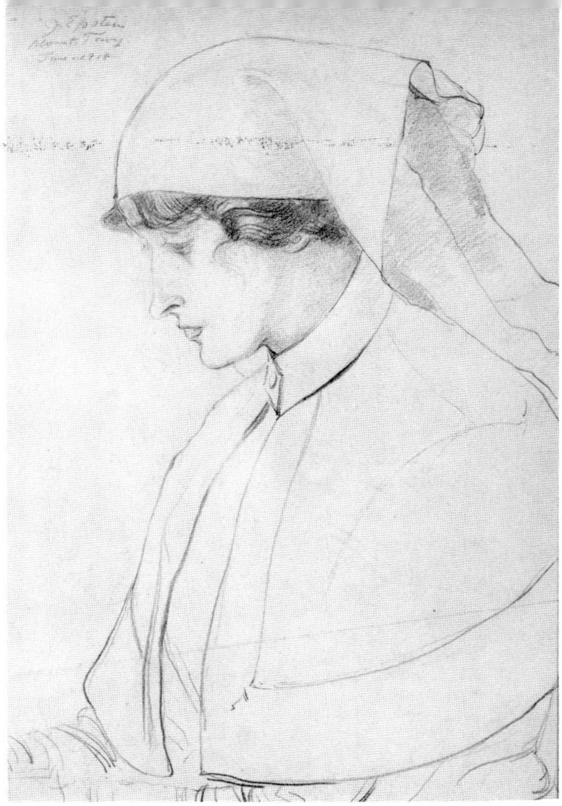

ARMY NURSE, 1919—*Drawing.* h. 14⅝″ x w. 10″

This pencil drawing is reminiscent of his 1906 sketches of women. The softness of the flesh is contrasted to the starched veil and cape. The sensitive treatment of the face corresponds to the subject matter.

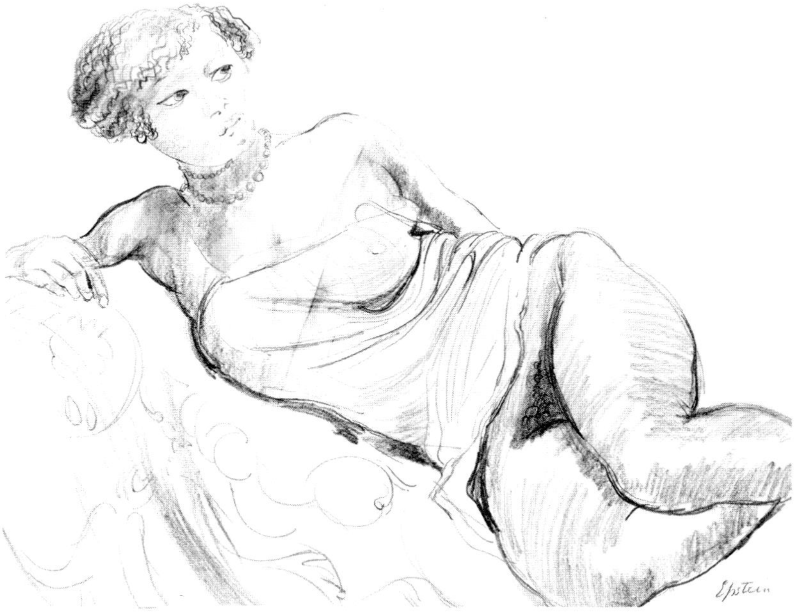

RECLINING NUDE, 1925—*Drawing* h. 18″ x w. 21½″

Epstein frequently used Negro models. The slightest change in pose was considered another drawing in its own right.

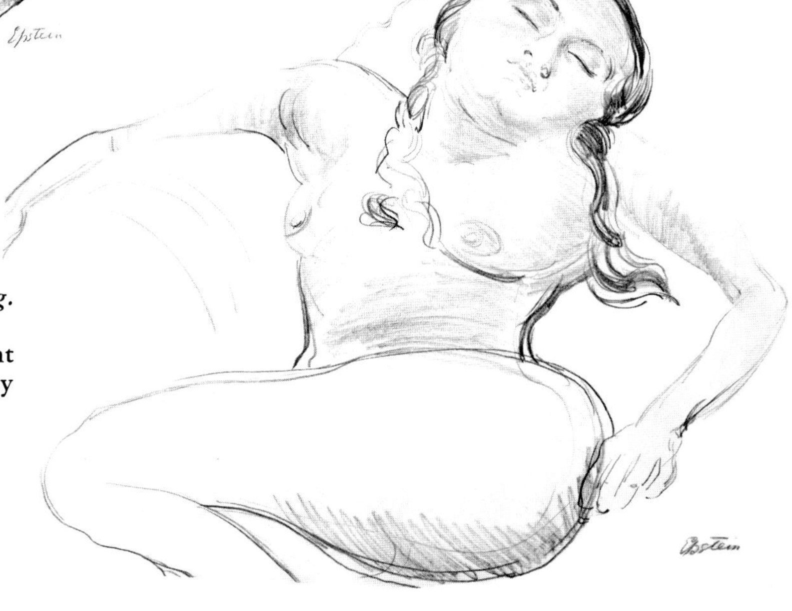

SUNITA ASLEEP, 1928—*Pencil Drawing.* h. 25″ x w. 23″

The feeling of complete abandonment is achieved, though the body is sharply twisted at the hips.

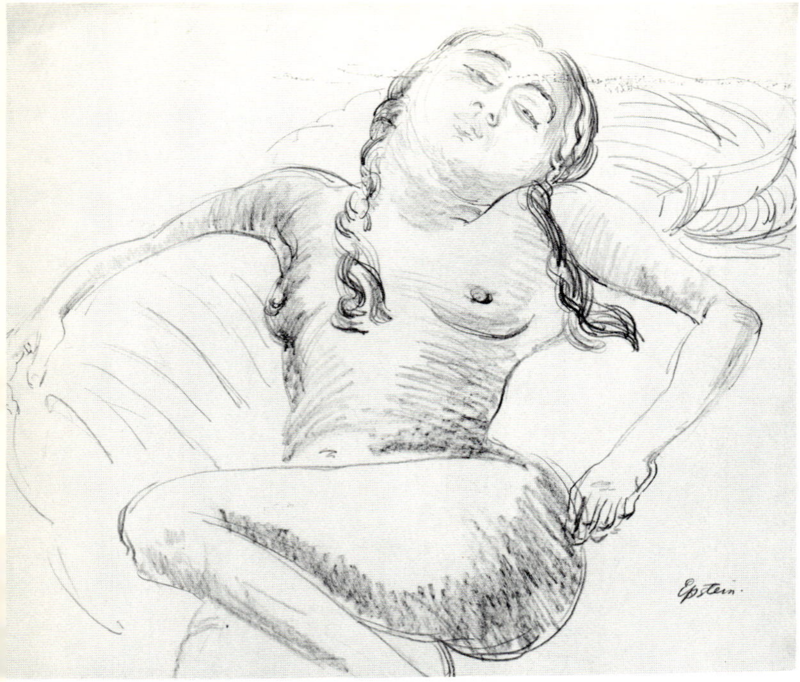

SUNITA RECLINING, 1928—*Drawing*
h. 18″ x w. 21½″

This drawing is nearly identical to *Sunita Asleep.* But here the model is awake and the couch is further delineated.

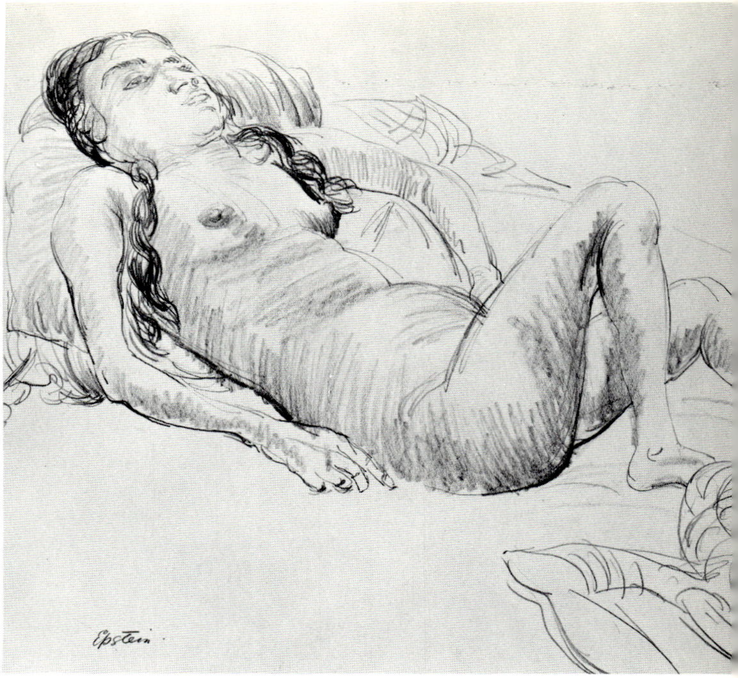

SUNITA RELAXED, 1928—*Drawing*
h. 19″ x w. 21″

Sunita, who came from India, became a part of the Epstein household. During the summer of 1928, the artist did numerous studies of Sunita in a variety of poses. Not always anatomically correct, these sketches evoke the warmth and vitality of the model.

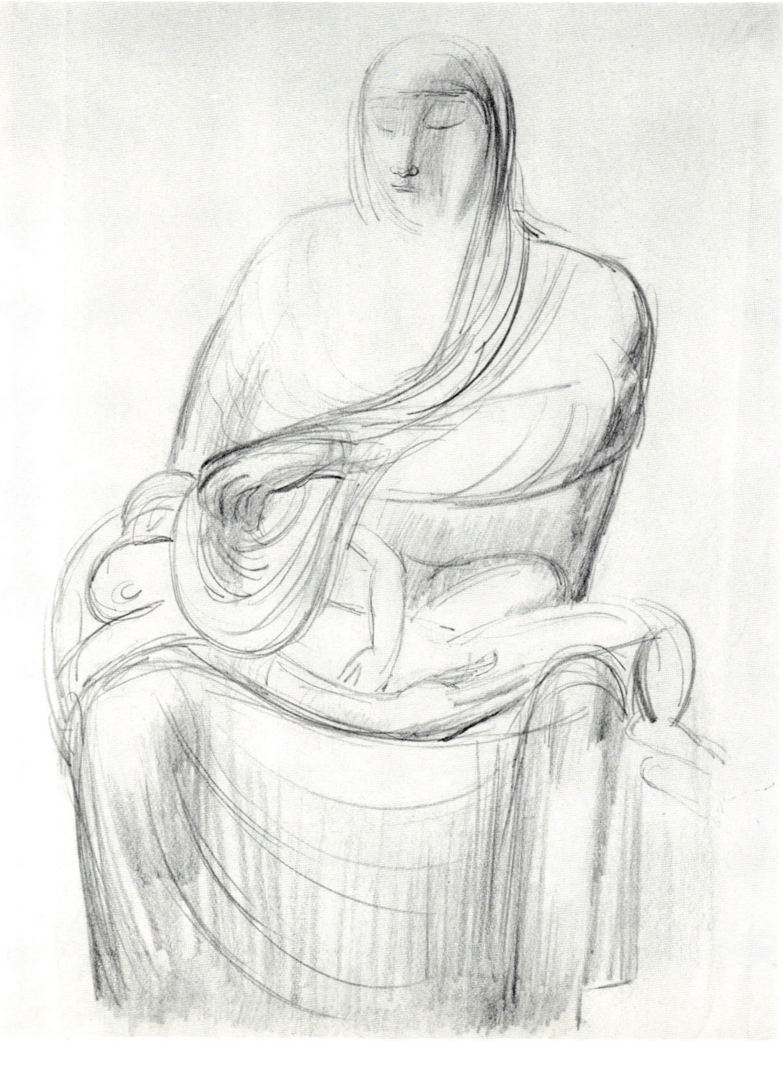

STUDY FOR "NIGHT," 1928—*Drawing.*
h. 22″ x w. 17¼″

Study of one of the stone groups at the entrance of the Underground (Subway) at St. James.

The long heavy arm of the mother hovers over her sleeping children. With slow moving curves this monumental carving evolves a quiet restful feeling.

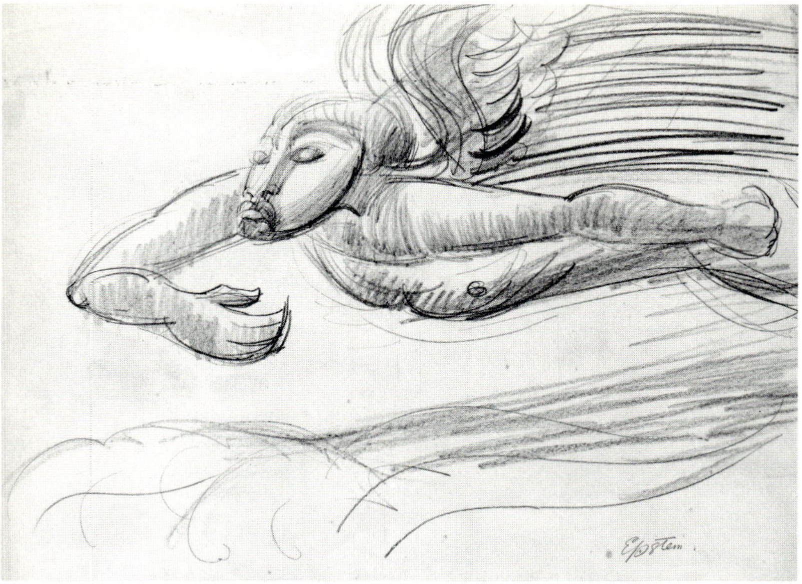

SPIRIT MOVING ON THE WATERS, 1930—*Drawing* h. 17″ x w. 22″

One of a series of drawings based on the Old Testament. The foreshortened body of the Spirit bears a marked resemblance to the earlier Vorticist figure of 1913.

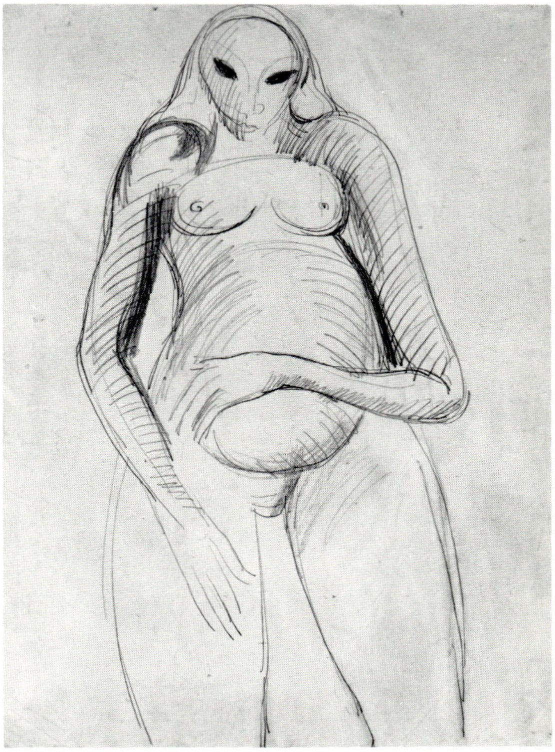

STUDY FOR "GENESIS," 1931—*Drawing.* h. 20″ x w. 15″

This unique sketch for the large carving of Genesis which was also done in 1931 portrays the stylized voluptuousness of an earth goddess.

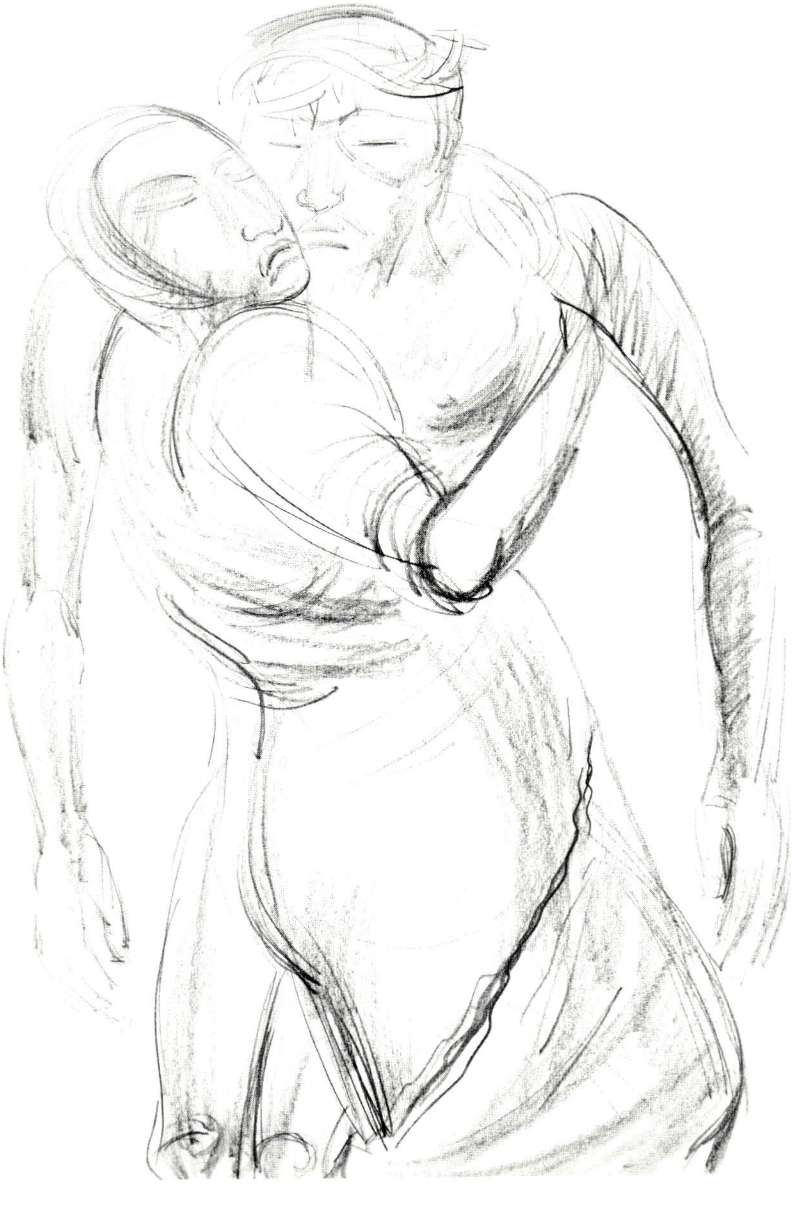

PIETÀ, 1932—*Drawing.* h. 22¾″ x w. 17½″

Epstein was about to model a Pietà when he was commissioned to carve the St. James' underground architectural sculptures. He adapted the intended seated Pietà to the Night group. The tension of a woman holding up her grown son is evidenced by the strain in her back and the grief in her face.

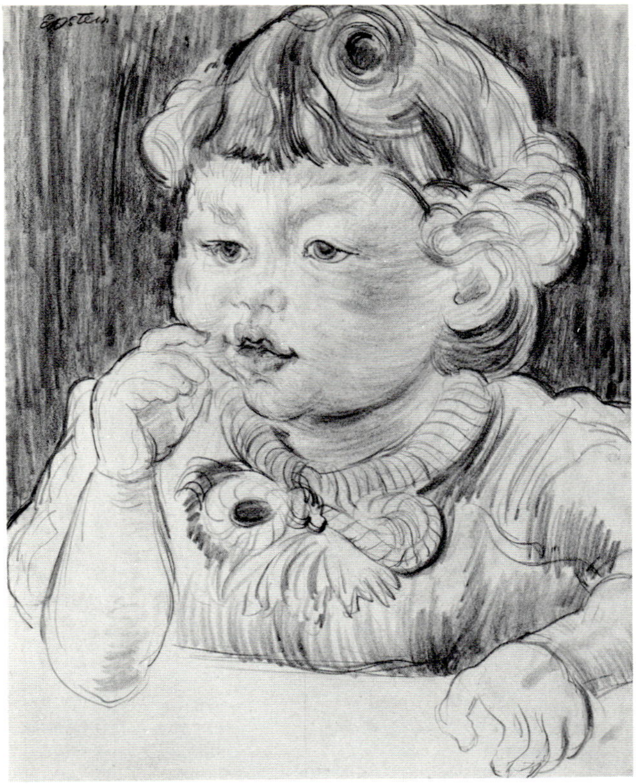

JACKIE—*First Portrait*, 1935—*Drawing* h. 22½" x w. 17"

These four portraits of his son Jackie, sometimes titled *Ragamuffin,* are representative of Epstein's loving handling of children both in his drawings and sculptured heads. The drawings exhibit the use of exciting energetic lines to create volume.

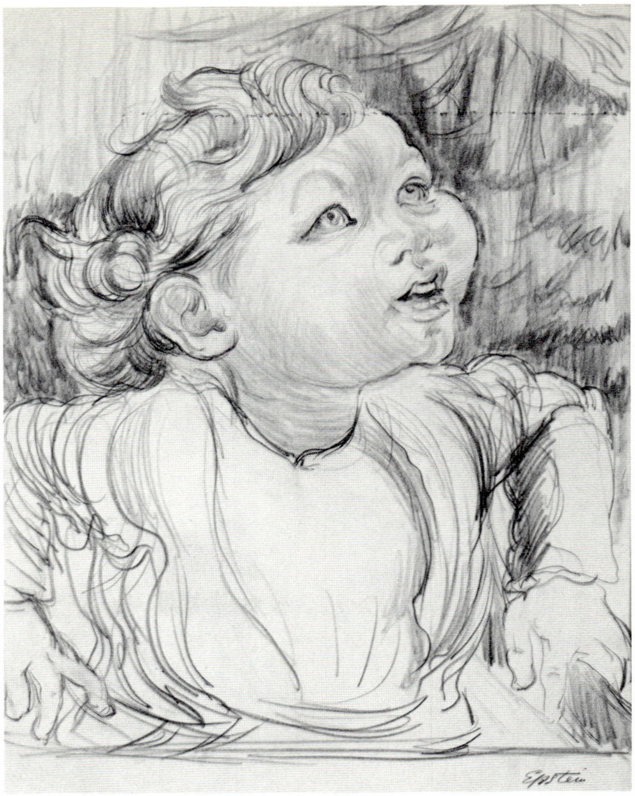

JACKIE—*Second Portrait*, 1937—*Drawing* h. 22½" x w. 17"

This is the most agitated portrait of the Jackie series. The active, sweeping lines of the hair are also used in the clothing. Epstein also enlivens the background by sketching in trees. He creates movement in the gesture of the arms, the tilt of the head, and the look of wonderment on the face.

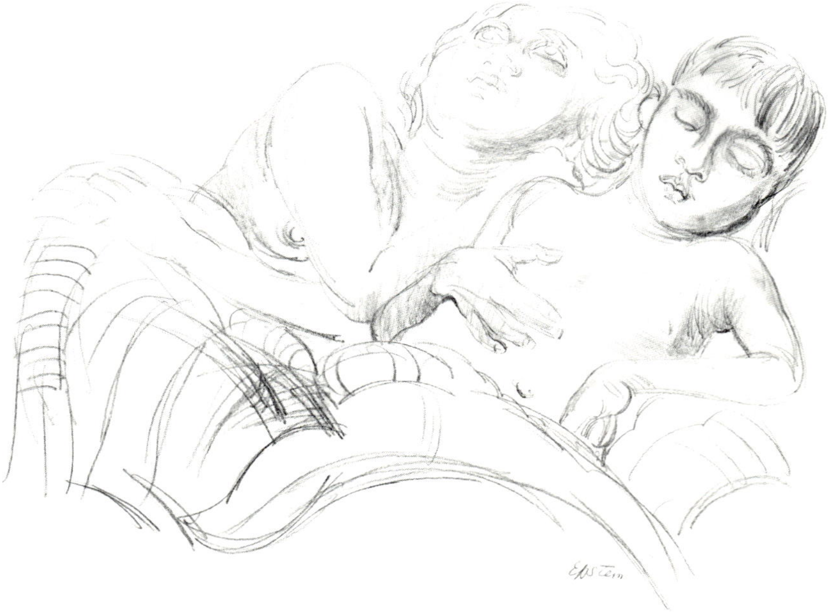

INDIAN MOTHER AND CHILD, 1932—*Drawing*. h. 21¼" x w. 26¾"

Sunita and Enver, her son, were the subjects of many sketches. They also modeled for the monumental bronze *Madonna and Child* of 1927.

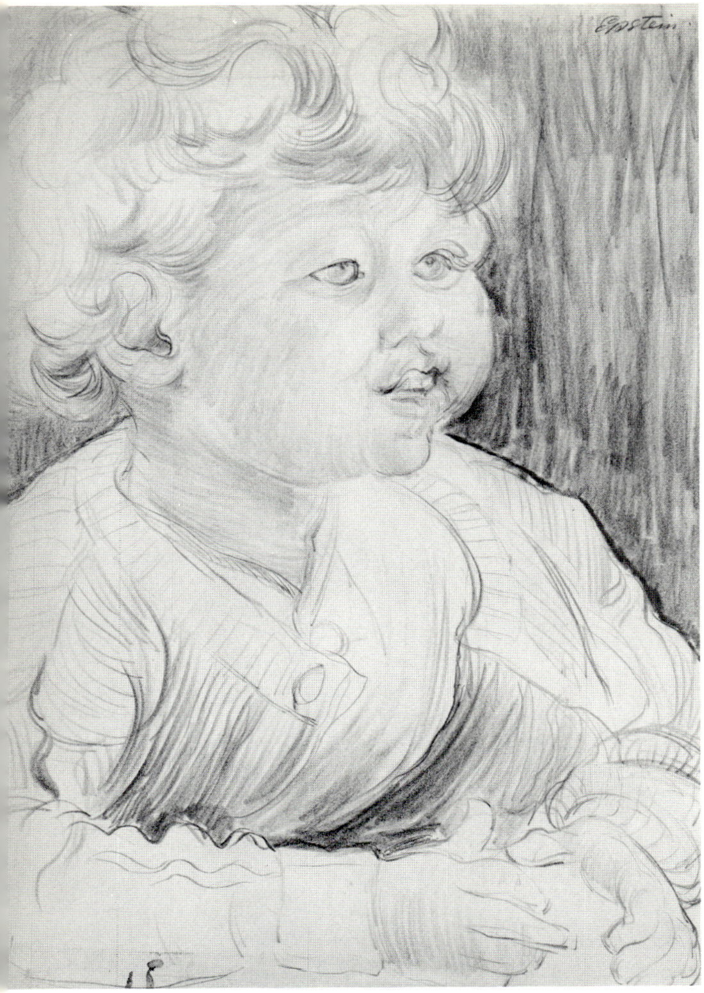

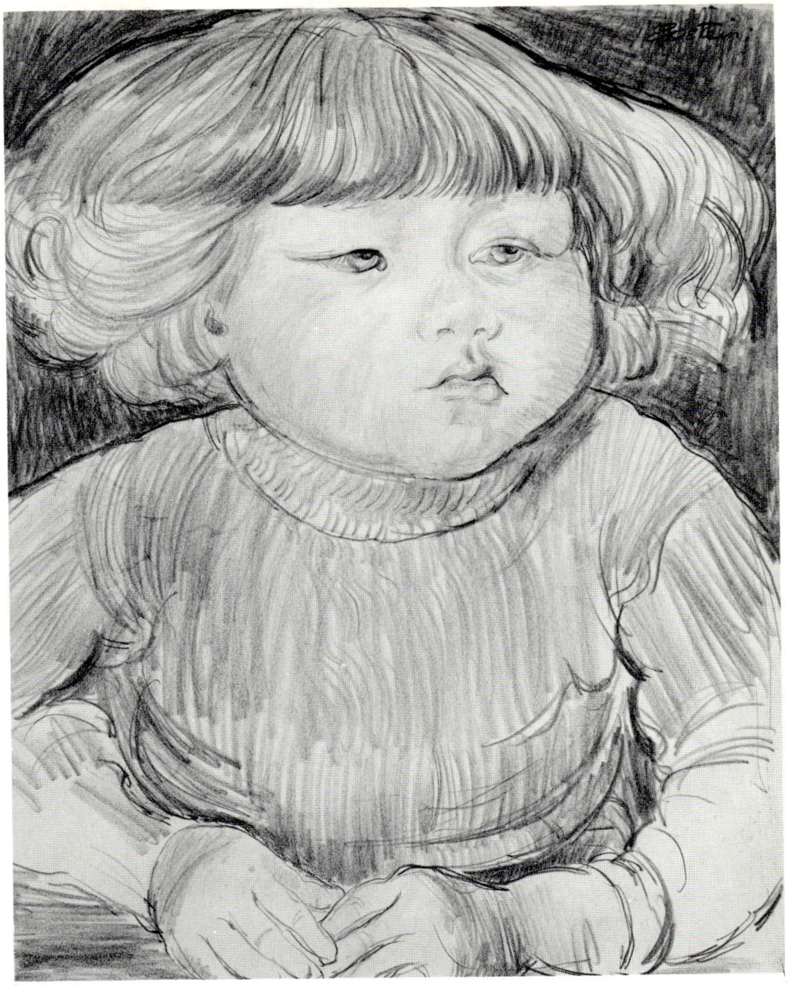

JACKIE—*Third Portrait*, 1940—*Drawing*
h. 22½″ x w. 17″

This the the most exaggerated and unidealized of the portraits. Strangely, he makes the eye closest to the viewer smaller and the other eye larger. As in all of the Jackies, Epstein exaggerates the smallness and curvature of the lips.

JACKIE—*Fourth Portrait,* 1942—*Drawing* h. 22½″ x w. 17″

The most stylized of the Jackie portraits, Epstein lets one part of the face sweep out and the other droop down. Feeling that the human face was never symmetrical, he exaggerates this point here. The apparent movement in the hair contrasts with the static casualness of the pose and expression.

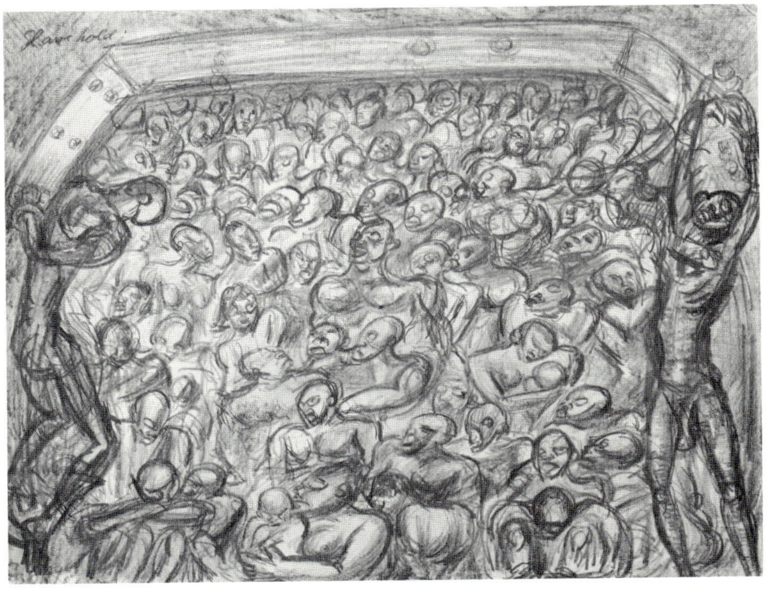

SLAVE HOLD, 1941—*Drawing*
h. 7″ x w. 9″

This drawing was never realized in sculpture except for a double portrait of a chained man and woman.

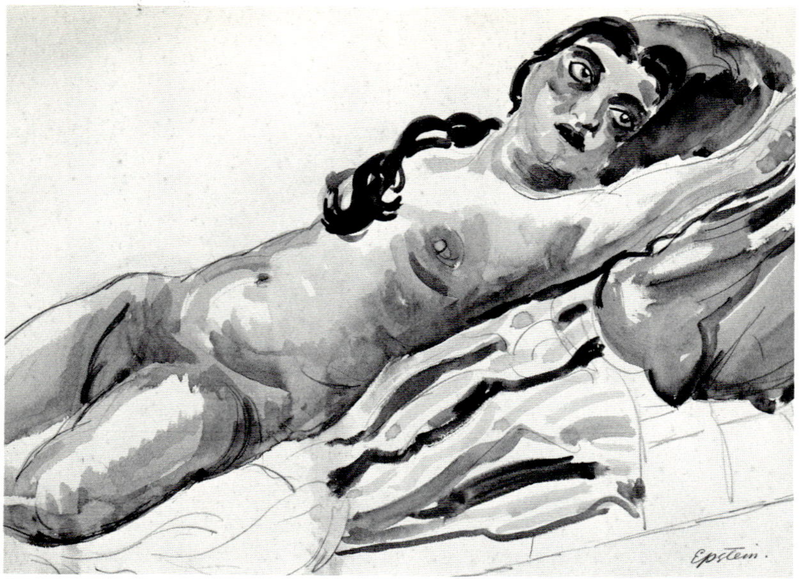

SUNITA DREAMING, 1928—*Water Color*
h. 16¾″ x w. 22¼″

Epstein communicates a dream-like mood in the hypnotic, faraway look of the model's eyes.

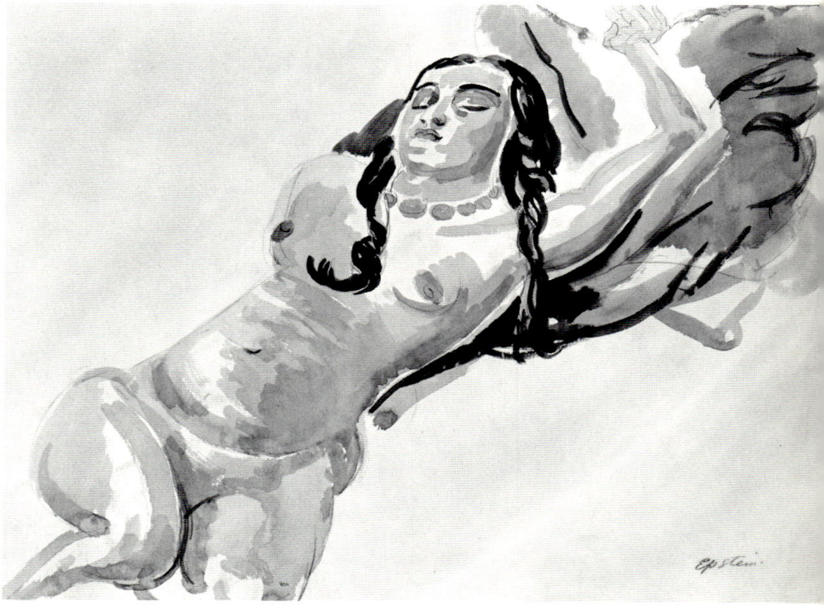

SUNITA RESTING, 1928—*Water Color*
h. 17¼″ x w. 22½″

In the water colors of Sunita, Epstein forgoes the line and uses varying shades of wash to model the figures. These were more successful and attractive than the drawings.

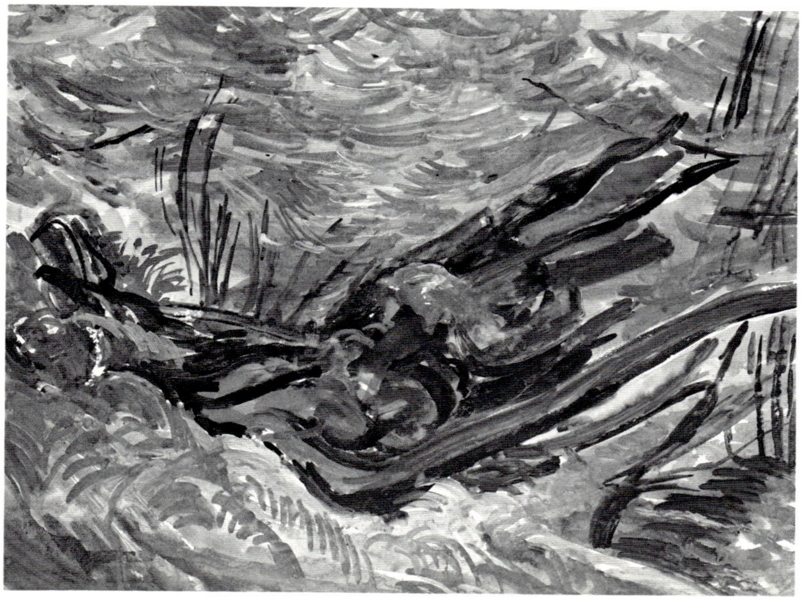

MYSTERY OF EPPING FOREST, 1933—*Water Color* h. 17″ x w. 22″

Epstein painted nearly a hundred water colors of Epping Forest, where he had rented a cottage. Emphasizing the play of light among the trees, he showed the forest in all its facets. Here he has depicted it in a violent mood by color and strong diagonals across the middle of the composition.

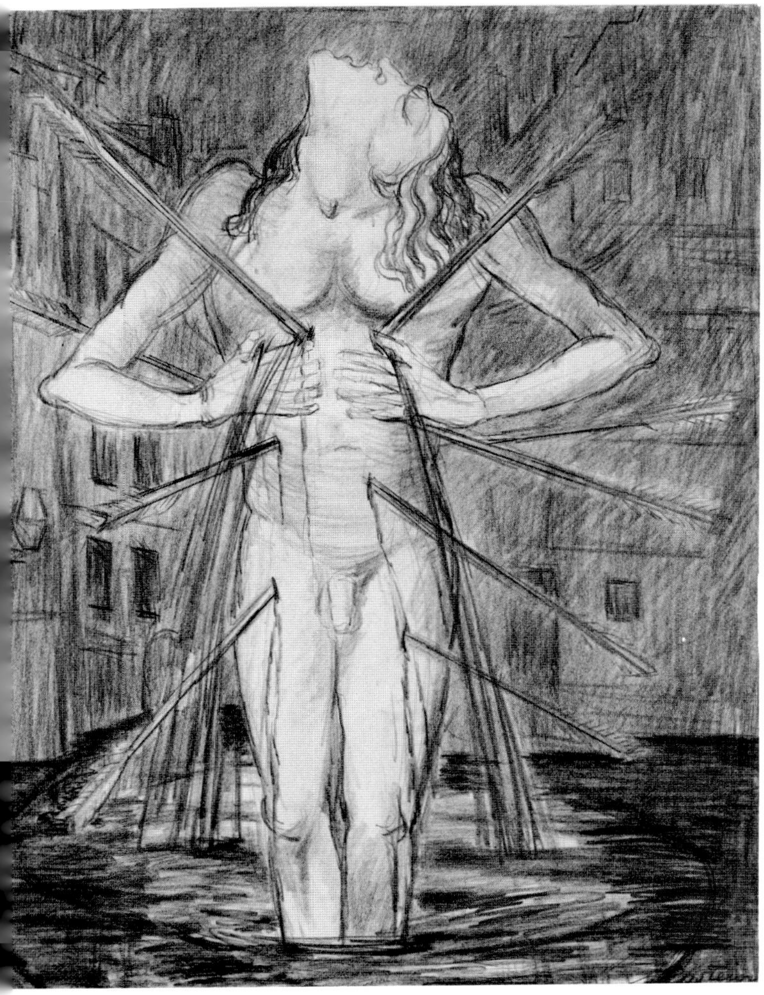

LA FONTAINE DE SANG, 1939—*Drawing.*
h. 30″ x w. 24″

This finished drawing is one of many illustrations for Baudelaire's book of poetry, *Les Fleurs du Mal.* The arrows focus the viewer's attention on the wounded body of the figure. The head is pathetically twisted to the side and is beseechingly turned toward the heavens.

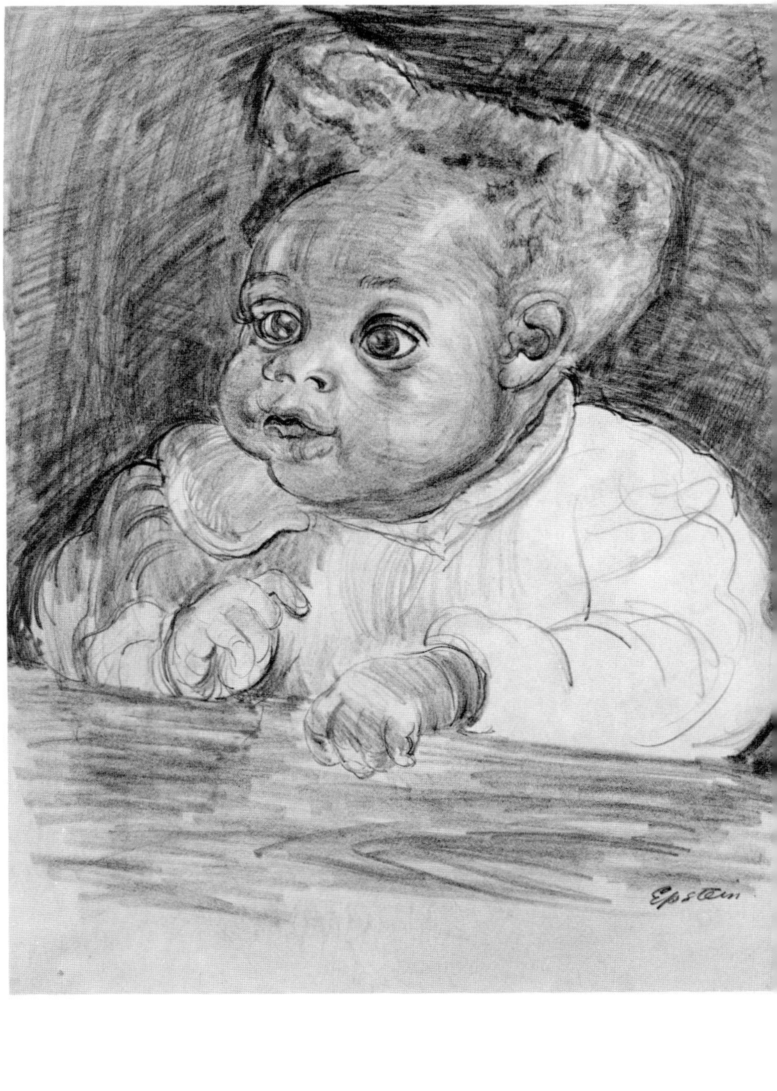

NEGRO CHILD, 1940—*Drawing*
h. 22½″ x w. 17″

This charming portrait shows Epstein's exaggeration of circular forms—eyes, cheeks, hands, and fists. The darkened background serves to project the child into the viewer's space.

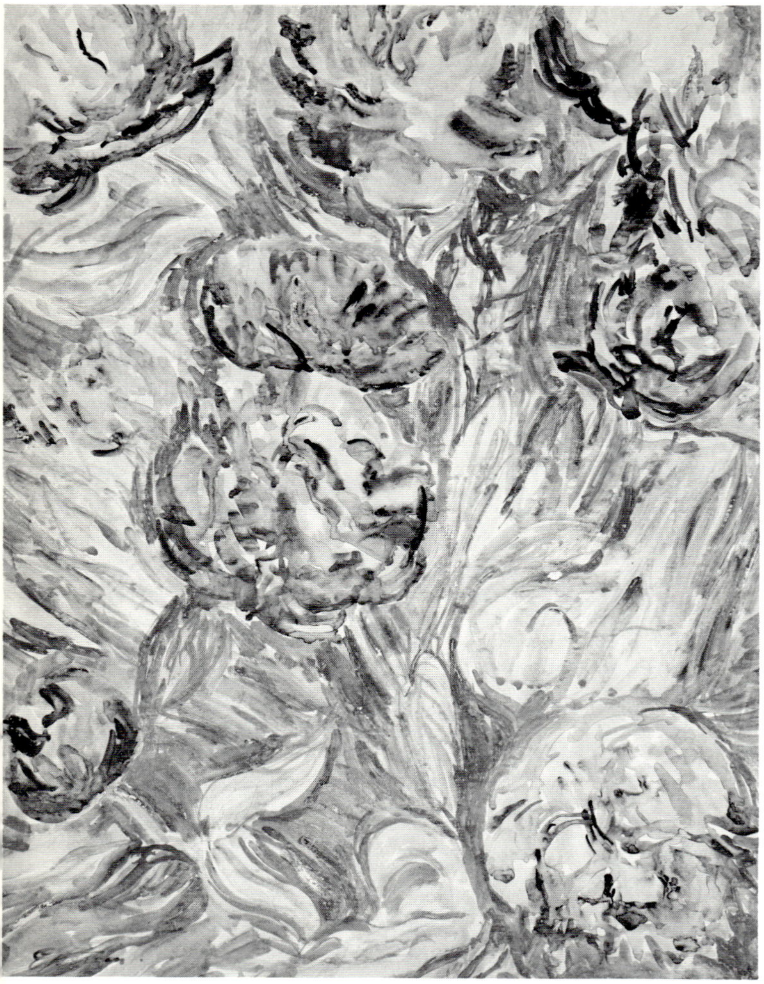

GARDEN PEONIES, 1933—*Water Color*
h. 22″ x w. 17″

A vivid floral splash of color and rhythm.

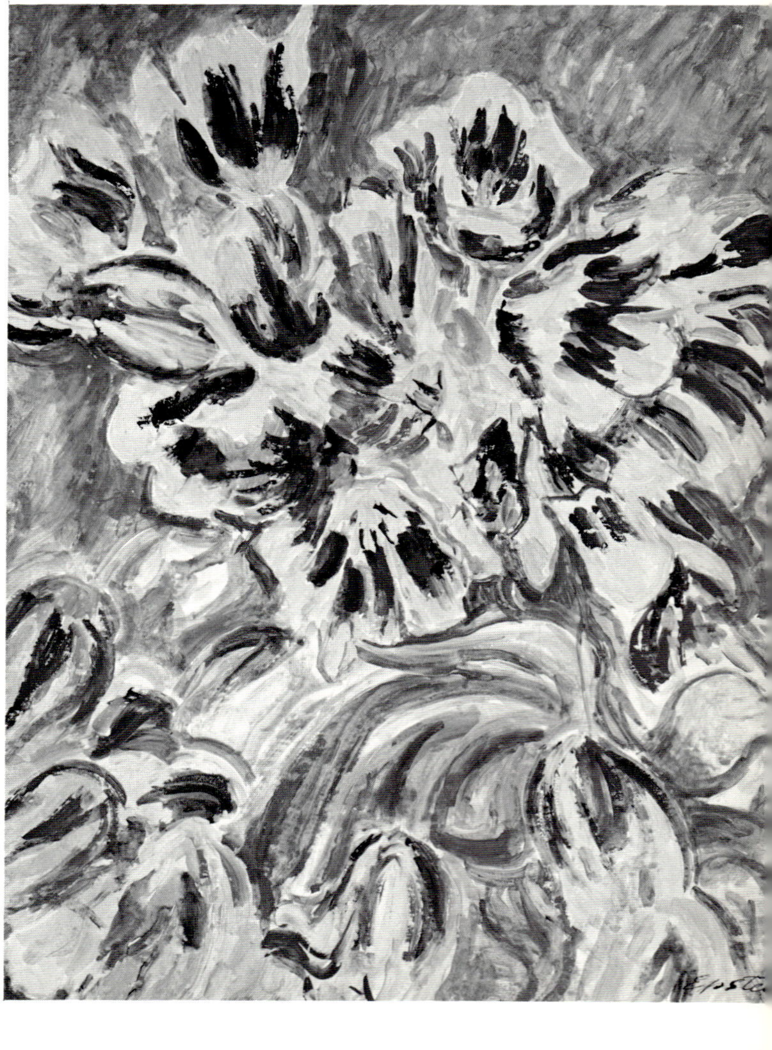

PROFUSION OF COLOR, 1933—*Water Color* h. 22″ x w. 17″

Epstein painted over 300 flower studies during this two-year period. The title of this one is a key to his fascination with design qualities in the colors of the flowers as well as in their graceful forms.

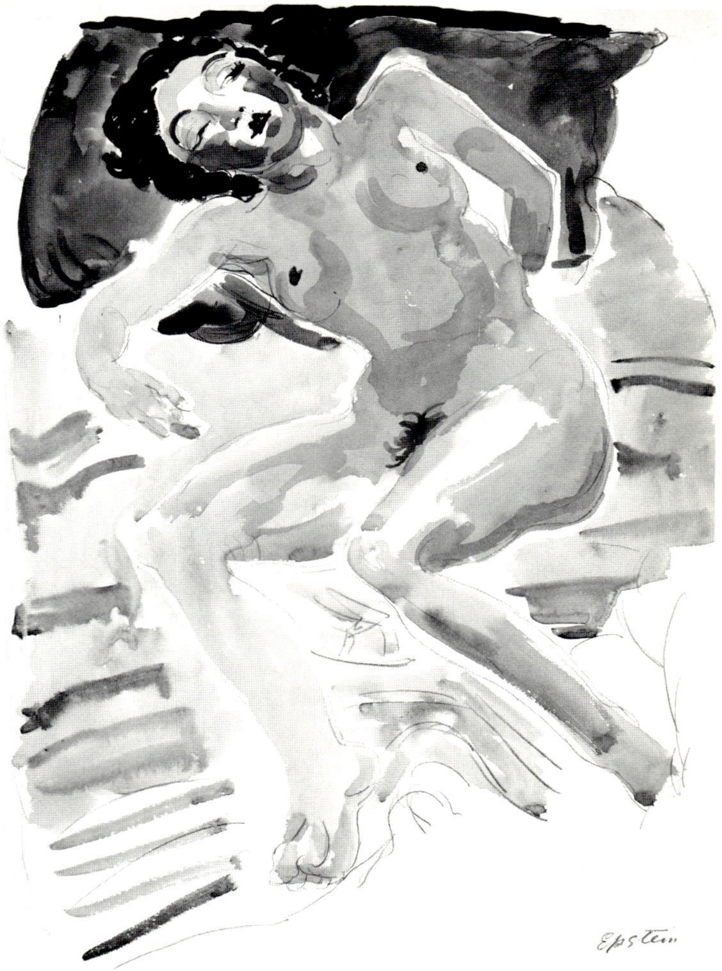

NUDE RECLINING, 1925—*Water Color*
h. 22″ x w. 16½″

This composition seems to be an unsuccessful study in comparison with the Betty Peters water color of 1945. The paint is washed on in an unsure manner and the figure is awkwardly posed.

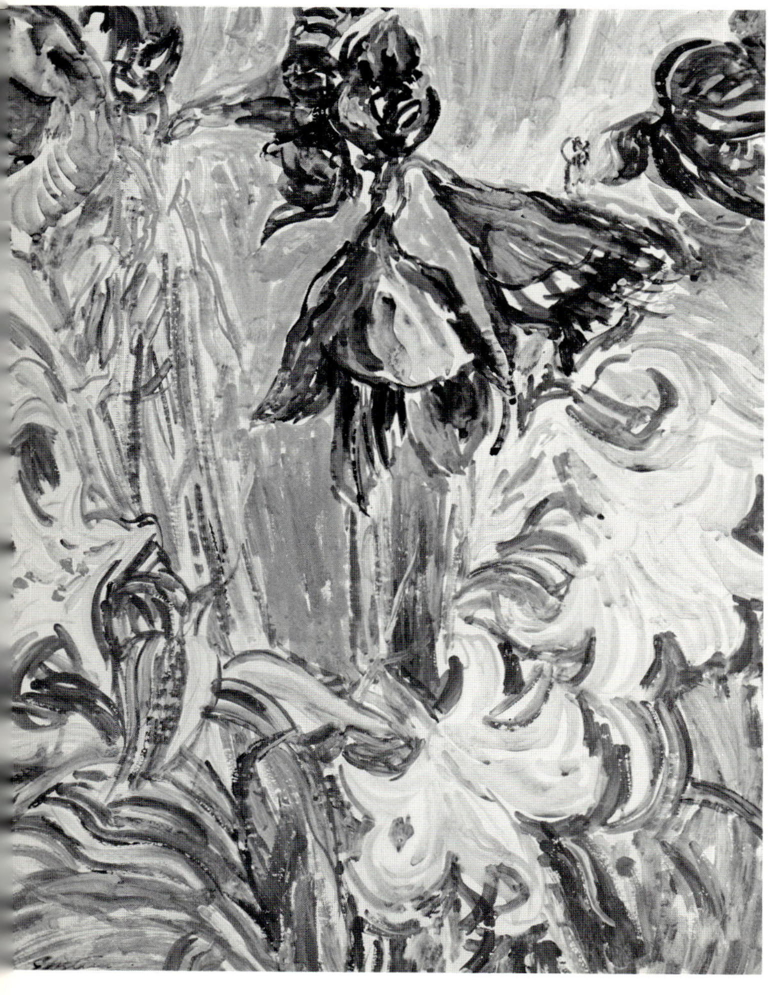

REGAL LILIES, 1933—*Water Color*
h. 22″ x w. 17″

The large series of flowers which Epstein painted burst forth with resounding joy. The brilliant colors are handled in long, parallel strokes reminiscent of the expressive style of Van Gogh. Epstein seems to abhor open space and fills each picture with echoing forms of leaves and flowers.

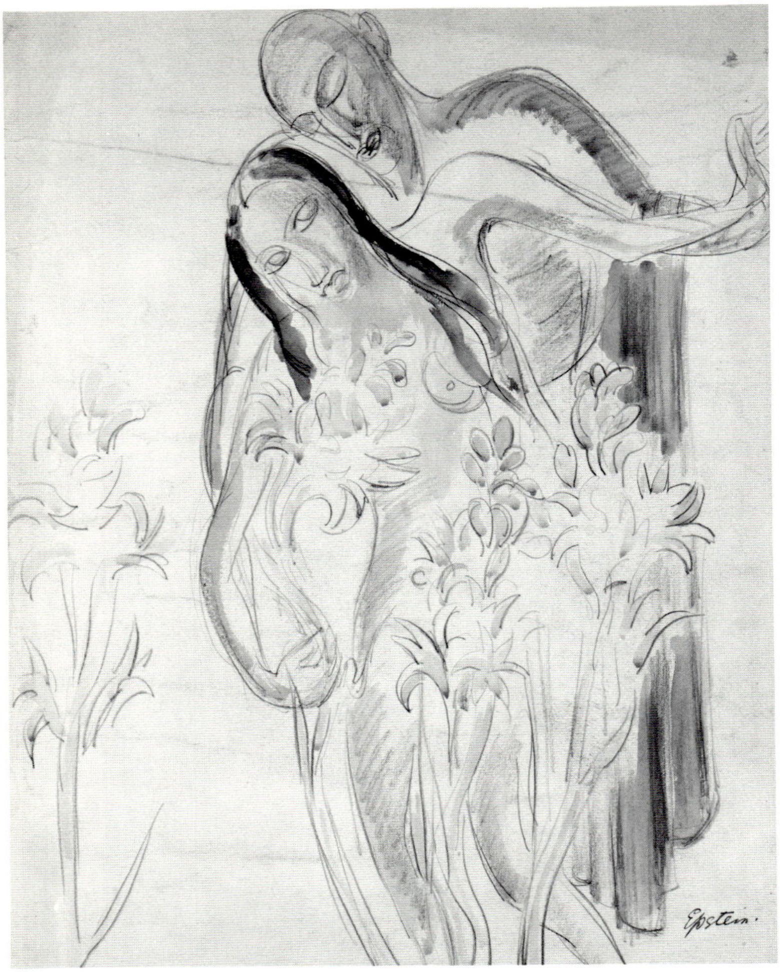

SONG OF SOLOMON, 1931—*Water Color*
h. 22¼″ x w. 17¼″

This is one of Epstein's more lyrical compositions. The two bodies echo each other in soft, dreamy curves as the plants sway to and fro before them.

THREE WISE MEN, 1932—*Water Color*
h. 17″ x w. 22″

The face of the middle Wise man in this sketchy water color foreshadows the face of the monumental carving *Consummatum Est* done in 1936.

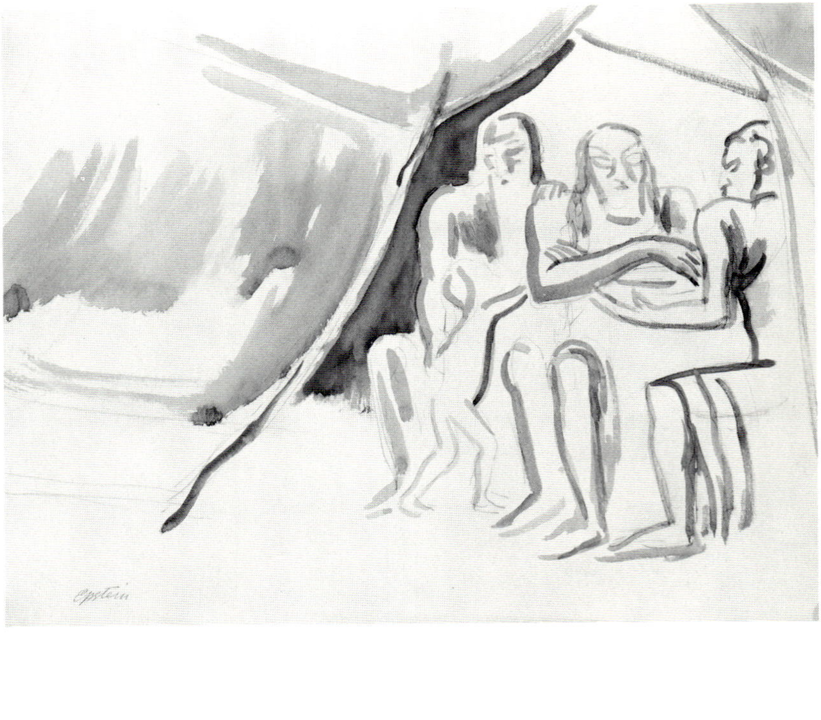

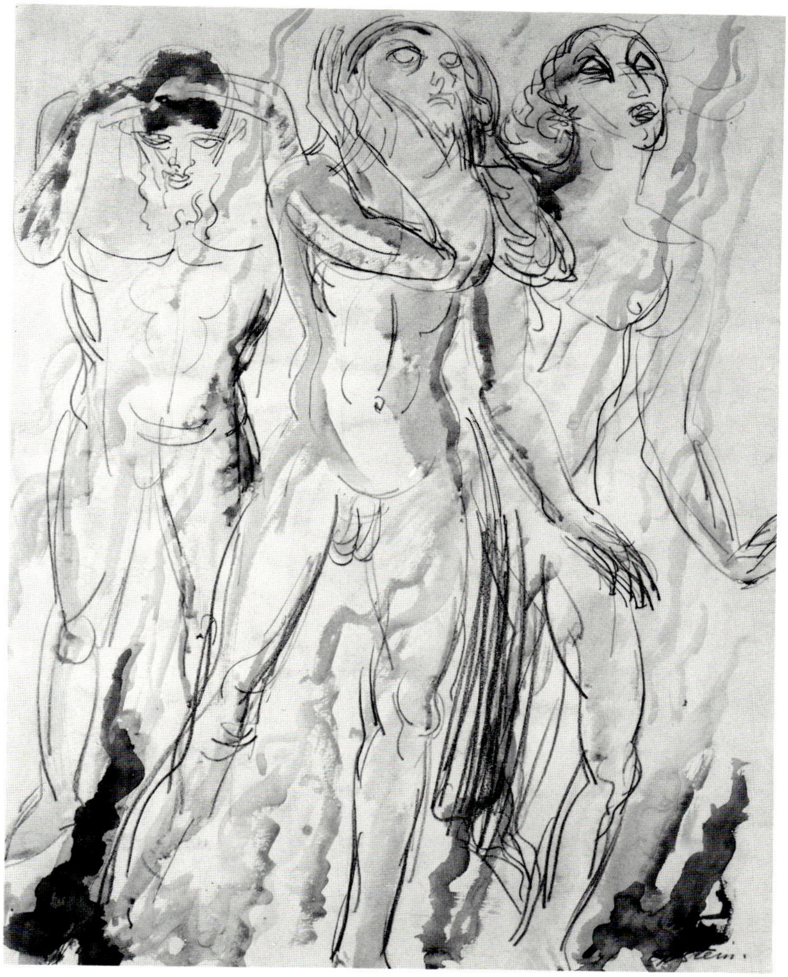

SHADRACK, MESCHAK AND ABEDNEGO, 1933. h. 22¾″ x w. 17½″

This pencil and wash drawing portrays the artist's vision of the three just men who walked through flames unharmed. The air of spontaneity is retained in the quickly traced curves of the three figures which contrast with the heavy flames of wash.

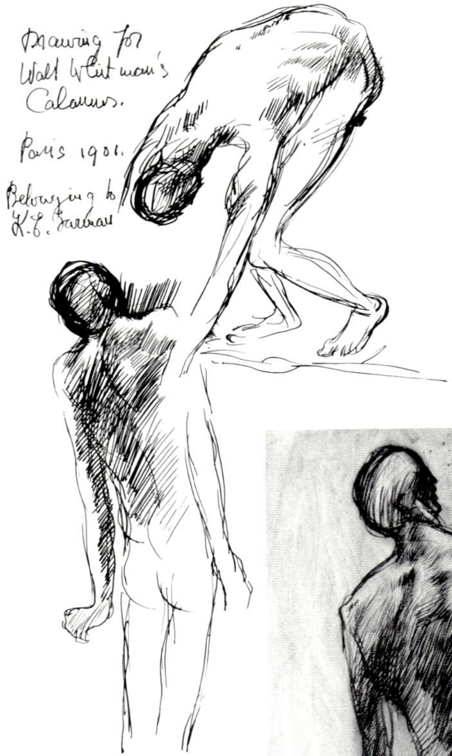

CALAMUS SKETCH, 1901—*Drawing*
h. 13½″ x w. 8″

These three pen, ink, and wash sketches are part of the series illustrating poems from Walt Whitman's *Calamus.*

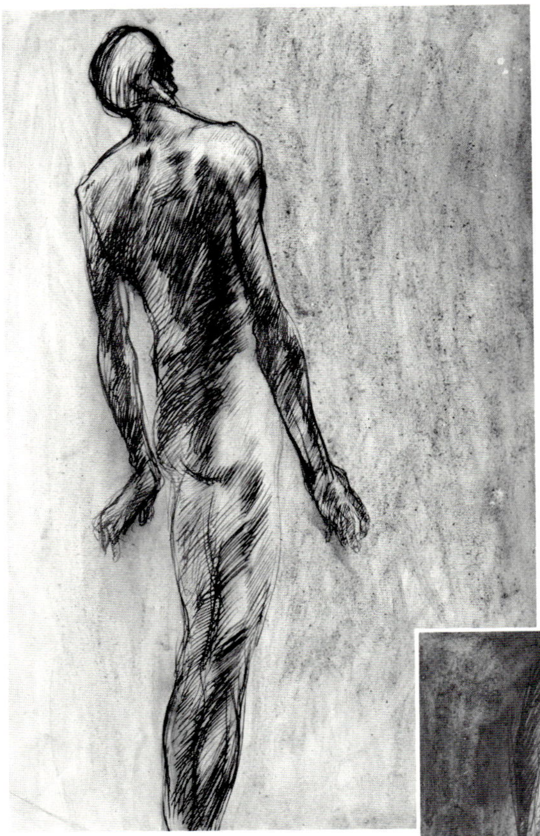

CALAMUS ILLUSTRATION, 1901—*Water Color.* h. 14¼″ x w. 9″

Having homosexual overtones, the title is named for a plant whose leaves and roots are considered a phallic symbol.

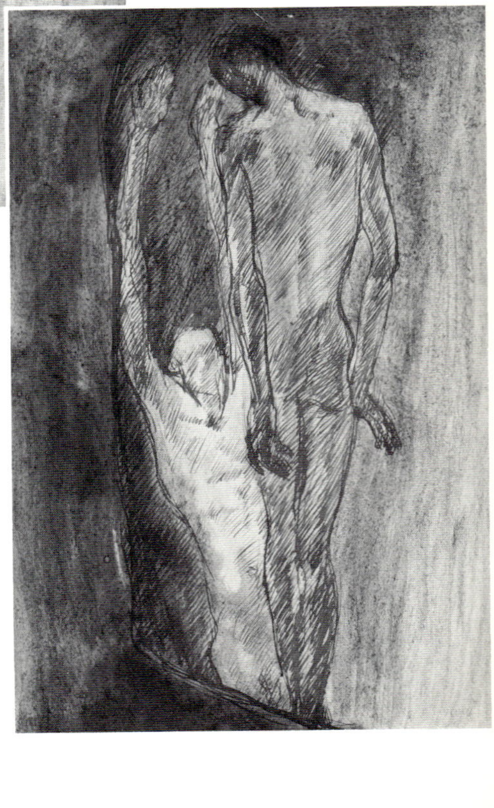

CALAMUS ILLUSTRATION II, 1901—*Water Color.* h. 12¼″ x w. 8″

Epstein translated from nature the long willowy leaves of the plant into elongated slender male figures.

The dark scratchy modelling used in these earlier drawings was later abandoned for a looser, smoother style.

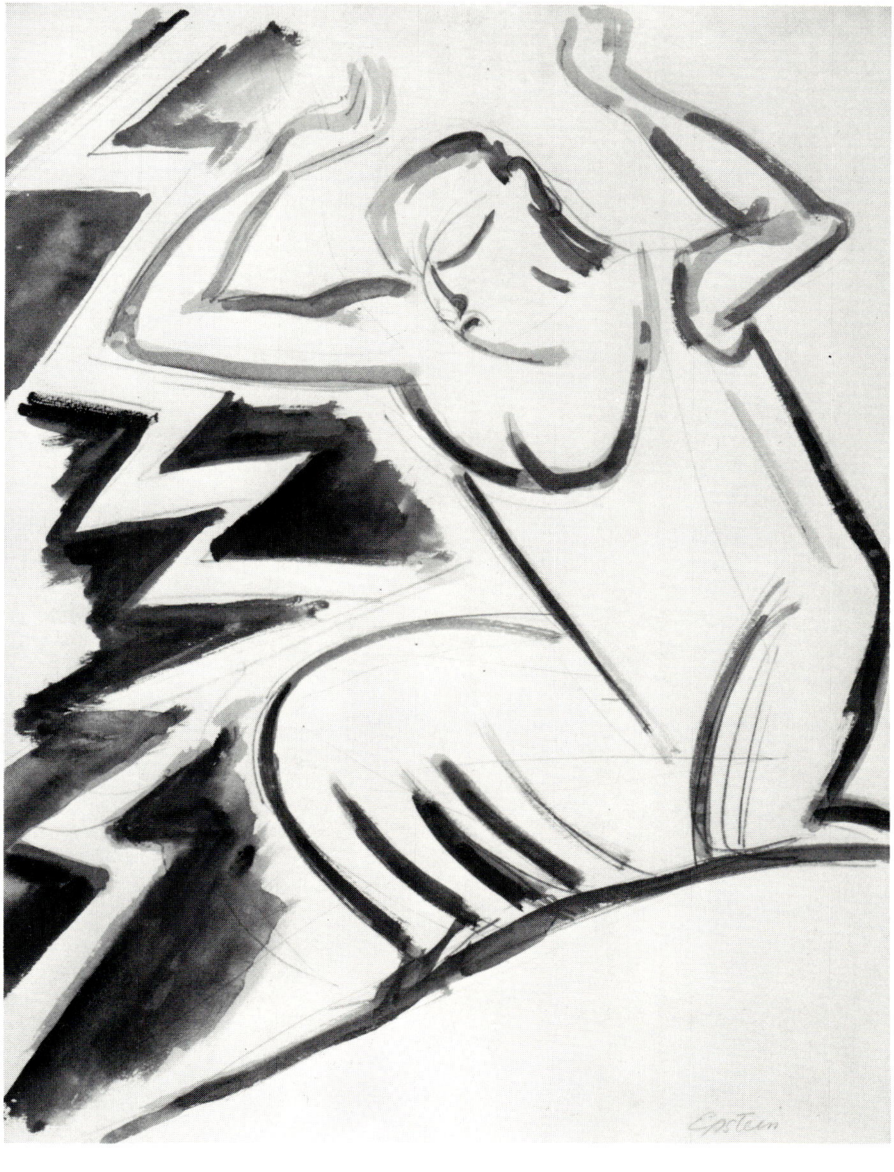

MOSES STRIKING THE ROCK, 1931. h. 25″ x w. 20″

This Old Testament illustration is powerful in its monumentality created by the gigantic figure whose arms and legs echo the zigzag strokes of lightning. The fierceness of the moment is underscored by the use of a purplish-brown monochrome.

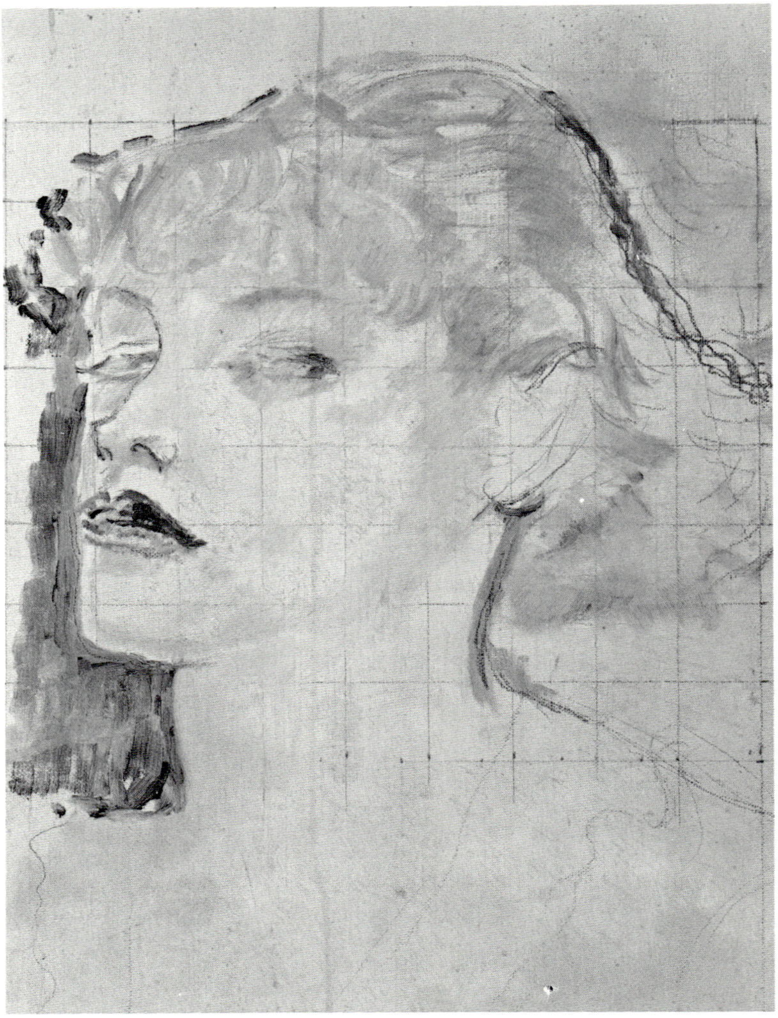

MEUM, *Oil Painting* h. 16″ x w. 12″

In this only known oil painting, date undetermined, Epstein seems lost. He could handle the contoured forms more easily in wash, pen and pencil which he himself must have realized in view of the painting's unfinished state.